Second

Searching For His Bloodline

✦ ✦ ✦ ✦

SECOND-JUMPER; Searching For His Bloodlines
by Sigfried Second-Jumper

Acknowledgments

I wrote this book in honor of those Apache and Seminole ancestors who so bravely lit and carried the torch that lights our path; their sacrifices must never be forgotten. It is up to their descendants to keep that torch forever burning.

I would like to thank the following people who supported me throughout the five years it took to write, edit, format and publish this book. First and foremost is my family, my Mother Ofelia, my children Emily and Lance and my friend Cristina Bilardello. It was Cristina's relentless perseverance that propelled me into starting something that became one of my life's biggest accomplishments.

On March 6, 2006, Cristina handed me a box of pens, a log book and a thesaurus. *"Here you go, no more excuses. You need to write your family's story as well as your life's journey for your kid's sake,"* she said. By the end of that year, I was done collecting information from my family, when I decided to approach other Chiricahua Apache descendants hoping to enhance and expand my Family Journal. Little did I realize what I was getting myself into. The response was overwhelming; within a short period of time, dozens of Apache memoirs exceeded the capacity of the one hundred page log book. A short time later, I was approached by my Seminole friends who also wished for their stories to be told and preserved.

It was at that moment that I realized I needed to go from a pen and paper to twenty-first century technology in order to accomplish such an immense task. My deepest appreciation goes to Carlo Soldevilla, Esther Luft, Lt. Rex Lehmann, Lt. Ruben Diaz, Alvaro Sanchez and Patrick O'Neal for helping me through that difficult transition.

To my brothers with the Miami Fire Department, Firehouse # 9, for their support and encouragement during the difficult times when I felt like giving up due to computer problems: Capt. Walsh, Lt. S. Landa, Lt. A. Arbolella, Lt. J. Maree, Firefighters L. Howell, O. Alvarez, S. Gibbs, G. Saab, M. Lindo, G. Borges, D. Perfumo, D. Alfonso, G. Morra, I. Chavez, Z Coronado, O.Tassy, C. Diaz, E. Rojas, A. Fernandez, A. Escoto, Lt. A. Chapman, Capt. Moye, G. Ingold, A. Stayton, Lt. M. Moore, V. Dominique, G. Martinez, Lt. R. Muñoz and E. Nuñez.

Support and contributions from my European friends, Barbara Holloway, Nancy Gregory along with Keith Bright, Jennie Hall, Henry Reina and Sonja Boekhurst are greatly appreciated.

Special thanks to my friend, published author and historian, Lynda A. Sanchez for her advice, guidance and encouragement during the editing process. Her contributions of rare captured moments from Eve Ball's photo collections are greatly appreciated.

My most sincere appreciation goes to the Mescalero Apache Tribe of New Mexico for opening their doors and hearts to my great-great grandfather, Jose Second in 1895, and later to all the Chiricahua Apaches in 1913.

I would like to thank all participants for their willingness to share their stories and for contributing in the preservation of the Apache and Seminole cultures.

My deepest gratitude goes to the two editors that helped shape all this information. They are Jose L. Fallad and Susan M. Dent. Half of this book was edited by Mr. Fallad in a period of a year. Through him I learned about editing, perhaps the most important and challenging part of any book. His patience and teachings are greatly appreciated. Susan Dent, my savior, stepped in when I needed someone the most. Her style of editing complemented my writing, making this difficult process into an enjoyable

Acknowledgements

experience. Within months, she finished the second half of the book, helped with photo selection, formatting and publishing application. To say that I am thankful to Jose and Susan for taking time from their families and daily endeavors would be an unfair use of the word. Thankful did not have enough synonyms to describe how I felt in regards to what they did for me out of kindness.

I am grateful to my friend Laure Marmontel for helping me through the publishing phase of this book and making a five-year dream become a reality.

With honor and humbleness I thank Mr. Robert Ove for allowing me to be the keeper of his 1948 White Tail photo collection.

Special thanks to Richard Bowers, President of the Seminole Tribe of Florida, for his unwavering support and encouragement throughout this process.

In memory of Betty Mae Tiger Jumper. Her encouraging words to *"never give up"* have echoed in my mind throughout the many difficult phases encountered in the past five years while writing this book.

I want to thank all my Miccosukee and Seminole friends for sharing their history, culture and memoirs. They have been an important and positive influence in my life. Most importantly they taught me what it was like to be a Native American and encouraged me on my journey to find my Apache family.

Last but not least, I will like to thank my Apache family and friends for allowing me to be part of their lives, ceremonies and keeper to their stories. Their warm welcome and acceptance was the force behind this project. Their teachings and guidance helped shaped the man that I am today. *The Author*

Sigfried Ruiz Second-Jumper

Introduction
A Broad Overview

This book pertains to the struggles, sacrifices, and accomplishments of two North American native tribes: The Chiricahua Apaches and the Florida Seminoles. Although many other books have been published about these two Nations, very few of them have ever been written from within. As a result, it is rare to find a truly accurate account expressing the views and feelings of the people themselves.

As the author, and a Chiricahua Apache descendant whose family was sent to Florida from New Mexico as prisoners of war, it is my pleasure and honor to bring to light the many untold stories and memoirs found in this book. These tales spanning from the mid 1800's to the present came from personal experiences, family members, as well as Florida Seminoles and Chiricahua Apaches from New Mexico, Oklahoma and Arizona.

Some of the participants that came forward and contributed to the preservation of these stories are directly related to great leaders such as Geronimo, the famous Apache warrior and Medicine Man and Chief Osceola, the proud and relentless Seminole war leader who stood as a trademark of the Seminoles' strong reputation for non-surrender.

Indeed these two legendary leaders rightfully deserve their historical recognition, but there were many others who participated equally in the protection of their people and their land. Unfortunately, their identities and contributions were either forgotten or poorly recorded. For the first time, descendants of those silent contributors such as Apache scouts and Seminole warriors have come forward to record and preserve their ancestors' courageous deeds along with recollections of their daily living.

Even though the Apaches and Seminoles lived far from each other, they shared something in common. They were both courageous freedom fighters who defended their people and their ancestral homelands against the invasion of Spaniards and other Europeans.

The arrival of the new immigrants to North America created conflict with the eastern tribes. At first, these nations welcomed the intrusion of white settlers, offering trade and information to help maintain order and peace in the region. Eventually the movement of these Europeans to the west created conflict between the native nations of the west and the ever-expanding white settlers of the east. Minor conflicts soon exploded into full scale wars forcing all Indian Nations to take up arms to protect their native homelands from invasion.

The Seminoles strategically migrated south to remote tree islands scattered across the Florida Everglades and the Big Cypress Swamps. Similarly, the Chiricahua Apaches sought refuge in the most inhospitable terrain of the rugged mountains and deserts of what are now the states of New Mexico and Arizona, along with portions of northern Mexico.

Despite the distance that separated the two groups, their struggles against extinction evolved in very similar fashion. The tragedy of the so-called Indian Wars reduced these proud nations to a mere fraction of their former numbers with hundreds of tribes crippled by poverty, disease, and finally by a military defeat that resulted in tribal disbandment, and in some cases total annihilation.

Like the Apaches, the Seminoles fought the U.S. Government, were imprisoned at Fort Marion, Florida, and sent to Oklahoma. Out of hundreds of native Tribes that took up arms against the Conquistadors and later against the organized war machine of

INTRODUCTION

the U.S. Army, only a few Nations earned distinctive titles in American history.

One of those was a group of Florida Seminoles who refused to neither relocate nor surrender. As a result of their unwillingness to negotiate with their enemy the U.S. Government, they became known as the *"Unconquered Nation"*. They remained aloof deep in the South Florida swamps until the late 1950's, when they filed for recognition with the Federal Government as the Seminole Tribe of Florida.

The other contender fighting for that distinctive title in American history was the Chiricahua Apaches. As a result of their superb fighting skills and ability to survive where others perished, they became known as the *"Tigers of the Human Race."* In 1886, they were the *"Last Indian Tribe"* to bear arms against the U.S. Government. Unlike the Seminoles, the group of Apaches that stayed behind fighting made one mistake, they negotiated with the U.S Government.

Under false promises they agreed to stop fighting and surrendered. As prisoners of war, they were ousted from their ancestral homelands. The entire nation including those Apaches that served (with honor and distinction) as scouts for the U.S. Government and those who remained peaceful were herded into trains and sent to Fort Marion and Fort Pickens, Florida; they were later transferred to Mount Vernon, Alabama and ultimately to Fort Sill, Oklahoma.

In 1913, after 27 years in captivity, they were set free by an Act of Congress. Sadly, only 265 had survived their imprisonment. Freedom came with a bitter taste, as those rag-tag remnants of a once fierce and powerful warrior nation found themselves homeless, a shameful and sad reality that remains to this day.

To their rescue came their kin, the Mescalero Apaches of New Mexico who offered a refuge deep in the mountains of their reservation, at a place called White Tail. Two-thirds (183) accepted their invitation while the other third (82) chose to remain in the Fort Sill - Apache, Oklahoma area.

On April 2, 1913, those who chose to relocate boarded a special train bound for New Mexico. Decades after their arrival in Mescalero, a small group of courageous Chiricahua Apaches, including Samuel Kenoi and Eugene Chihuahua told their stories to a reputable writer by the name of Morris Opler. Their actions were criticized by their peers. The importance of these revelations became clear to other Chiricahuas many years later, when sixty seven of them revealed their stories to Eve Ball, a respected writer and historian.

Both writers told the stories of their interviewees using their words and versions of events. Little did the participants know that their accounts would one day become the pride of their tribe's recorded history. It was Samuel Kenoi and Eugene Chihuahuas stories that helped to validate mine. I am grateful for their courage and wisdom.

It is my wish as the author, and someone who grew up among the Seminoles, to share the struggles encountered by my Apache family as they were taken from Arizona to Florida as prisoners of war. Shortly after their arrival in 1886, my great-grandparents were separated from the bulk of the survivors and sold to Cuba as slaves.

Decades later, their offsprings began migrating from Cuba to Miami, Florida. In the mid 1970's, they moved from the inner city to the outskirts of the Florida Everglades. It was there that I began learning the art of breaking-in horses and capturing alligators. In time, my activities led me to discover an Indian camp and its inhabitants, the Miccosukee-Seminoles Indians. As a result of that encounter, a friendship was born and so was my desire to learn about their ways of life.

INTRODUCTION

In time, I was asked to join them in their travels as a singer and a traditional dancer. Shortly thereafter, I began to experience an irresistible calling to seek out anyone or anything related to my own Apache native blood.

Motivated by that awakening, my family and I embarked on a trip across-country hoping to discover that missing piece that my heart ached for. That journey ended in The Mescalero Apache Reservation, located in the rugged mountains of southern New Mexico. There I met face-to-face with one of the last surviving Chiricahua Apache ex-prisoners of war. The warm reception led me to return a year later, where I was taken to a remote Apache camp to meet with the rest of the Chiricahuas.

Besides being accepted, I was welcomed into the Medicine Circle, where I was inaugurated into their most sacred and powerful singing group, The Chiricahua Apache Crown Dancers. Having been a member of such an elite group for over a decade has allowed me to learn the ways of my ancestors and the spiritual power that guides all traditional Apaches.

In time, I was taken to a remote canyon within the reservation to meet my long lost relatives. That special reunion, along with other unique historical events, is part of the many recollections found in this book.

Many times, when inquiring about something, I was told that the only person with that knowledge had passed away. Because of that, I was encouraged by friends to record my family's story for my children's sake. What started as a personal journal developed into a massive contribution of similar memoirs from other Chiricahua Apaches and descendants like me.

A short time later, I was approached by my Seminole friends who also wished to have their stories told and preserved. Honored by their request, I included their parallel stories, beliefs and hopes for historical documentation. Because I was a true friend of the Seminoles and a respected member of an elite group in my family's reservation, it created a level of trust that allowed the participants to reveal their deepest feelings on sensitive subjects long suppressed. They include issues such as spirituality, ceremonies, and sacred places along with the sharing of many photographs never before published.

In order to maintain the trust bestowed upon me, I wrote the stories word-for-word without judgment as all participants would want their children's grandchildren to hear it. To insure accuracy, everyone involved had the opportunity to review their contributions prior to publishing.

I hope that the reader will not only enjoy the fresh and exciting material found within the pages of this book, but gain a clearer understanding of these two cultures and of my own heritage as a Native American descendant.

Although both groups have blended into mainstream America, they still value and practice their religious beliefs as well as their old ways of living. Preserving their traditional ways and their native language is the only wish among the elders. Perhaps for fear of losing those things, a sad reality in this fast-paced world that we are living in today, is the reason for their coming forward and allowing me to record their most intimate tales.

It is a great honor to have been involved with the preservation of all these memoirs and recollections. I am extremely proud to be associated and related to such unyielding people. My intent is to not only preserve in writing the culture and traditions of both nations, but to encourage present and future generations to seek, practice and preserve the old ways and to follow their hearts' calling. It is my wish to dedicate this book to my family and future Apache and Seminole generations.

TABLE OF CONTENTS

End of the War Cries

Chapter One

In November of 2004, I received a phone call from my friend Chris, an Oklahoma Seminole. Chris worked at the Ah-Tah-Thi-Ki Seminole Museum, located in Big Cypress, Florida. Big Cypress is one of six Florida Seminole Reservations. He informed me that an Apache Cultural dance group from Arizona, called Yellow Bird was hired by the Seminole Tribe to perform at the museum. Chris said that he had talked to them about me, and they were looking forward to meeting me.

The next morning, I woke eagerly and drove to the reservation, where I met up with the leader of the dance troop. His name was Ken Duncan, a Coyotero-Chiricahua Apache from San Carlos, Arizona. Ken was wearing cowboy boots, jeans and a multicolor vest over his red long sleeve shirt. His dark eyes complimented his long black hair and olive skin. He introduced me to his wife and kids, who doubled as his dance group. After getting acquainted we sat down to talk. During our dialogue, I learned that Ken's family was also sent to Florida as prisoners along with mine. Our conversation ended at around noon when the time came for Ken's group to get ready for their scheduled show. Ken asked if I was going to watch them perform. *"Of course"* I replied.

At one o'clock, I walked into a huge tent that sheltered the stage from the elements. Inside, I took a seat in the front row. Soon dozens of spectators filled the aisles near and around me. After the opening Prayer, Ken recited the following story accompanied by his oldest son playing the flute.

"Not that long ago in 1886, our Country received the Statue of Liberty; Americans celebrated this monument as a symbol that stood for freedom, liberty, and justice for all. At the same time, across the frontier, in the deserts of Arizona and New Mexico, Apaches were being tortured and murdered. While millions of immigrants from all over the world rejoiced at being welcomed to the 'Land of the Free,' these brave warriors and their families were stripped of their dignity and freedom. Shamefully, they were herded into trains and sent far from their homelands to a place call Florida, thousands of miles away. Many if not most, never saw their homelands again. Shamefully to this day they remain without a piece of land to call their own."

The prevailing speech was part of a song called 'Come Home.' Its lyrics, also talked about those Apache prisoners that were sent to Florida, and how the time had come for their scattered descendants to make their way back home to the mountains of New Mexico and Arizona. Shaken by emotions, I stayed paralyzed in my seat as tears ran down my face. Little did I know Ken's speech had touched me so deeply that those echoing words were the first thing that came to my mind a year and a half later when I began to write this book.

All I could think as I heard Ken end his introduction was how *"shameful but true."* As fireworks lit the skies of the northeast country, the Chiricahua Apaches of the southwest lands were entering the darkest chapter in their history. Decades of fighting the Mexican and U.S. Government had taken their toll. The endless loss of blood and a continuous decrease in the number of fighting men, made the once mighty and feared Chiricahua war cries come to an end. "The Tigers of the Human Race," a title earned and given by a U.S. General, had finally laid down their arms and surrendered.

That dreadful year was 1886. The site was Cañon de los Embudos, Mexico. There, on March 26 and 27, the four Chiricahua Apache leaders, Chihuahua, Geronimo,

Naiche, and Mangas, met in conference with U.S. General George Crook to discuss surrendering terms.

The first to surrender was Chief Chihuahua. Among his group of seventy seven, only fifteen were warriors, the rest were women and children. According to military records these were the men: Cathla, Shoie, Nezulkide, Nahdozin, Eskinye, Seeltoe, Lensee, Ni-losh, Nezegochin, Tisna, Dahkeya, Ulzanna, Nana and Jose Second.

Among the warriors was Chief Chihuahua's brother Jolsanny, also known as Ulzanna. "Jolsanny was especially noted for the raid he led up from Mexico through and behind General Crook's lines into Arizona and New Mexico Territory with 10 warriors, November-December 1885, when in 4 weeks under constant pursuit they raided 1200 miles of country and escaped safely back into Mexico.[1]"

Another significant prisoner was Nana, known as the Desert Fox, regarded as the most powerful Medicine Man the Apaches ever had. Both Jolsanny and Nana were masters of guerilla warfare and considered extremely dangerous. To have them in custody must have brought a sigh of relief not only to the new settlers of Arizona and New Mexico but to the U.S. War Department's budget.

Among the men in Chihuahua's group was an individual by the name of Jose Second, my great-great grandfather. He and another Apache were captured by Mexicans at an early age and each was given the name Jose. In order to distinguish one from the other, the Mexicans decided to call them Jose Primero and Jose Segundo, which translated to Jose the First and Jose Second. After many years in captivity, these two men, both full-blooded Chiricahuas, escaped and found their way back to their specific band, the Chok-anen.

The Chok-anens were known as the true Chiricahuas, easily identified by their traditional and trademark band of white clay drawn across a warrior's face. Their homeland was located in what is today southeastern Arizona. Their vast territory included some of their sacred mountains, such as The Dragoons, Dos Cabezas, and The Chiricahuas.

It remains unknown the exact year that the two warriors masterminded their escape and the location where they settled. It is safe to assume that both men returned while Cochise was still in power and living in the sanctuary known as the 'Stronghold' deep in the Dragoon Mountains of Arizona. What is documented is that Jose Second was inaugurated under Cochise's son Naiche in 1884.

After marching for days, Chief Chihuahua's group arrived at Fort Bowie, Arizona. There, the new Prisoners of War or P.O.Ws. awaited their fate unaware that they would maintain that status for nearly three decades and to this day would still not have a piece of land to call their own. A few days later, they were forced to march again for over two hundred and eighty miles to Holbrook, AZ.

On April 6, 1886, under armed guard, the rightful owners of this land were herded aboard an eastbound train. The arduous journey across the 'land of the free' had just begun. One can only imagine what those once proud people felt like. Half starved, half-naked with no sanitary conditions, and the heat and humidity increasing with every mile, they endured the two thousand mile crossing.

On April, 13, after a week of the torturous conditions, the train and their human cargo arrived in Jacksonville, Florida. The next day the group arrived via ferry in St. Augustine, Florida. As they marched down the city streets, crowds watched as they were taken to Fort Marion, an old Spanish Fortress located on the eastern coast of the State.

2

Fort Marion, St. Augustine, FL.
Imprisonment for Chiricahua Apaches
Courtesy of St. Augustine, Florida public library.

Local business traders, mostly Spaniards, saw the arrival of the prisoners as a possible opportunity for exploitation. Import-Export was big business between St. Augustine, Florida's main port of commerce and Cuba, a rich Spanish-owned Caribbean island, located ninety miles south from the Florida Straits. Because the Apaches already spoke Spanish with a basic degree of fluency, also understood and accepted many aspects of Spanish culture, it made them very valuable to the business-minded Spaniards. These characteristics will later come to play a major role in changing the life of some of the prisoners.

Apache Prisoners, Fort Marion, FL. ca. 1886. #1-Colley,#2-Jose Second,#4-Chief
Chihuahua,#7-Lancey?,#8-Nana,#11-Jolsanny
Courtesy of St. Augustine Historical Society Library

Soon after Chihuahua's group arrived in Florida, other Apache groups began to arrive as well. Within months, the entire Chiricahua Apache Nation found themselves confined within the walls of the old fort. Out of more than five hundred prisoners, only eighty-two were men. Among them were those that remained peaceful, as well as those who served the U.S. Government with honor and distinction as U.S. Army Scouts.

Prison records stated that one hundred and thirty to one hundred and forty cone-shaped Sibley tents were erected on the north rampart, an area of approximately one acre of square footage. Perhaps due to lack of space, other groups were taken to Fort Pickens, another Spanish Fort located in Pensacola, Florida. Imprisoned there, were the other three principal leaders - Chief Naiche, Chief Mangas, and the notorious warrior and medicine man, Geronimo.

The prisoners at Fort Marion were allowed some freedom to move about. It was common for women and children to walk the streets of St. Augustine. Men enjoyed the same privilege, but preferred to travel in groups. Jose Second became the translator for the prisoners who did not speak Spanish. His Indian name was Itsa-Dee-Tsa, meaning 'speaks two tongues'.

His wife was a Chiricahua from the Chienne's (Red Paint People) band. They were known for their traditional band of red clay drawn across a warrior's face.

The Chiennes were the eastern-most band of the Chiricahuas. Their territory covered what is today the southwestern part of New Mexico and parts of northern Mexico. Hidden deep in the mountains of their territory were their most sacred areas, Red Paint Canyon and Ojo Caliente (Warm Springs). The Chiennes were known to outsiders as the Warm Springs Apaches, named after a small spring-fed pool that flows down the high rocky walls of the Cañada Alamosa Canyon. Some of their leaders were Mangas Coloradas, Victorio, and Loco. Their sacred spot can be found near what is today the town of Monticello, New Mexico.

Jose's wife name (*perhaps Huana*) remains unknown, as women were assigned a number or simply known as someone's wife. During this early period of captivity, Jose's wife and children disappeared from Fort Marion. Like them, dozens of other prisoners, mostly children, vanished without a trace. It became common practice for the U.S. Government to declare someone "*to feeble or dead,*" a policy statement officially transcribed in fort records, which made these victims, disappeared. Although the lack of specific prison records make it impossible to account for the fate of all the missing children, the history of two of the many children, who supposedly died there, will come to light and be revealed in the pages of this book.

One was an Apache boy named Florentino, the other, a girl by the name of Kukah, also Apache. Both children boarded a sailing ship and disappeared into the horizon. The event(s) became well known among the Chiricahua prisoners. Many decades later, in the 1940's, two Chiricahua ex prisoners, Samuel Kenoi and Eugene Chihuahua, were the first to come forward to reveal the hardships they lived and witnessed to a respected writer, Morris Opler. Years later their courageous acts were followed by others when they gave their accounts to another writer/historian by the name of Eve Ball. Both writers did an outstanding job by telling the stories of their interviewees using their words and versions of events. Like most Chiricahuas at the time, Samuel and Eugene were under the impression that the prisoners aboard the sailing ship(s) were thrown overboard and left to drown. What they didn't know was that the ship(s) and their human cargo were sailing to Havana Bay; a major port of entry into the Spanish-owned island of Cuba.

END OF THE WAR CRIES

Long ago, Spain had established Cuba as the primary port of embarkation for black slaves from Africa's Ivory Coast, and many years later, Apache prisoners from Vera Cruz, Mexico, and later Fort Marion, Florida. Thus Havana, Cuba became known as the main port of commerce for the trade of slaves and prisoners. The following numbers shamefully reveal Cuba's unquenchable thirst for slavery. Between 1513 and 1886, more than seven hundred and thirty thousand slaves were greeted by their Spanish owners and kept in the Island.

Florentino and Ku-kah arrived at Bahia de la Habana (*Havana, Bay*) to be greeted by Spaniards, who eagerly waited for the arrival of their goods and human cargo. Also awaiting the newcomers was the conversion of what the Spaniards perceived as *"savage little demons"* into good Catholics. This was all the Spaniards knew, *"Convert or burn at the stake."* This cruel method started in Cuba centuries earlier when a Taino Chief by the name of Hatuey was burned at the stake for refusing to be baptized. The legendary event was executed in front of his followers as a teaching lesson.

Unaware of these atrocities, Florentino and Ku-Kah found themselves boarding a train. He was taken to Las Minas de Guanabacoa (*The Mines*), which was about fifteen kilometers southeast from Havana's Bay. She was taken a little further to the town of Tapaste. Both were rugged country towns with clear rivers running through a landscape of rolling hills. The land was dotted with swaying palm trees and a variety of fruit trees native to the tropical forested island. A paradise indeed to the eye of the beholder, but to Florentino and Ku-kah, it must have looked like another planet when compared to the deserts of their native land. Either preteens or teenagers, both were old enough to fear, but young enough to adjust and convert to the new ways of their new world.

Very little is known of Ku-kah and Florentino's personalities, and how they adjusted to their new ways of living. The one thing that could have helped them through that difficult period, was the fact that Cuba had great cultural influences from other indigenous people. Among them were Cuba's own natives, the Tainos. Like the Apaches, many other groups of Indians were also taken to Cuba from Florida. Among them were the Seminoles, Timucuas, Yamasees, Tequestas and Caloosas.

The town of Las Minas and its neighbor, the village of Tapaste, were no strangers to the arrival of Apaches. Earlier groups shipped from Vera Cruz, Mexico were taken there. Florentino worked in a cattle ranch in Las Minas. Ku-kah who initially settled in Tapaste, was later relocated to Las Minas, where she became a rope maker; a trade that remained in her family for generations.

Apaches from Las Minas made baskets using grasses found in the area. Most handmade crafts were taken to nearby towns and left on consignment at the general stores. Some of these towns were La Gallega, Santa Fe, Becuranao, and Guanabacoa, all of them easily accessible on horseback. Whether Ku-kah was allowed to participate in these interactions is unknown, as women did not have that kind of freedom. Was she able to brain-tan leather, do beadwork, and make baskets? It is probably safe to assume that she did. Men on the other hand traveled freely, as the risk of escaping from the island was minimal to non-existent.

Life on the plantations of their Spanish masters was not easy. Although they were technically not considered slaves in the traditional sense, the young couple's position as indentured servants carried other hardships. Prejudice to the Indian inhabitants ran deep and much effort was spent on maintaining a strong process of assimilation into the dominant culture.

Ku-kah was often caught and punished for speaking the Apache tongue to Florentino. The couple was forced to speak Spanish only. However, in the quiet of the night, by the light of a harvest moon, stories were passed on and many of the old ways maintained. In this way, the history of others like them was discovered. That's how the young Apache couple became familiar with the ways of the indigenous Indian Tribe of the island of Cuba, the Taino People.

The Taino People:

"The Tainos were among the first to meet the Spanish Conquistadors including Christopher Columbus. They were also the first of all Native Tribes to suffer slavery and almost complete annihilation. A legendary Taino Chief by the name of Hatuey left his native land of Hispañola (*known today as Haiti-Dominican Republic*) and paddled his canoe westerly to warn the Tainos of Cuba led by Chief Guama of the atrocities his people suffered at the hands of the Spaniards. The two Chiefs formed an alliance that lasted a decade.

In the end both leaders gave up. After their surrender, a Spanish Friar wanted to baptize them. Chief Hatuey refused. As a result, he was burned at the stake. Chief Guama was also killed. Without leadership, the Tribe became easy targets for enslavement. Legend has it that many Taino families committed suicide by climbing the cliffs of the mountains and jumping into the Yumuri, a river that flows into the Atlantic. It was the only way to defeat the Spanish. By killing themselves, they were not humiliated and they died with their dignity.[9]"

By 1550, Spaniards reported to Spain that there were no Indians left alive in Cuba. Such reports led social scientist as well as the Cuban people, especially those in exile here in the USA, to believe that there are no Indians left in Cuba today. I am hoping that my book will enlighten their knowledge.

LAS MINAS DE GUANABACOA APACHES

The Tainos of Cuba have endured through the centuries and are very much alive today. They can be found throughout rural areas from coast to coast. "The majority of them are found residing on the Island's eastern most regions, from Baracoa to Maisi Point down to El Pico Turquino and Sierra Maestra. The area or refuge is known for its rugged mountains and dense rain forest. "Tucked deep in those mountains are the *Villages of Guirito and Yateras.* Within Yateras there is a community called *Caridad de los Indios.*

These villages remain today as they did centuries ago. The Tainos still cook in open pit fires called *Barbacoa.* Slow cooking stews called *Ajiacos* provide the main course meal. Their cooking oil comes from coconut. They still drink from *Jicaras,* a clay pottery vessel similar to a pitcher. Their traditional bread, *Casabe* comes from the yucca plant. The *Hutia,* a four-legged creature similar to a possum is considered a delicacy.

During special gatherings, a call is made across remote valleys and Maniguas (*wilderness*), through a calling shell called *Guamo.* In these remote villages the Tainos still keep alive the *Areito* and "*Guiriba,* a communal dance passed down from generation to generation. During these dances the singers recite cosmologies that speak of stars, moon and the heavens above.

The dugout canoes, *Yolas,* are still used for fishing expeditions down the Tao and Yumuri Rivers. Their favorite fish is the *Teti,* which is caught according to the cycles of the moon. The Tainos are known as excellent wood carvers. Their favorite material for carving is the *Guayacan,* a soft black wood native to the island.""

A New Generation
Chapter Three

As the years passed, the people of Cuba began to rebel against the tyranny of the Spaniards. In February of 1895, they declared a war of independence from Spain. By December of 1898, the Spanish flag came down as the people of Cuba took control of their Island with the rising of the American flag and later theirs. No one knows for certain, but it is believed that Florentino was involved in that movement. Regardless, these were exciting times, especially for Cuba's minorities, as the aroma of freedom lingered in the air.

Ku-kah had developed into a beautiful young lady, approximately five feet, two inches, stocky build, with a dark complexion and straight black hair. Florentino was a little taller, perhaps five feet, five inches, and slim. He had high cheekbones, black eyes, dark complexion and silky black hair. Timing could not have been better, both Apaches were in their prime and they were free to express themselves and make choices.

In late 1899, Florentino proposed marriage to Ku-kah. When the time came to get married at their local church, they discovered a harsh reality. They were simply too poor to pay the fee and had no choice but to have the marriage ceremony at home. In the presence of a small group of friends, the couple exchanged their wedding vows and join in holy matrimony. With the help of other local Indians or *Guajiros*, the couple built their home using the Island's natural resources, such as the Royal Palm and the Guano Cano Palm. The two bedroom dwelling became the first thing they ever owned in their new world.

Typical dwelling of Cuba's poor working class during the 19th and 20th century, commonly referred to as *Casa de Guajiros* or *Casa de Guano*.

The newlyweds remained active in the rope-making business, and as a result, were able to acquire horses and few head of cattle. Once all the basics were taken care of, the couple felt ready to enter the challenging stage of parenthood. Based on results, it appears that they took this phase with lots of enthusiasm. Soon the young couple began having children, ten in total. Among those children, was Francisca Segunda, my grandmother. Segunda, as she was called, was born in 1907.

Chiricahua Apaches in Cuba
Segunda's Family (circa 1917)
L to R - Upper row Rita, Lucio, Francisca
L to R - Bottom row Ku-kah, Paloh, Florentino

By 1915 or so, the family had expanded both their rope making business and the small head of cattle they had acquired years earlier, into a small but lucrative cattle enterprise. Florentino was in his forties when he died in 1917 from alcohol related problems. One can only wonder if a lifetime of hardships at the hands of the U.S. and Spanish governments contributed to his excessive drinking and ultimately in his death.

Losing the head of the family at such early age created a hardship for young Segunda and her siblings. In order to make ends meet, all the children were force to work at the family ranch. Not much is known of the children and Segunda's childhood other than they were very quiet and reserved.

A NEW GENERATION

By 1920, the business had picked up enough that an extra set of hands was needed to deliver the goods. As a result, Ku-kah hired a young man of Spanish-Arabian descendant by the name of Angel Cabrera. His job consisted of delivering rope to the nearby towns. Although his time at the ranch was limited to a couple of hours each morning, it did not prevent him from noticing Segunda's older sister Rita. It has been said, that a relationship existed between the two.

As time passed, Segunda began to develop into a beautiful young woman. She was about five feet three inches tall, slim build with long straight black hair, and beautiful black eyes. Angel, seven years older, began to court her and within a short period of time they fell in love. The relationship created animosity between the two sisters, a loathing that lasted a lifetime. Due to criticism by family and neighbors, the young couple had no choice but to elope. Segunda was fifteen when she ran away and married Angel.

With the help of friends Angel built a new home. It was located next to his mother's Pepilla, on a half looped dirt road called *Callejon de los Tramposos* (*Trickster's Road*), named after those who traveled through it in order to avoid paying their overdue accounts to the businesses stores on the main road. Their home was similar to the one Segunda was born in, *Casa de Guajiro,* a term commonly used to describe dwellings of Native people. The two bedroom house was rectangular in shape and measured approximately five hundred square feet. The front door was located in the middle of the house, which separated the two rooms. From the main entrance, a straight path led to the back door. This style of construction allowed for maximum ventilation. Beyond the back door, a wood burning iron stove was the center of attraction. In time, a small addition was added next to the stove, which served as a pantry and dining room. The furniture consisted of a homemade wooden table and wood/rawhide chairs. The walls were made from the trunk of the Royal Palm tree. The tree trunks were split in half and stripped of its inner fibers. Each half was placed on top of the other, like the typical wood slat construction of today. The roof was made from the fronds of Guano-Cano palm (*an indigenous tree similar to the Florida Cabbage Palm*). The fresh cuttings were weaved through horizontal wood ribs that made up the "A" frame roof. The top of the roof was covered with *Yaguas* (*The self-peeling part of the Royal Palm*). The natural material was known for its durability and water repellent qualities.

These roofs lasted on an average between seven and ten years, depending on weather conditions. All materials were easily accessible and abundant in the area. The wood had to be cut during *Cuarto Menguante* (*waning quarter moon*). If the wood was cut during that time, it remained termite and bug free.

By late 1922, Angel and his newly wife Francisca Segunda Cabrera became the proud owners of their new home. Behind their house, ran the Calvo River. The cool and steady stream was the source for all the young couples water needs. Other natural resources such as *Palmiche*, (*the fruit of the Royal Palm*) provided an excellent source of food for the animals. *Pinon de Botija*, a native island tree similar to the Castor tree found in Florida was used as fence posts. These posts along with barbed wire made excellent holding pens for the various farm animals. Once all the essentials were taken care of, the newlyweds started their own rope making business. Knowing all the ins and outs of the trade, made the transition to self employed smooth and easy. After all no money was needed up front, their experience and a strong desire to prosper were all the ingredients needed to succeed.

Original Francisca Segunda's home (circa 1950's)

Francisca Segunda's Home with front porch added, ca. 1980's

In time, their marriage produced ten children. The first was Ta-Tah, born in 1923. Ta-Tah was known as *Sapatico*. The name was given because at birth he slept in a small shoebox. This tiny crib was perfect for his size since he was born premature and was small by any comparison, thus, the given name, which literally meant *Little Shoe*. The fragile newborn's skin was thin as paper, a condition that scared his young mother. To the rescue came his grandmother Pepilla, who nursed him until he was strong and healthy.

The second child born was Tinoh followed by Titeh, Rene, Aurora, Bejoh, Pichin and my Mother, Ofelia, who was born in 1937. Born after her were Bertha and Ruben, thus making her the third youngest of the ten. The family grew up in an almost illiterate world. Outside information was rare and specific news about the Chiricahua people was non-existent. To make matters worse, Angel prohibited any practice of Apache customs and so with time, Segunda lost track of her heritage and her Native spirit.

Whether the marriage was a happy one from the beginning no one knows for certain. By the time my mother was old enough to remember, it did not appear to be such. Neither my mom nor my uncles Ta-Tah and Rene remembered Segunda as ever saying much. She appeared unhappy, and depressed. Her home ran like a military academy. In command was my grandfather, Angel.

My mother remembers her father Angel as being very abusive, not only to his wife but also to the children. His abuse toward my grandmother Segunda was not only verbal but physical as well. The beatings were often and the verbal threats were constant. To make matters worse, it was done in the presence of the children, who watched horrified and fearing for their lives. When mad, Angel had a habit of calling my grandmother *India* as well as other names that were perceived as degrading. Because of the underlying stigma attached to being *Indios* (*Indians*) and *Negros* (*Negroes*), these constant insults served to cripple Segunda's self-esteem.

Another form of abuse had to do with Angel's fishing, which he did often into the late hours of the night. Upon his return, he would wake my grandmother and the children, and force them to clean his catch. It was something Segunda detested doing. The stench of raw fish lingered in the stale air and underneath their fingernails. The smell persisted regardless of how many times they washed their hands. When the cleaning was done, Segunda and the children would all go back to bed. The next morning, Angel, would give the cleaned fish fillets to the neighbors. This made him feel generous and important, even though Segunda knew better. Later, my mother, Ofelia, explained to me that fish was abhorred by her mother Segunda, an Apache custom that had been passed on to Segunda and her siblings by her parents, Florentino and Ku-Kah.

My mother remembers the daily routine in Angel's house. By 6:00am everyone was up and ready for work. Breakfast was meager, only cocoa mixed in water. Then the workday began. Mom's job was turning the tourniquets. A tourniquet was described as a piece of round stone with an attached metal handle, like a spool if you will. This constant turning provided the twisting of the Mira-Guano fronds, resulting in a braid called rope. At 1:00pm was lunchtime. It consisted of bread, cornmeal mixed with cinnamon and sugar. After lunch the task changed from turning the tourniquet, to cutting the fronds for the next day's work. The frond from the Mira-Guano palm was split with a knife, the center vein was removed, and the two soft sides of the leaf were collected and made into five-inch bundles, then tied and stacked. The splitting and bundle making went on until 6:00pm. Dinner was rice, beans, and squash.

12

Francisca Segunda (1907-1955)
Her turquoise necklace was described in detail by her children.
Painting by Sonja Boekhurst

The menu rarely changed. As a matter of fact, my mom does not remember eating anything else. My Uncle Ta-Tah, on the other hand, remembers earlier days when his Mother Segunda cooked *Tasajo* for him. It was made from horsemeat; which was cut in thin layers and hung to dry in the sun. Later, it was soaked in salt-water until it became tender. It was then shredded by hand into thin fibers and fried in oil with sautéed onions and yucca. It was a treat that he enjoyed greatly.

Ta-Tah told me of being a little devious when young. He remembered one incident, when his mother Segunda, was cooking a cheese meal for some special occasion. While the food was cooling off, Ta-Tah came and ate most of it. His mother was furious, especially when no one came forward to take responsibility for it. The next incident he remembered was over a pot of tomato soup left on the stove. That time he fell in the trap, as his mother hid behind a door and caught him with his hands in the cookie jar. *"Did she hit you?"* I asked. *"Oh no,"* he answered, *"She would never do that. She had a talk with me and said all you need to do is ask."*

Ta-Tah explained to me that he did it mostly for fun and not out of hunger. He also got caught drinking his father's coffee. After drinking some of it, he would add water to the rest of the coffee. The results were predictable, his Dad would complain to Segunda because the coffee was cold and weak. He also told me of sleeping arrangements. Because the big family lived in a small house, sacrifices had to be made. Ta-Tah and Tinoh being the oldest of the children had to sleep outside. They both slept in a *Bohio*, a structure very similar to a wickiup. It consisted of a small (*perhaps four to five feet tall*) wood dwelling covered with Guano-Cano fronds. The door was made from a piece of an old canvas material. When I asked what he used for a mattress he laughed and said, *"Anything you could find, but mostly wool blankets."* He also explained that he preferred the soft dirt of the Bohio floor, instead of the hard dirt floor throughout the house. *"The dirt floor in the house, looked like a polish stone from daily foot traffic and sweeping,"* he said.

On cold nights, Ta-Tah slept at his grandmother's house. Other siblings slept in the living room, either on cots or on the floor. The younger ones slept in the second bedroom. The doors were closed at night to keep the animals out. The locking mechanism consisted of an iron ring on the door's edge that went over a nail on the door's frame. Electricity was not available, lighting was provided by kerosene lanterns and candle light. Water either came from the Calvo River or from a well in Pepilla's backyard.

When Ta-Tah turned thirteen, he bought his first horse, a Palomino gelding, for $1.78. Soon after, he became his father's helper. That meant riding long distances looking for the right Mira-Guano, a much smaller member of the palm family (*very similar to the Saw Palmetto Palm found in Florida*). Mira-Guano was used to make rope. Ta-tah explained that the Mira-Guano had to be picked when it was young and green, any kind of dryness, made it undesirable. Searching for the right palms was a long and tedious task. Traveling through thick and dense woods meant possible contact with poisonous plants. In order to protect himself from skin outbreaks, Ta-tah had to recite a *Guao (wow)* prayer. An oration taught by his mother and done prior to entering the dense and hostile terrains filled with toxic plants, such as poison ivy, sumac and oak.

By noon, both packed horses were back home. The fresh material was unloaded and made ready for cutting. Once the rope was made, it was sold to nearby towns, but mostly to the town of *Bacuranao*. Angel was in charge of sales and delivery, a job he had done since he was Ta-Tah's age. Ta-Tah explained the dimensions and prices for the rope. Each roll of rope was ten Baras. One Bara equals two yards. Twelve rolls, sold for thirty cents. A more expensive rope was made for those who specialized in climbing the Royal Palms to cut the *Palmiche* seeds. That rope was very tight and was made by using heavier weights. It had to be strong and stiff so that it would not slip when tied around the smooth palm trunk.

The tools of this trade consisted of a big and small tourniquets. At times Ta-Tah turned the big tourniquet called the male end. That job had to be done by a grown up, as it required strength. Ta-tah became so efficient that he was able to do twelve sixty foot ropes in an hour. The family also sold brooms and brushes. These were made from *Raiz de Jata*, a Cuban native medium size palm.

By 1945, the grown children began establishing relationships of their own. Ta-Tah fell in love and married Curucho. Rene also fell in love and married his present wife Margo, a light eyed Spanish girl who lived nearby. Rene's marriage made Segunda very happy, as she wanted the couple to marry since they were children.

A NEW GENERATION

During my interview with Rene and Margo I discovered the following about my grandma and her siblings. Margo remembers a different side of Segunda. *"Although she seemed quiet and reserved to others, she had a sense of humor she didn't often reveal,"* said Margo. My Uncle Rene remembered when his mother, Segunda, made all of the children hide if a stranger came to the door for fear of giving them the *"evil eye,"* he said.

Rene also remembers his Aunt Guillermina as being the only one who could make wine by fermenting potatoes and corn. The end result was an alcoholic beverage similar to *tiswin*, an Apache beverage made from the Century Plant, also known as Agave.

Ofelia and Sigfredo Ruiz, ca. 1992

In 1952, my Mom Ofelia was fifteen years old and with each sunrise she began to look more and more like a woman. She was five feet two inches tall. Her light olive skin matched her soft and shiny brown hair. With each passing day, she became more and more attractive to the young men in her native town of Las Minas.

It was during that time that a young cowboy by the name of Sigfredo Ruiz, my Dad, visited her house to purchase rope. It was love at first sight, and he found excuses to return. Soon after, he began courting my mother. Riding in on his liver chestnut stallion, must have made him looked like a prince charming to my mom. My Dad was ten years older and measured almost six feet in height. He was a gentle giant, soft spoken and extremely humble, the total opposite of my mom's father, Angel. It was perhaps those qualities that attracted her the most.

Sigfredo was no stranger to hardships. By the age of eight he began to face immense responsibilities after the death of his father Rafeal. At that early age my Dad began helping his mother Encarnacion and his three brothers with various chores at the family's three hundred and forty acre farm. Young Sigfredo grew up and became a gentleman. He was sensitive to my Mom's needs. Falling in love happened fast and easy. With no objections and family approval, their love grew stronger and stronger. In the spring of 1955 they married.

By then, Segunda had become terminally ill. Rene's wife, Margo, remembers her ambulating with a walking stick prior to her death at the end of that year. After her passing, some of my Mom's siblings began to leave the Island. Six out of the ten Cabreras' decided to stay, while four took a chance and migrated with their families to Florida.

Among the six who chose to stay was Pichin. He left Las Minas and moved about 60 kilometers east to the town of Guajay (*Wa-Hi*), where he served the community as a medicine man *(Curandero)* until his death in 2006. *"Among his gifts, he had the power to clear corn fields that had become plaque-ridden with bugs. He accomplished that by tying a knot on the southeastern stalk, followed by a recited prayer. Within four days, the once infested fields were bug free."* As stated by his son Alberto Cabrera.

Out of the four siblings that left the Island, Rene was the first one to arrive in Florida, followed by a sister, his brother Ta-Tah, and finally my Mom, Ofelia. They all settled just blocks from each other in the northwest section of Miami, near the Orange Bowl football stadium and a short distance from the beach.

Miami *(meaning sweet water in the Tequesta language)* was a busy city full of opportunities for those willing to work. My Uncles Rene and Ta-Tah began working in the restaurant business. Mom and her sister began working in factories while my Dad went into in the booming construction industry. With everyone working, prosperity soon followed. In a short time, each family flourished beyond their dreams.

Tatah Cabrera, ca. 2009 seen here during his 86 birthday
Redland, Florida
****

I was born in 1960. My sister Sonia was born five years later. Perhaps due to our gender and our age difference, we never really spent a lot of time together. I loved her and protected her like a hawk, but when the time came to play, we had very little in common.

The two male cousins in my family were older than me. My oldest cousin named me Cowboy for my love for horses and a pair of cowboy boots that I wore daily. My second cousin Rene was five years older than me. He was the one I spent most of my free time with. Those fun days came to an end when he joined a band as a drummer. Without having anyone to hang out with, evenings and weekends seemed long.

Because I was different and not Anglo, the kids in my neighborhood didn't really hang out with me. My dark skin, brown eyes and jet black hair, was something they couldn't or didn't want to get used to. As a result, I became used to being by myself. Trapping lizards and hunting birds was something I did for entertainment.

In 1971 my Dad purchased his first new car, a Pontiac Ventura. He spent every day after work hand-washing his pride and beauty. In order to entertain myself, I helped by washing the bottom half, so that he wouldn't have to bend over and further hurt his aching back. For a while that became the extent of my daily activities besides going to school Monday through Friday. In those days we walked to school, something that is unheard of today.

On my first day at Riverside Elementary, the entire class was taken on a mandatory tour through the principal's office. The objective was to show us all the different style paddles hanging on the wall. They came in all sizes and shapes. Some had drilled holes in them to intensify pain. That was the way discipline was handled. Something like that is not even conceivable today.

In 1972, after getting jumped by a group of kids older than me, I began taking judo classes after school. There I found other kids similar to me. Most of us felt under-privileged and discriminated for the color of our skin and or creed. Shortly thereafter I formed a small gang. It consisted mostly of Judokas and Karatekas. Our group was not formed to cause problems, but instead it offered us protection. In time, other kids wanted to join our band, thus forcing us to form an initiation ritual. It was simple, prove that you can fight and you are in. Half way through the school year a new boy arrived from New Orleans. His name was Ulyses Garcia, also of Indian descent.

Immediately, I sent Ernesto to test the newcomer. Ernesto, a green belt in karate, was the last member to join the gang and therefore assigned to carry any assignment given to him by any of the members. His task was to provoke and or challenge the new-comer into a fight to find out if he was worthy of joining us. Ernesto came back saying, *"You fight him. Have you seen what the guy looks like? He is all muscles."*

A few days later I met face to face with Ulyses. Indeed, I had never seen anyone so muscular. To top it off, he was street-smart and a smooth talker. Within hours he had me wrapped around his little finger. Ulyses and I bonded immediately. In a matter of days, we developed a friendship that still exists today. Although slightly older than me, he acted a lot more mature. A short time later, he gifted me an old ten speed bicycle. Underneath all the nicks, dents, and scratches, a faded golden yellow was seen. The bike had no brakes and just a few gears worked.

This made riding the bike quite an art. Once I felt I had mastered it, I decided to take my first trip to visit him.

Ulyses lived near an area known as the projects, since nearby low income government housing were easily found. It was in the northwest area of Miami, near 18th Avenue and 17th Street. Our neighborhoods were divided by the Miami River. Although we only lived a few miles away from each other, our homes seemed like they were worlds apart.

The most exciting part of that trip was crossing the bridge over the Miami River, especially on the way down with no brakes. After surviving a near accident, I made it to his house. Once there I was able to relax. I found the people on that side of town, a lot friendlier and less prejudiced towards me.

To add to the excitement, Ulyses had converted his backyard into a gym. He had all kinds of exercise equipment made from old pieces of steel pipes welded together by his dad. The vita-course consisted of dip and pull up bars. An incline strip of plywood was used for sit-ups. It had an old car seatbelt to tie up your feet, making the sit-ups more effective. For a chest workout, Ulyses had an old bench that was missing most of its foam padding. Next to the bench was a squat rack made with old galvanized threaded water pipes. Weights were plastic filled with sand. All these items completed the gym's inventory. Not bad for a homemade gym in those days!

Between taking judo twice a week, competing on weekends, working out and my Mom's good cooking, I developed big muscles quickly. Ulyses and I loved my Mom's cooking, specially her home-made tamales. She did this by grinding the corn grain down to a meal and mixing it with water into a soft paste. When she wanted to make them spicy, she simply added hot peppers. Occasionally she added pre-cooked meats to the mix. Once done, she wrapped the soft cornmeal in the husk and left it to cook either in an underground fire pit or in an oven. This method of preparation and cooking had been passed down for generations.

Like my Uncle Ta-Tah, my favorite meal was Tasajo made from horsemeat, cooked in olive oil and sautéed onions. The tasajo was later added to rice and beans and fried or boiled yucca. Soon, Ulyses and I began to roam into other neighborhoods.

In time we discovered Brickell Key, a forty four acre deserted tropical island covered with trees, native grasses and sandy trails. It was located many miles away from our homes. Our newly found playground was connected by a bridge to downtown Miami. A hole in the fence allowed us to trespass into the immense paradise. Once on the Island, we played for hours through the endless trails. When tired, we rested under the shade of the many Australian Pines and Coconut Palms. A peanut butter and jelly sandwich was all the fuel we needed to carry on. Needless to say, we were happy kids, doing simple things.

Today I look at Brickell Key with sadness. The once tropical and beautiful island is filled with concrete and high rises. Ulyses and I were the last generation to see it as it was meant to be. Sometimes I think we were the last generation to have lived when life was simple and choices were easy.

We also spent a lot of time playing at Sewell Park on 17th Avenue and South River Drive. Across from the park were two caves. People called these natural wonders the Indian Caves. They were located inside a high limestone ridge next to a creek. Each cave had two entrances big enough for a human to walk upright. One of the openings led to a spring fed creek that flowed into the Miami River. According to local folklore, those caves once provided shelter for the true Miami Natives, The Tequesta Indians.

Miami River Indian Caves, ca. 2006 ****

Miami River Indian Caves
Cave's side view that leads to creek off the Miami River
****

Each cave measured approximately twenty by thirty feet. Although we could walk to them, Ulyses and I preferred the silent approach of our canoe. This drew less attention from the neighbors and it gave us more fun time without being harassed by police.

One of the caves, sat adjacent to a creek. Once inside that cave, we would tap on the water and waited for manatees to appear. Upon the arrival of the gentle sea cows, Ulyses and I enjoyed the thrill of a short ride by jumping on their backs. Once done with the ride, the playful animals returned over and over as if they enjoyed the activities as much as we did. Today the caves are owned by the Miccosukee-Tribe of Indians of Florida. Hopefully they will remain unchanged for future generations to appreciate.

Another Tequesta cave was found in the small town of El Portal, just north of Miami's eastern city limits. The cave had a small entrance and it was about six square feet inside. It was tucked inside a huge Tequesta burial mound located about one hundred and fifty feet from the edge of the Little River.

Most of our adventures occurred either on weekends or during school breaks. While in Junior high school, Ulyses and I began playing football. As a result our popularity increased, especially with the girls. Ulyses and I had more girls than other kids our age, which meant trouble. Fighting over them was a common thing. Assault and battery was a foreign language to us. In those days people simply fought things out.

Those fun days ended when I turned thirteen and began working every weekend as a dishwasher at The Racket Club, an upscale restaurant located on North Bay Village, adjacent to the City of Miami. Both my uncles worked there. It was also the place where I got my nickname 'Siggy'. I made forty-five dollars before taxes for my two eight hour days.

When there were no dishes to wash, I helped my Uncle Rene in the kitchen and my uncle Ta-tah with the setting of the tables for the weekend buffets. As the meals were consumed, it was my duty to replace the food trays when empty. That was the part I hated the most. While all the rich customers wore their fancy suits and expensive dresses, I wore my dirty apron. I felt as if the whole world was staring at me, especially those beautiful women that were dressed to kill.

In 1974, I began working at a print shop after school hours. It was great having weekends off, which gave me free time to hang out with Ulyses. Things got even better when I purchased my first motorcycle. It was a 1973 Honda SL 125 Enduro, which meant it was made to ride in the streets as well as on the dirt. Because of that versatility, I was able to convince my parents to keep it at my aunt's house.

My aunt had moved out of the city limits and onto the western section of rural Dade County, in the vicinity of West Flagler Street and 129th Avenue. The swampy area was known as Mosquito Country, due to its proximity to the Florida Everglades, home to the Miccosukee and Seminole Indians.

The Everglades, considered a national treasure, is one of the largest wetlands in the world. It consists of a shallow sheet of fresh water that flows slowly over the lowlands and through billions of blades of sawgrass. The movement of water causes the sawgrass to ripple like waves. As a result, the Everglades are also known as the "River of Grass." Originally, this natural wonder extended over 3,000,000 acres from Lake Okeechobee to the Florida Bay. The vast body of water began to change after the arrival of new settlers in the early 1900's.

In 1948, Congress authorized a multi-purpose project that provided flood control, water supply for municipal, industrial, and agricultural uses.

The primary system included over a 1,000 miles of levees, over 700 miles of canals and almost 200 control structures. This project went on for decades. By early 1970's, it had successfully dried out over 1,000,000 acres of land, thus giving birth to Mosquito Country, which later became known as Horse Country. The small rural area was full of dirt roads and rock pits, which made it ideal for horseback riding and off road four wheeling. The newly discovered haven became my playground, and I took full advantage of its rich resources, horses. They were always my true passion.

In 1975, armed with a restricted driver's license, I began driving my motorcycle on the streets of Miami. That allowed me to pick up Ulyses and bring him to my newly discovered oasis. Within a short period of time, the area became the victim of our somewhat delinquent lifestyle. Together, we began to perfect the art of 'borrowing' horses.

Unlike today, open pastures were very common; even more ordinary was finding herds of horses along with cattle in those fields. Most parcels of land were divided by poorly constructed scrap wood fences. As a result it was not unusual for the owners to have a few animals missing. Most horses we took found themselves back home after we released them, which made them available for us to take at a later date. The few that didn't make it back, we doubt seriously that they were missed, or so we thought. That justified our actions and took our guilty feelings away. We borrowed every grazing horse and rode them until they got tired, or should I say we got tired.

Our favorite spot to take breaks was on a coral ridge next to a canal that was canopied by Australian Pines. It was located near Krome Avenue and Tamiami Trail. It was during those breaks, that Ulyses would always ask me about the Apaches, *"Siggy tell me about the Apaches? Do you know any words?"* Unfortunately, I did not have much to share, other than the little that my Mom knew of her past and heritage. I spoke to him of those times and her knowledge about herbal medicine.

Our breaks were short, consisting of watering the horses and stretching our legs. Heading back was our favorite part of the trips, as the horses ran full gallop, knowing that they were returning home. These were fun times for Ulyses and me, leaving very little time for anything else.

Ulyses' girlfriend at the time, a rich white girl by the name of Laura, did not agree with the way we borrowed horses. In a fruitless attempt to stop our criminal activities and/or spend more time with Ulyses, she bought us our first legally owned horse. We named the Appaloosa gelding 'Apache'. Unbroken, high spirited and very strong, it became the first horse we broke. Not knowing the right way to break a horse in, we took turns running him in circles around the corral until he began to show signs of wearing down. After that, we tied him to a pole and saddled him up. Then we released the rope and watched him run and buck wildly. The next step was to hold him by the holster while Ulyses and I took turns riding him. Surprisingly, we had discovered another way to satisfy our need for a thrill. I loved the explosive power in which the horse took off. The bucking was the icing on the cake. The hard to describe rush was addictive. We repeated this process until the horse was subdued to our satisfaction. At times our actions may have seemed harsh and maybe even cruel, but deep inside we loved the animal that so clearly expressed our own restless spirit.

Soon after, Ulyses and I began to break in horses for the many ranches in the area. One in particular was the Golden Eagle Ranch. The facility was well known to locals for their hourly horse rental. The prosperous business provided us with a way to supplement our income.

This allowed me to work fewer hours at the print shop and spend more time doing what I really loved.

In time, our expeditions into the outer areas of Mosquito Country became longer and our adventurous spirits led us deeper and deeper into the western swamps. There we found an abundance of wild life, in particular, the American Alligator. It was perhaps its vicious reputation that encouraged us to start messing with the prehistoric beast.

By the age of fifteen, I was sure that I could catch an alligator by myself. Encouraged by Ulyses, I jumped into the shallow, murky water and successfully caught my first gator. In a short period of time our confidence grew and so did the size of the alligators we picked on. Looking for bigger ones, meant riding deeper into no man's land.

One day as we rode further west, in search of alligator holes, we came across a high levee *(manmade barriers, built by the Corp of Engineers to dry out the land)*. After climbing it, we noticed something unusual in the distant horizon. As we rode closer, the concealed structures began to reveal themselves. Indeed we had discovered what turned out to be a Miccosukee Indian camp.

The village consisted of clusters of Chickee Huts, (*traditional dwellings unique to the Seminoles and Miccosukee people.*) Because it was late, we turned back, but my curiosity was peaked. The following weekend, instead of going to the beach with Ulyses in his newly purchased 1967 GTO, I broke away and decided to ride west into the swamplands in search of the Indian village.

On a cool early morning in February of 1976, I saddled up Apache and rode west for about ten miles. About two hours later, I arrived at a Miccosukee camp, where I met a welcoming family. I am not able to recall all of their names other than they were Tigers' and Osceolas'. The first one to greet me was a slim older man with short hair parted on the side and combed backwards. He was sitting under an open Chickee wearing a patchwork long sleeve shirt, blue pants and barefooted. After introducing myself, I proceeded to tell him about my ancestors being Apaches and their journey to Florida and Cuba.

Traditional Miccosukee Village along the Tamiami Trail ****

23

Traditional Miccosukee Chickee homes along the Tamiami Trail ****

He seemed to have known about it and began telling me about a journey that he and other Miccosukees made to Cuba in 1959, in an effort to pressure the U.S. government into signing their independence. He also explained how his ancestors were kept as prisoners at Fort Marion. He asked me if I had ever visited the Fort. *"No, it sounds like a long ride,"* I said jokingly, as I pointed to my tired horse. The Miccosukees did not show great interest in horses. Their mode of transportation had gone from horses and dugout canoes to modern airboats and swamp buggies. When the memorable visit ended, I was invited to return and learn more about their history.

Two weekends later, I eagerly rode west towards the Miccosukee camp to meet with my new friends. During that visit, I leaned about two Seminole leaders, a warrior named Osceola and a Medicine Man named Abiaka. It took many years before I understood how the two legendary leaders had contributed to the very existence of my newly found friends.

Osceola, a master of guerrilla warfare, not only masterminded many successful battles against a handful of baffled U.S. generals, but took punitive action against any Seminole who cooperated with the enemy. He stood as a defiant trademark of the Seminoles' strong reputation for non-surrender. In 1837, Osceola was captured under a flag of truce; he was put on a horse and taken prisoner to Fort Marion, Florida along with 76 warriors and 6 women. He was later taken to Fort Moultrie in Charleston, South Carolina, where he died on January 30, 1838.

Abiaka (AKA Sam Jones) was the inspirational and powerful spiritual leader, who used his 'medicine' to provoke and mentally prepare his warriors into battle. His relentless objection to removal kept a strong fight before and after Osceola's period of prominence. When the fighting concluded, Abiaka was the only major Seminole leader to remain in Florida.

24

SIGGY'S CHILDHOOD-ADULTHOOD

On later visits to the Miccosukee camp, I got to ride on one of their airboats for the first time. The boat had rows of seats, where some of my Miccosukee friends and I sat. The driver sat up high above us, on a single pedestal seat. That was the first time I saw the swamps from a different perspective. During later visits, I began to learn the history of the Everglades and appreciate the love that the Miccosukees had for the beautiful place they called home.

In the spring of 1976, I bought my first car, a 1968 GTO; it was yellow with a black vinyl top. Ulyses and I spent endless hours detailing our "Goats" before driving out to teenage clubs. One club in particular was called 'Skips'. It was located on old Davie Road, in the town of Davie, about an hour north from our homes. One Friday, prior to going to Skips, Ulyses and I decided to dye our hair blonde. We figured that by doing so, we would fit right in with the other guys at the club. Most of them were blonde and had light colored eyes, even more so in Davie, a town well known for cowboys and good old boys driving pickup trucks and flying Rebel flags.

After buying the hair dye, I was chosen to try it first. I remember Ulyses donning plastic gloves and massaging my head with the foul smelling chemical. A few minutes into the procedure, Ulyses began to laugh. Although I was not able to see what was so funny, I knew that things were not going well. I remember walking to a mirror hesitantly, almost afraid of what I was going to see. To my surprise, my long black hair had turned bright orange. We both looked at each other and said the same thing. Holy shit! Not knowing what to do, I drove home in a hurry before my Dad got home. My Mom gave me a big lecture on how beautiful my natural color hair was, as she proceeded to re-dyed my hair black. Needless to say, that was the last time I attempted a stunt like that.

In the summer of 1976, my family moved from Miami to the neighboring City of Hialeah (*Miccosukee word for High Prairie*). Its landscape was dotted with cattle and horses. Nightlife consisted of country western clubs and bars, but I was interested in other things, like martial arts. I had just received my brown belt in judo and to top it off, the Junior Olympics sponsored by Chevrolet were going to be held in Florida. I made the team and won the gold medal in my class. Distance and my busy schedule meant less contact with my old pal Ulyses. Although he only lived fifteen miles away, our time together went from seeing each other almost daily to just hanging out on occasional weekends.

During my high school years I began to spend a lot of time at a place called Lost Lake, a hidden oasis known only to locals. It was located in the town of Miami Lakes, west of 12th Avenue and south of the Dade/Broward County line. The area was full of muddy trails that cut deep into the Everglades. The place was a true haven for off-road enthusiast. On any given weekend, dozens of sand buggies, dirt bikes and every make and model of 4x4 pickup trucks were found there. A hidden lake the size of two football fields was the favorite spot for local girls to sunbathe. People brought their horses and dogs and camped for days on end, free of any hassles.

Although everyone was friendly, most people stuck to their relevant groups. Those with dirt bikes like me rode in big packs, while the other groups in ATV's, and Sand Buggies went on their separate ways. The trails cut through heavy wooded areas, mainly consisting of Brazilian Pepper Trees, Melaleucas and Australian Pines. Some of these trails seemed endless, going on for miles and miles. One of the most challenging bike trails ended on Krome Avenue and Okeechobee Road. There, an old wooden-shack general store sold homemade lemonade and snacks.

After hours of splashing mud, getting stuck in the mud and a sustained brutal physical beating caused by my Kawasaki KX 420, nothing tasted better then that cold homemade lemonade! Today Rancho Okeechobee sits where the old wooden store used to be. That kind of weekend activity went on for years. My bike was a two-stroke powerhouse very few could tame. I had graduated to it after having many other smaller bikes. On the streets I rode a Honda CB 750 and later a Yamaha RD 400. Airbrushing was a big thing in those days. Most of my bikes and helmets were custom painted. My helmet had Geronimo's face painted in the back of it.

In 1980, I moved on to the track and began drag racing. My bike was a Kawasaki Mark II 1000 with an 1105 Yoshimura kit, running at approximately 115 mph and low 11's in the quarter mile, pretty good numbers for those early days.

Siggy Second-Jumper in the near lane drag racing his 1979 Kawasaki 1000cc
Moroso Speedway, Palm Beach, FL. ca 1982

At age nineteen I started college and began working as a bouncer at a couple of strip nightclubs in the Miami area. I used to get off work in the morning and go straight to school. It was amazing that I was able to maintain a passing grade. Working the night shift and trying to maintain such a crazy schedule was exhausting. As a result, I switched jobs and began working in the auto leasing industry during the day, and going to school at night.

My major in college was Optometry, but after learning more about it, I knew it was not for me. Soon after, I realized that I wanted to be a doctor (M.D.). I began making arrangements to go to medical school in the Dominican Republic. Those dreams came to an end when the U.S. stopped accepting credits from that country's medical schools. The closest thing to my dream of being a Doctor was to be a paramedic, or so I thought.

In 1982, I started the EMT-Paramedic program and two years later, I had graduated with honors. Ulyses opened his own gym; he went on to win many major titles in bodybuilding, including Mr. America, Mr. Southern States, and Mr. Florida, just to name a few.

SIGGY'S CHILDHOOD-ADULTHOOD

In 1984, I became a Volunteer Firefighter/Paramedic for the City of Miramar. In exchange for my free services, I was enrolled in Fire College. By late 1984, I had graduated as a certified firefighter. My hard work and sacrifices paid off and in 1985, I was hired as a professional Firefighter on the southern west coast of Florida.

The relocation created a complete separation from my old pal Ulyses. Because I was different and not Anglo, I found myself once more isolated from social groups. That loneliness opened a desire in me to seek out people like myself. As a result, I began to look for local Pow Wows. I was thrilled to find a few that were sponsored by a Seminole lady from Naples, Florida. These events were staged meetings where people sold crafts, sang, danced, and socialized. There I felt more at home and easier in spirit. Over time I began to learn the art of Northern traditional dancing.

In December of 1986, I was hired by the City of Miami Fire Department, where I am presently employed. While attending their Fire Academy, I was forced to cut my hair short. That was the hardest thing for me to do. My long hair made me feel proud and it represented to the outside world, a statement of my roots as an Apache descendant. Because of those feelings, it really felt strange going from long hair to a crew cut. It was mandatory and without malice, even the women were forced to cut theirs.

After graduating from Miami Fire College, I was assigned to a district to start all over again as a rookie. It didn't take me long to see the kind of work force I had joined. It was a true 'good old boys club.' The hateful looks I got, reminded me of my younger days. Some Officers did not even talk to me, the ones that did, belittled and insulted me. The hostile environment continued through the nineties. Most of those good old boys have since retired and the ones that remained had no choice but to hypocritically hide their true feelings after a great influx of different minorities groups were hired.

The privilege of being a Firefighter/Paramedic/Registered Nurse has allowed me to touch and/or help people in their greatest times of need. It has also permitted me to raise my family with comfort and dignity and enjoy many things that my parents were unable to provide for me. I give thanks to the Creator every day for such a gift.

In early 1990, I began nursing school at Miami-Dade College. While attending a mandatory nursing skills lab and in the process of bathing a mannequin, a group of female nursing students walked in. Among them was a young girl by the name of Ana Cossio, who began to make fun of me. She got my attention and in a very short time we began dating. Our relationship grew stronger and we fell in love. Ana and I got married in late 1990. We both graduated from nursing school in 1992 as Registered Nurses. It was a big milestone, since I was the first member in my family to attend and graduate from College.

After marriage, we moved into my townhome in the City of Hialeah, we later bought a bigger house on the outskirts of the Everglades in west Broward County. Ana and I traveled through Indian country while I sang and danced. It was an incredible experience that we both enjoyed.

In 1993, I experienced the most powerful moment in my life, the birth of my daughter. That special moment was enhanced by the fact that I delivered her myself. Seven years of experience as a medic, and a few deliveries, gave me the confidence to welcome her into this world. I was proud to know that my hands were the first to touch and carry her to her Mother's breast.

I named her Emily, after a hurricane that was menacing to hit the South Florida area. The news had made a big deal out of it. After all, it had only been a year since South Florida was devastated by a category 5 hurricane named Andrew.

27

By the time my daughter was one month old, she had attended her first Pow Wow in Jacksonville, Florida. It was called Discover Native America, or DNA and it was sponsored by the Seminole Tribe of Florida. In time, Emily became so used to them, that she was able to fall asleep next to a contest drum

Bloodline Search

Chapter Six

The birth of my daughter Emily inspired me to look deeper into my roots. In 1994, I learned through a cousin living in Cuba what my ancestors looked like and where they were from. My cousin had researched the information through the Civil Department and Catholic Church records. Through her I learned that my great- grandmother Ku-kah was born in Cañada Alamosa, Mexico. My great-grandfather Florentino was from Sierra Madre, Mexico. Some of the names found in various documents were Chenesgue (Cheneske), Jumper, Segunda, and Jose Segundo. Although the information did not change my daily activities, it affected me each evening as I attempted to sleep. With each passing day, my desires to find anyone or anything related to me grew into an obsession.

In the summer of 1995, while driving in the streets of Miami, I noticed a Mitsubishi Eclipse with an Eagle on it's out of state license plate. The unusual and beautiful tag caught my attention. I pulled up next to the car and noticed what appeared to be an Indian woman driving it. I waved at her and signal her to pull over. Her name was Jana Stacey and she had just moved to Miami from Indiana. During our short conversation, I told her I was an Apache and a traditional dancer. She told me she was a Lakota and a fancy dancer herself. Jana and I became good friends. Soon we discovered that we had much in common. To begin, we were both non-reservation Indians, with no language or ties to our ancestor's tribes or clans. Despite all the things that we were not, Jana and I were part of a small percentage of Native American descendants that were interested in connecting or reconnecting with their past. On a minor level, we discovered that we both were interested in Native American beadwork as a hobby and a craft. With Jana's help, I learned different styles of beadwork, and the tricks and shortcuts of the trade. The result was that my own work with beads simple in scope and design expanded and became more refined.

As we got to know each other on a deeper level, Jana began telling me of her search for her biological family. She and her siblings had been adopted as infants by different white families from the Lakota Reservation in Pine Ridge, South Dakota. After the birth of her daughter, Jana felt it was her responsibility and obligation to find her roots. She visited Pine Ridge in search of relatives. Unable to find anyone related to her, she consoled herself with dancing and joining different Indian groups. She became very involved in the studies of Tribal Law. Later, she joined the American Indian Movement (AIM) in protest of the grave desecrations that were going on in Union Town, Kentucky. Jana was a very strong and proud woman, but most of all, she was a teacher and a motivator who believed, *that if one has even a drop of Indian blood running through their veins, then it is the duty of that person to search out the legacy of the past and come to understand one's role as a Native American and the ways and traditions of one's people.* Her ideas and encouraging words, along with those of my Seminole friends and the birth of my daughter were the contributing factors that truly motivated me into doing something about my obsession of finding my Apache roots.

While growing up, I had so many unanswered questions. Who were my ancestors? What did they look like? How did they live? Although my Cuban cousin had answered those questions, my curiosity ran deeper. I knew in time my daughter would start asking similar questions of her own. Not only did I want to give her more information than it was given to me by my mom, but I also wanted to tell the story with a sense of pride, instead of pain, tears, and shame.

Siggy Second-Jumper, Northern Traditional Dancer, ca. 1995

In March of 1996, a Pow Wow was held in the City of St. Augustine, Florida. I saw it as an opportunity for my family and me to learn more about Fort Marion, the last place that saw all of my ancestors together. After a five-hour drive, we arrived in St. Augustine in the late morning hours. After driving a few miles through congested and narrow cobblestone streets, we arrived at one of the many Trolley stations that were part of the charm of the city. We boarded the train and began our tour of the sights in the oldest city in the U.S.A. I found the trip to be very informative, and a much more practical way to visit the many tourist attractions. As the tour continued, I couldn't help to notice all the statues throughout the city that commemorated the Spanish Conquistadors. As a result, I experienced feelings of ambivalence. After all, their blood also ran through my veins. How could these people be regarded as heroes after all the destruction they had caused? Their cruel actions destroyed civilizations. I felt ashamed.

Our next stop consisted of various attractions such as the oldest school-house and the oldest pharmacy along with a modern restaurant. We decided to go to the restaurant, but the stress from so much inner turmoil prevented me from eating. After a quick tour of the school and pharmacy, we got back in the trolley and proceeded to our next attraction.

The conductor stated that our next stop was going to be Castillo de San Marcos, formally Fort Marion. From the street, the old stone fort appeared to be ancient, like a timepiece. Upon arriving at the gate, I realized there was a fee to get in, which I refused to pay. A park ranger was called to solve the dilemma. I explained that an entrance fee was something that my Apaches ancestors had paid long ago. After some thought on the matter, he agreed to let us in for free. We crossed the bridge and entered the Fort. Its massive, dark gray stone walls gave me a sensation of having entered a prison. Once inside, it felt cool and humid, and there was a repugnant smell of mold.

After visiting half a dozen cells, we climbed some stairs that led us to the rampart, where a soft and cool ocean breeze rolled in from the east. When I looked down, towards the center courtyard, I saw the room where the Apache prisoners had to bathe in full view of the guards. That shameful experience has been orally passed down for generations.

From there, we walked over to the eastern perimeter wall where the breeze seemed to intensify. As I looked down, I began to observe the cannon ball damage sustained throughout the entire defensive fortification. It appeared that the old fort had seen a lot of action in the past.

My thoughts took me back to 1886, as I tried to picture in my mind what my family must have felt like, living among five hundred plus Apaches in one hundred and forty Sibley tents in an area of approximately one square acre.

Coned shaped Sibley tents on Fort Marion's north ramparts, ca. 1886 From the F.W. Bruce Collection, photos provided by Mr. Cleve Powell.

While facing east, I began to pray for my ancestors and thanked God that I had made the trip. My daughter, oblivious to the history of the place ran and played innocently. How ironic, a place that witnessed so much sadness and pain from my ancestors had turned into a playground filled with joy and laughter for my daughter!

Tents used to accommodate the Apache P.O.W. at Ft. Marion, FL ca. 1886
From the F.W. Bruce Collection, photos provided by Mr. Cleve Powell.

At that moment, I began to think about life and realized how lucky I was to be standing here as a free man. I looked to the sky and humbly prayed again. After spending hours there with mixed emotions, my family and I left the fort. Once back in the trolley, we skipped the rest of the attractions and checked into a hotel.

The next day, we woke up to a crystal clear blue sky and eagerly drove to the park where the Pow Wow was being held. Upon arrival, we were welcomed by a cool, gentle ocean breeze. The smell of salt and water seemed to energize me with every breath I took. I stood under an oak tree and began to pray for a strong dance. I wanted the crowd to see that the Chiricahuas had persevered. After entering the arbor (*the traditional round dancing arena*), I felt as if I had gone into a trance. At that moment, I realized that despite all government efforts to annihilate the Chiricahuas, they had failed to succeed. I was filled with pride and in a small way I felt unconquered. I danced hard, trying to hurt myself. I wanted to pay homage to my ancestors for the agony they had suffered and the pain they endured. They never once gave up, and their will to live was the reason I was dancing that day. Looking up at the blue sky, I felt a wave of emotions so powerful that I cried out a prayer. Later I was told that I had danced like never before and that it seemed as if I was floating, as my feet barely touched the earth.

In the spring of 1996, shortly after the St. Augustine Pow Wow, I met two individuals who became very influential in my life. The first was Kevin, a Southern Paiute, who was visiting Florida from the state of Nevada. He was a Sun Dancer many times over, a great singer and drum maker. Kevin taught me a great deal, from running sweat lodges to making pipes and drums.

He also gifted me with many Sun Dance songs, which I still know to this day. Kevin spent a lot of time fine-tuning my dance style and teaching me how to conduct myself in the dance arena.

The second individual was the late Boo Boo Ann Jumping Eagle. She was a Lakota Indian from Pine Ridge, South Dakota, and a descendant of Crazy Horse. She lived in the Tampa Bay area in Florida. Her teachings and support guided me further into the Native American Circle, also known as the Pow Wow Circle. In time, we referred to each other as Mother and Son. Under the watchful eyes of these two wonderful mentors, I grew and prospered to competitive levels. In time, I became a true dancing machine. I am thankful for their guidance.

L to R: Boo Boo Ann Jumping Eagle and Sonja Boekhurst
Orlando, FL, ca. 2000
****

From 1996-98, I danced at two of my favorite events. The first one was held at the Cherokee Ceremonial Grounds in the state of North Carolina. What made this Pow Wow special to me was the warm welcome I received by the Cherokee People and the beauty that surrounds their country.

The second event was the Schemitzum Pow Wow, hosted by the Pequot Indians in their reservation in the state of Connecticut. It was considered to be the biggest gathering of Indians in North America, with thousands of dancers from all over the continent, along with more than seventy invited drums.

Siggy Second-Jumper,Northern Traditional Dancer, ca. 1996

Because of the enormous amount of competitors, I only danced a few songs per day. The short lasting experience was priceless, as I found myself competing against the best in the world.

Just when I thought things couldn't get better, my wife informed me she was pregnant again. Shortly after, on a hot summer night I had a dream where I saw a boy carrying a lance and a pipe. The next morning I told my wife of my dream and my desire to name our unborn child Lance, if it turned out to be a boy.

In 1997, my son Lance was born. Like his sister, he was also delivered by me. Again, it was my hands that first touched and carried him to his mother's breast. I felt like I was the luckiest man in the world. Both my children were healthy and that's all I had prayed for. I was a happy Dad. My world revolved around going to work, spending time with my family, singing and dancing. What else could anyone ask for? Both my children were growing up listening to the cries of lead singers, the sound of jingles and beating drums.

In March of 1997, along with the birth of my son, came another blessing. I was invited to join a northern singing group out of the Hollywood Seminole Reservation. There are two styles of singing in the competitive circuit. They are referred to as Northern and Southern.

Drum practice at the Seminole Village, Hollywood ca. 1997
L to R: John, William Cypress, Siggy Second-Jumper

The Northern style has a much higher pitch sound than its counterpart. The Southern style has a deeper and lower tone of voice. The singers surround a large drum on which they pound a baton as they chant the songs associated with their style.

The name of Our Northern style group was called Red Bear; the drum keeper and lead singer was Ray, a Navajo from the Mud Clan out of Window Rock, Arizona. Among our singers were my friends William Cypress, a Florida Seminole and a member of the Panther Clan, John, a Dakota Sioux from Minnesota, and Duke, an Apache from Colorado. Practices were held on Tuesdays and Thursdays at the Hollywood Seminole Reservations, either at William's home or at the Seminole Native Village.

Our Drum traveled the southeastern circuit, which consisted mostly from Florida to North Carolina. We were all dancers as well as singers. William, Duke, and I were Northern Traditional dancers. Our style of dancing mimicked a scout or a hunter tracking the enemy or game.

Ray and John were Grass Dancers. Among them was the youngest member of our dance troop, a young Seminole by the name of William K. Osceola. Little William, as we called him, was welcomed into the sacred circle as a Grass Dancer. That particular style of dancing goes back to the old days when nomadic tribes arrived at a new campsite. The Grass Dancers danced the tall grass down, thus clearing the area prior to setting camp on it. Along with their dance were their prayers and blessings. It is a Medicine Dance. Little William went on to become a Grass Dance Champion; his devotion was proudly supported by his parents, William Sr. and Peggy, who attended many of his competitions. William Osceola Sr. was a Traditional Seminole and member of the Panther Clan. *(Traditional, meaning he maintains and follows the lifestyle of his ancestors).* Peggy was an Oklahoma Seminole.

William K. Osceola, Seminole Panther Clan, Grass Dancer, ca. 2000

William Osceola Sr. Seminole Panther Clan, ca. 2007 ****

In time, I felt the responsibility and obligation to search deeper into my past, not only for the sake of my kids, but for my very own. With each passing day, my desire grew stronger and stronger, like a calling if you will. *Are there any others left alive?* I asked myself. I grew up similar to my mother and grandmother, not knowing of any other Chiricahuas that had survived. By 1998, I was determined to find out. I planned a trip with my family across the country, from the east coast of Florida to the mountains of New Mexico and Arizona. I figured somewhere along that path; I was going to find someone or something that was left behind. Our first destination was 'Castillo De San Marcos' (*formally Fort Marion*) in St. Augustine, Florida.

Emily and Lance ****
Fort Marion, FL

On that second visit, my attitude was quite different than on my previous one. Upon arrival, I introduced myself to a park ranger. I was polite and paid attention to his tour, where I learned the following information:

1) On April 16, 1886, Chief Chihuahua arrived at the Fort with 14 warriors, 33 women, and 29 children ages 7 to 20.
2) September 18, 1886, Chatto's band of 10 men and 3 women arrived.
3) Two days later another 383 prisoners arrived including 68 men, 159 women and 156 children.
4) On October 24, 1886, Geronimo, Naiche, Mangus were left at Fort Pickens, Florida, while their 11 women, 6 children and 2 men were sent to join the rest of the P.O.Ws. at Fort Marion.
5) November 7, 1886, 3 women, and 7 children arrived.
6) 12 infants were born in captivity at Fort Marion.

Warriors in captivity at Fort Pickens were: Chappo; Perico; Fun; Yahnozha; Ahnandia; Hunlona; Besh; Zhonne; Nah-bay (Na-pa; Nahi); La-zai-yah (Laziyah); Motsos; Kilthdigai; Tissnolthos

Apache Chiefs in captivity at Fort Marion were: Chihuahua; Nana; Joana; Cathenay; Catia; Josonna; Hosannah; Karntnea; Dutchy; Jose.

Apache Scouts at Fort Marion were: Gout-kill; Izilgan; Toklanni; Noche; Chatto; Martinez; and Keita.

Some of the Apache women in captivity at Fort Marion were: Ha-o-zinne, Naiche's wife. Bi-ya-neta, Perico's wife. Tah-das-te, Ahnandia's wife. Nah-chlon, Chappo's wife. Belle, Fun's wife. Ugohun, Besh's wife. Huana(?), Jose Second's wife. Maria Jose, Jose First's wife. Yahnozha's wife. Nahbay's wife. Laziyah's wife. Tisnolthos's wife.

Some of the Apache Children born in Fort Marion were: Coquina, daughter of Chihuahua and Marion, daughter of Geronimo (*name changed to Lenna later*).

After an enjoyable and informative experience in St. Augustine, my family and I returned home.

A week later we flew out to Las Vegas, Nevada where we rented a car for our trip across Arizona and New Mexico. The first place we visited was Fort Apache and the San Carlos Apache Reservations. Unfortunately the four-day visit did not go well and the outcome was not positive. The Apaches I met there were either unable or unwilling to discuss their past or answer my questions. Disappointed but determined, we headed east on I-10. We were about to reach the New Mexico-Arizona state line when we came upon the Fort Bowie area. It was there that my ancestors were taken after surrendering to U.S. General Crook.

I was amazed and disappointed at how desolate the area was. With no one to talk to and nothing to do, I felt that my quest had reached a dead end in the state of Arizona. *"Will my luck change in New Mexico?"* I wondered. Feeling optimistic, we pushed on. Shortly after, a sign welcomed us to the State of New Mexico. After driving for a couple of hours, we decided to stop for a much needed rest in Deming, a small town in New Mexico. There we found the majority of the residents to be of Mexican descent with limited knowledge of Apache history.

The next morning we woke up to a blue and cloudless sky. To the south, the Florida Mountains rose majestically in the horizon. Little did I know that I was looking at one of the most sacred mountain range of the Chiricahua Apaches. After breakfast, we left Deming and headed towards our final destination, Monticello, New Mexico, formally known as Cañada Alamosa-Ojo Caliente. Monticello was approximately two hundred and twenty miles northeast of Deming.

An hour later we reached Las Cruces, New Mexico, where we merged onto Highway I-25 north in search of the tiny hamlet of Monticello. After driving seventy five miles or so, we noticed a billboard on the side of the highway that read, "Next exit, Geronimo Springs Museum." The sign lifted my spirit and gave me hope. *Could that be where Ojo Caliente was located?* I asked myself. It made sense to me, when translated into English, Ojo Caliente meant Hot Spring. The spring was definitively historical enough to become a museum and adding Geronimo's name to it made it more attractive. In my mind, I had it all figured out. My wife, on the other hand, was not so optimistic.

Without hesitation, I exited and entered the small town of Truth or Consequences, where Geronimo's museum was located. I don't think I saw more than one traffic light during my search.

What I saw in abundance were dozens of hotels advertising their sacred hot springs. I remained vigil in hope of finding the one that was meaningful to me. A short time later, I spotted the museum. I parked my car and was about to enter the facility when I noticed a young white man working on a sign. Hanging from his pocket was a beaded key chain with long leather fringe. That led me to believe he was Indian-friendly. I approached the young man and introduced myself as Siggy Jumper, a Warm Springs Apache descendant. I told him that I was traveling with my family in search of Ojo Caliente, the sacred springs of the Chiricahuas. *"Why do you want to go there?"* he asked. Based on his answer, I realized that I was in the wrong place. *"Cañada Alamosa/Ojo Caliente were places mentioned by my ancestors as their homeland. We would like to go there and see if we can find anyone or anything related to them or at least any reminisce of their existence,"* I replied.

I explained to the young man that during our week-long trip across three states we had not found anything but disappointment. *"I was hoping maybe you might be willing to help?"* I said. The young man wiped the sweat from his forehead and set down the sign. *"I wish I would have known about this earlier. It would have been my pleasure to take you guys out there myself,"* he said as he pointed to his faded yellow Dodge Ram 4x4 pickup truck. *"You won't make it out there in that!"* the young man said, as he referred to my rental car, a Dodge Stratus. By the look of his truck I realized that it had seen some rough country in its days. I told him I was willing to give it a try. He began to give me directions, but then decided to take me inside the museum to show me on a map. He appeared to have known all about the history of the Warm Springs-Chiricahuas, including their journey to Florida. Later, as the events of the future played out, it became clear just how significant this young man's knowledge and help would become.

Once inside the museum, I was greeted by an older lady working behind the counter. The young man asked her if he could borrow a few Apache books to show me a map and/or picture that would help me get there. The kind lady agreed and handed him a handful of books. I was shocked to see so many Apache books in one place. Back home at the book stores, the entire Native American section contained half of what they had there. After looking through a couple of books, he found one that contained a picture of a mountain range that was divided by a gap. He then pointed to a very distinctive round formation on the left side of the gap and said, *"That is what you are going to look for. That is where Ojo Caliente is located"*.

With some directions and that picture in mind, I headed out. I got back on highway I-25 and headed north. It was at that precise moment in time, when my life changed and my quest began. Caught in all that excitement, I had failed to ask the young man what his name was. Later I would fix that.

After driving a few miles on Highway I-25 north, I noticed a sign on a bridge that read Alamosa River. *"Could Alamosa River be related to Cañada Alamosa?"* I thought. After all Cañada means River or Creek in English. *"Could it be the town where my great-grandmother was from?"* I wondered. I was so excited over finding the Alamosa River sign that I almost missed the next exit, which read Cuchillo/Monticello.

According to the young man's directions, it was there that I needed to turn. I exited and headed west down what seemed to be an endless road. After driving for a few miles, the signs of civilization completely disappeared from my rearview mirror. We soon found ourselves surrounded by pure barren desert. Those were some of the most isolated roads I had ever traveled. In the horizon, a mountain range, tall and majestic, filled the landscape.

Isolated highway somewhere between T or C and Monticello, Sierra County, NM
**

Once I reached those mountains, I realized that it was not going to be easy locating the sacred spring. I was almost done driving through that mountain range, when I saw two small villages located in a remote valley below us.

As I approached the first of the two villages, a sign read Placitas. I estimated its population to be under twenty five. The small village was littered with abandoned vehicles, trailers, and homes. A few hundred yards further down the road, I entered the town of Monticello. It was also small but more populated and much cleaner. The first visible buildings were mainly made of adobe. I had gone no further than the center plaza, when a blonde lady in a white truck stopped me to find out who I was, and what if anything I was looking for. After a formal introduction and telling her my story, she suggested that I stop and see a gentleman by the name of Frank. According to her, Frank had a great deal of knowledge about the events that took place during and after the Apache removal. She escorted us to Frank's house, but unfortunately he was not home. After that, I asked her for directions to Ojo Caliente. *"Well you are not going to make it in that car. The spring is up the canyon and you will need a four wheel drive to get to it. I suggest that you go through the town of Cuchillo instead,"* she said. After giving me directions, I thanked her, and watched as she drove away.

Before leaving Monticello, we got out of the car and gave ourselves a self-guided tour. Most of the homes appeared to be very old, dating back to the 1800's. I wondered if some of those structures were around during the friendly interactions between the Warm Springs Apaches and its residents. I couldn't help but wonder if it was from there that my Mom's recipe for tamales originated. I wanted to stay longer and interact with the residents, but I didn't feel like I had enough time to do it all.

After looking inside an old church, we drove out in search of Cuchillo. Shortly after leaving Placitas and Monticello, I stopped the vehicle on a mountaintop and took one last look at the two small towns below. Suddenly I was filled with sadness. *"Will I ever see this place again?"* I wondered.

A while later I reached an intersection where a sign read Cuchillo. I made a right turn and headed west towards it. By then my daughter was beginning to get cranky. *"Daddy, I am bored. Can we please stop somewhere to get ice cream,"* my daughter Emily stated. *"Sure, Honey! We are going to get you some ice cream soon."* My wife Ana replied. Ana was also starting to get irritable and was beginning to show signs of restlessness and anxiety. She expressed being very uncomfortable with the terrain and its isolation. It was by far the furthest she had ever traveled away from civilization. I must admit that I took many glances at my fuel gauge and wondered if three quarters of a tank of fuel would get us there. After all, I had no idea where I was going, nor how far I had to go. In time, even I began to experience feelings of grouchiness, as my daughter kept asking for ice cream. We had all kinds of goodies in our cooler except ice cream of course. Oh how I just wanted to snap my fingers and come up with it. Trying to stay calm, I said, *"There is no ice cream here, Honey, can't you see we are in the middle of the desert?"* Emily quickly replied, *"Ok, Daddy, I can wait."* The look on my wife's face told me that she did not care to wait for anything anymore and that she felt the journey was getting out of hand.

After many miles, we reached the town of Cuchillo, named after Cuchillo Negro (Black Knife, in Spanish), a Warm Springs Apache Chief who lived, fought and died there. The village of Cuchillo consisted of a dozen or so old homes. Most of the structures were worn out by weather and time, showing cracks on their walls from many years of exposure. In the middle of town was a bar/store also called Cuchillo. I parked the car on the main street in front of the establishment and stepped out with my daughter.

Upon entering the store I saw an elderly lady with gray hair and large glasses standing behind the counter. *"Hi!"* I said. *"Do you have any ice cream by any chance?"* I asked. *"Well, of course we do!"* she replied while pointing to an ancient freezer with a solid lid in the middle of the store. As my daughter and I walked towards it, the old wood floor squeaked with each step we took. Somewhat embarrassed by the noise, I stopped in front of the freezer only to realize I did not know how to open it. *"Excuse me, can you help me here?"* I asked. *"Sure, give me one second"* she replied, as she came over and made it look easy. Once the freezer was opened, my daughter grabbed three ice cream sandwiches while I searched for sodas and chips. When I got to the counter, I was amazed by the cash register. It looked like an old typewriter with bells and whistles. I suppose the sweet old lady read my facial expression when she asked. *"Where are you folks from?"* *"Florida, my family and I are looking for Ojo Caliente Spring."* *"Son, you have a long ways to go."* She said. *"How far would you say?"* I asked. *"I am not sure, but a few more miles than you probably expect. I'd take some more provisions for your daughter if I were you,"* she replied with a tender smile. *"Thanks, I will."* I replied as I grabbed a hand full of goodies.

After our purchase, Emily and I walked back to the car where my wife sat quietly, listening to a country western station on the radio. *"How'd it go?"* she asked. *"Good, we found some ice cream and I bought you some chocolate."* At that she smiled, as I reached over and gave me a kiss on the cheek. Then we drove away. Within a few minutes, the ¾ inch layer of ice around the ice cream wrappers had melted. Once exposed, the ice cream sandwiches felt hard like a brick. They were old and tasteless.

My wife and I looked at each other and began eating ours without comment. We were both afraid that our daughter would pick up on the fact that we were eating some of the worse ice cream we ever had. Luckily Emily continued chipping away slowly without any complaints. That was a blessing indeed. The frozen concoction brought some peace and quiet to the car.

We continued our trip driving up and down some very steep rolling hills. Many miles later we arrived at Winston/Chloride, two small towns which stood nearly side-by-side. In the center of Winston was an old gas station that also served as a general store. Not wanting to take a chance of getting lost, I decided to go inside and ask for help, which was hard for me to do. Like a lot of men, asking for directions was something I hated to do. To my surprise, I found a lady behind the counter using a computer. I never expected to find such technology in a place like that. After all, it was 1998 and neither I nor anyone in my family owned a computer yet. *"Good afternoon. I am looking for Ojo Caliente; any chance you can tell me how to get to it?"* I asked. *"What is going on out there? Lately, there have been a lot of people looking for the spring as well."* She stated. *"I have no idea. It was my ancestor's home, and I would like to see it and talk to the people that live there."* I responded. *"Honey, no one lives there and I really don't know how to give you directions to get to it. I have not been to that spring in years. All I can tell you is that it is many miles away once you get on the dirt road."* Disappointed, I went outside to fuel up the car.

The gas pump was old style, with a huge glass window covering the actual manual rolling numbers. On the side of the pump casing, was a metal knob and handle to manually reset the pump. It was very similar to the ones used when I was a lad. The whole task was accomplished in less than ten minutes and away we drove.

A few miles later, the paved road turned to dirt, and with it came the sound of rocks hitting the bottom of the car. The only thing in sight were mountains and free roaming cattle. Some of them sat on the road while others got spooked and ran away. Determined to find the spring, I drove on. To my right was a continuous range of mountains that filled the landscape. To my left, open prairies stretched into the horizon. As the isolation and the noise from the rocks hitting the car increased, my wife entered a state of panic. *"What's going to happen if we break down over here? What are we going to do?"* She asked. I begged her not to talk like that, as I believed that not only by saying, but to even think of things like that can bring one's negative thoughts to a reality. *"Stop please, we are going to be just fine,"* I kept telling her in a fruitless effort to calm her down. It became harder to convince her as the road conditions continued to deteriorate. The loud banging noise made it feel ten times worse than it really was. Because I had grown up four wheeling, I knew the sound was insignificant. My wife on the other hand kept trying to convince me otherwise *"Siggy, look where we are! You are never going to find that place by looking at a picture. All these mountains look the same to me. We need to turn around now,"* she said. *"No, they are all very different, can't you see?"* I said, as I point out to different characteristics found throughout the mountain range. *"I am telling you, Siggy, you are not going to find anyone here to help you. It has been a week and yet you have found nothing or no one with any helpful information."* She said. Her truthful statement, almost had me convinced, but something inside kept me moving forward.

About half an hour later, I noticed a distinctive color on the walls of a distant canyon. The green-moldy looking gorge was very different than any others in the area. Immediately I saw the resemblance to the picture that the young man had shown me.

Sierra County, NM
View from the Box Canyon and Ojo Caliente
**

Full of anticipation, I kept driving towards the ravine. A short distance later, I noticed a side road that appeared to lead towards the place of interest. I proceeded to get on that path and quickly found out that it was in very bad shape. The rocky trail was extremely bumpy, full of potholes and huge rocks. I knew I had to slow down, or else the bottom of the car truly ran the risk of peeling off of like a can of sardines. The rough but slow ride had a calming effect on my wife Ana. Driving about a mile per hour, we continued our approach towards the distinctive canyon.

About an eighth of a mile later, I came up to a fence with a no trespassing sign on it. I ripped it off and threw it out like a Frisbee, hoping to play dumb in case I got stopped by a rancher or a ranger. My action triggered my wife to panic all over again. *"Siggy, let's turn around and leave before we get shot out here in the middle of nowhere,"* she said.

Determined to reach my target, I continued driving until I came upon a creek that ran across our path. I knew better than to cross it in a Dodge Stratus. I stopped there and got out of the car with my daughter. My wife, who was still in a state of panic, chose to stay behind, while Emily and I walked away towards the canyon. With each step we took, the sound of running water seemed to intensify. About a quarter of a mile later, we came upon an area where three streams of water came together to form a shallow river.

In time I learned that was the Alamosa River, its water ran through a mysterious corridor that cut through the middle of the canyon. I stood at the edge of that river in total amazement. Not knowing what to do in the presence of so much beauty and power, I held my daughter's hand and began to pray. After my prayer, I looked back toward the car, only to find it surrounded by cattle.

43

Without hesitating, Emily and I ran back to rescue her mom. By the time we reached the vehicle, most of the livestock had left and did not appeared interested in returning. Not surprised, I found Ana laying down in the front seat of the car covering her head with a blanket.

Siggy with Daughter Emily at Ojo Caliente, NM, ca. 1998

Even after the cattle cleared, she refused to step out of the car. She appeared frightened and speechless, and based on the look she gave me, furious. After giving her some time to compose herself, I asked if she wanted to join us. Again, she chose to remain in the car. A few minutes later, Emily and I began walking back towards the canyon again. Shortly after, we reached the spot where the three creeks met. As the cool water ran through our feet, I began to feel the essence of a mysterious power coming over me. Suddenly, I knew I was in the right place. Filled with emotions, I knelt down and brought myself face to face with my daughter. While holding her little hands, I said *"This is it; it is from here that our bloodline comes from. This is the place that witnessed the birth of our ancestors. I am glad you are here with me to share such a special moment and place."* Even though she was only four years old, I felt she cared because she remained quiet and attentive as I spoke to her. I felt a great sense of accomplishment knowing that I had reached a place in time as far back as I could trace my family.

The area was beautiful and peaceful, like what I pictured heaven might be, where God and man might come to hold hands. Influenced by so much beauty and power, I humbled myself and began to pray again. Once done, I cupped my shaking hand and proceeded to drink the holy water that rushed beneath us. I repeated the motion and gave some to my daughter as well. This was my way of baptizing ourselves, if you will.

It was at that moment, that I began to pay attention to my immediate surroundings. At that time, I was unaware that the trinities of water were independent and that only one originated from Ojo Caliente. Intrigued, I chose to follow one of the streams up a mountain in hopes of finding its origin as the true Ojo Caliente spring.

After climbing one hundred yards or so, I realized it was probably not a good idea to enter unfamiliar territory in the company of my little one. With some hesitation, I decided to turn around and head on back. By then my wife had come out of the car and was heading our way. Once she reached us, it was the same thing all over again. She kept looking over her shoulders, obviously uncomfortable and unable to relax. Even though the place was tranquil and beautiful, she continued nagging on for us to leave. After pleading with her for few minutes, we reached an agreement. With regret, I accepted not to stay longer than twenty more minutes.

With little time to spare, I looked at the mystifying corridor and decided to unveil its mystery. Against my wife's wishes, I walked into the mouth of the canyon by myself. I must admit that I felt overwhelmed. As I peeked through, the sheer walls curved to the left. The cold water running at my feet sent chills down my arms, as I continued to walk into the unknown.

A short distance later, I reached an area that resembled a *"Cathedral."* The jagged walls of the canyon seemed to be at its highest and adorned with pinnacles that resembled musical organ pipes. Because of the way the corridor twisted, it seemed as if I had reached a dead end. In a way, I felt I had entered God's Kingdom. The echo from the rushing water was loud, and honestly, even spooky. As a result, I felt small and vulnerable. With water running above my knees, I looked up to the skies and began to pray to the Creator. I thanked him for allowing me to be there and for all his blessings bestowed upon me and my family. After my prayers, I felt completely satisfied. I slowly began to walk back and realized I had made the most out of my limited time. A few minutes later I was welcomed by my family. My wife wanted to know what I had found. Still under the influence of so much beauty and power, I answered her question with the following statement, *"I think I found a Cathedral of Sacredness."*

Siggy and Emily visiting Cañada Alamosa/Ojo Caliente, NM in 1998

After taking some pictures, we began to head out. I remembered walking back to the car and feeling a sense of euphoria like I had never felt before. Everything around me looked so inspiring and full of life. Only those fortunate enough to have experience real love can relate to the way I felt that day. In just minutes, I had fallen in love with Ojo Caliente and its surrounding beauty.

Under a partly cloudy sky and a beautiful sunset, I grabbed my hand drum from the trunk of the car and began singing a song. The sound of rushing water complimented the echo of my drumbeat. Again I gave thanks to the Creator for all his gifts and blessedness. With limited sunlight to spare, we all got back in the car and I began to drive away. Through the rearview mirror, I saw the whole canyon getting smaller and slowly fading away. I soothed my sadness knowing that I would be back some day.

Once on the main dirt road, I drove north towards the town of Socorro. Luckily the road conditions improved with every mile driven. Sometime later, we passed the only visible home. It was an enormous hacienda located on a sprawling track of land. As we continued our drive, the landscape remained beautiful with majestic views of rolling hills and open prairies. We saw many longhorn sheep and cattle along the way. Deer crossed our path every now and then. About an hour later, we came across a very impressive sight. In the vastness of the landscape, some entity, government or otherwise, had installed many satellite dishes all perfectly spaced in row. We were all impressed with how giant they were and equally upset at how they destroyed the beauty of the prairie.

Shortly after, we came up to a paved road that led us to the town of Socorro. We then headed north on Highway I-25 to Albuquerque, where we met with my Navajo friend Ray and his Seminole wife at a Restaurant. While having dinner he and I spoke of the good old days in Florida when we sang and danced together. Our wives paid little attention, absorbed by their own topics of conversation

The next morning we flew back to Florida. In the safety and comfort of our home, my wife began to comment on all the beauty we had seen. We also talked about the young man at the museum who went out of his way to help me find the spring. I wanted to thank him, but shamefully realized that I didn't even know his name.

Late that afternoon, I decided to call the Geronimo Springs Museum to thank the young man personally. Ironically, the person that answered the phone was the lady that had provided him with various Apache books to show me Ojo Caliente and its surroundings. She remembered me and asked if I had any luck in finding the spring. *"Yes I did, I am calling to thank you and the young man for helping me out with my search."* I asked her if it was possible to speak to the gentleman. She informed me that he was a former museum employee, hired to do a single detail job on the day we met. I asked her if she knew his name. *"Yes of course, that's Apache Jack, but his real name is Jack Wood,"* she said. To my surprise she told me to hold on while she looked for his phone number.

I called Jack that evening and thanked him for his help. Little did I know that he would become one of the most significant people in the search for my Apache relatives. He was happy to hear that I had found the spring. Before hanging the phone, I asked him for his address. I wanted to make something for him to show my appreciation.

About a month later I mailed him a handmade leather bag with a small cross and a crescent moon beaded on it, a design I noticed on an old picture of Kukah and Florentino. That particular picture which I saw in 1995 went back to Cuba. Besides being old, it was hidden and mistreated for many years as my grandfather Angel did not allow my grandmother Segunda to display it.

46

As a result, it had sustained damages deemed too expensive for restoration. Jack and I stayed in contact through phone conversations. In time, our friendship grew and he began inquiring about my family's history in detail. Jack became sympathetic and began sending me Apache books from the museum's bookstore. Through those books, I learned about Morris Opler and Eve Ball, two respected writers who had chronicled a number of stories related to the Apache experience, specifically pertaining to the Chiricahua group. In reading those books, I learned about the Chiricahua prisoners of war, like Sam Kenoi and Eugene Chihuahua. They were amid the Chiricahuas who witnessed Apache children aboard a ship leaving Fort Marion, Florida.

In early 1999, I purchased a computer and e-mails made communication a lot easier between my new friend Jack and me. Shortly after, he informed me that his best friend and roommate, Carlos Enjady, was a Chiricahua Apache from Mescalero. They both lived in Truth or Consequences, New Mexico, also known as T or C. Through Jack's teaching I learned about the history of T or C, which was formally known as Hot Springs, New Mexico. For hundreds of years, humans have enjoyed the various medicinal benefits provided by the hot springs found throughout that town.

Legend has it that the Warm Springs Apaches, who called the region home, honored and respected the sacred hot spring so much that even their enemies were allowed to soak without fear of the consequences. It was great learning about something I knew so little about. In return, I began to share with Jack more specific information regarding my family's history.

In March of 1999, Jack e-mailed me saying that my family story had sparked an interest in his friend Carlos Enjady. An expert in the art of bead work, Carlos sent me a beaded key chain and a book called *The Mescalero Apaches* by C.L. Sonnichsen. It was through that book that I learned about the fate of the Chiricahua Apaches that were imprisoned in Florida in 1886. In 1913, after almost twenty eight years in captivity, they were set free by an act of Congress. Out of the two hundred and sixty five that survived, two-thirds chose to join their kin, the Mescalero Apaches, at their reservation in New Mexico. The rest chose to stay in or around Apache, Oklahoma, not far from Fort Sill, the last place that held them as prisoners.

In time, I learned that Carlos' family was among those that chose to relocate with the Mescaleros and that his grandmother Catherine Kenoi was one of only a handful of the surviving ex-prisoners of war. After learning her name, I thought of Samuel Kenoi. *How are they related?* I asked myself. *Was Catherine his wife, sister or daughter? Could she possibly know the stories, especially the one, where Samuel Kenoi witnessed young Apaches sailing away from Fort Marion, Florida.*

A few weeks later, Jack informed me that Carlos was inviting me to meet his grandmother during a family feast. I accepted his invitation with eagerness and without hesitation. Later I learned that the feast was held annually at the Mescalero Apache Reservation on the Fourth of July. The celebration is commonly referred to as The Maiden's Puberty Ceremony Feast or Sunrise Feast. It is done to honor those Apache girls who reached puberty. The four-day event was equivalent to "Quinces" or "Fifteenth" in the Spanish tradition, or what we know in America as Sweet Sixteen.

It was also a time of laughter and reunion, as Apaches from all over the country came to rejoice and celebrate. I was overjoyed with the invitation. How could I not be! Not only was I was going to meet Carlos, a Chiricahua, but his grandmother, an ex-prisoner of war who was related to the Kenois'. Filled with anticipation and enthusiasm, I patiently waited for the month of July to arrive.

As if that wasn't enough, another friend of Jack Wood, a gentleman by the name of Jack Noel, had started working for Denny and Trudy O'Toole, the owners of a ranch in the upper Monticello Canyon. According to Jack Wood, the O'Toole's property was either the same or near the ranch that I had visited a year earlier with my family. *"I believe their property is the one I showed you in the book at the Geronimo Springs Museum, the one with the distinctive mountain formation that led you to Ojo Caliente. I am going to ask Jack Noel if something can be worked out with the owners of the ranch in order for you to visit the canyon without fear of trespassing,"* Jack Wood said.

A few days later I received an email from Jack Wood. It read, *"Jack Noel asked the O' Tooles if a Warm Springs Apache descendant would be allowed to visit the birthland of his great-grandmother. Guess what? It's a done deal! The new owners welcomed you."* Delighted with his email, I wrote. *"I don't know why you are doing all this, but I can't thank you enough."*

These were truly blessed times for me. I could not believe that I was going to be allowed to enter the old homeland of my family. To top it off, I had been invited to meet a P.O.W. who belonged to my ancestor's group, and who could possibly be related to me.

While waiting for July to come around, I stayed busy by going back to the Seminole Native Village, located on State Road 441 and south of Stirling Road in the Seminole Reservation in Hollywood, Florida. The Native Village sat in a two acre oasis that preserved the original and native Florida landscape. It was designed as a tourist attraction. It consisted of a few wood structures and a cluster of Chickees. These Chickees were built on a frame made from Cypress logs and a roof covered by Sabal Palm fronds. The main building was approximately two thousand square feet with an 'A' frame galvanized tin roof. Inside, visitors enjoyed arts and crafts made by Seminoles. The large variety of souvenirs consisted of cabbage patch dolls, grass baskets, jewelry, woodcarvings, beadwork, and the famous patchwork clothing, the trademark of the Seminoles.

For a small fee, the tourists were allowed to enter the back of the village, where they found Seminole women working on those crafts. Among them was my friend Sally Tommie Billie, a Seminole and member of the Bird Clan. She sold her traditional patchwork to the tourists that came in by the busloads. Sally was hired in the 1970's by her old time friend, the late Michael "Skeet" Johns. The two had worked together at Okalee, another Seminole Village, where Skeet wrestled alligators and Sally sold her handmade crafts. That village was located where the Seminole Hard Rock and Casino sits today, on State Road 441 at the intersection of Stirling Road in Hollywood, Florida. Working at Okalee were exciting times for Skeet and Sally, but it didn't compare to the Native Village.

The new place was done right, and it had a good feeling to it. In the center was the Fire Chickee, in it, was a fire that never went out. The embers were rekindled every morning keeping it endlessly alive, a responsibility that Sally did with pride. On the higher grounds of the property was a crystal clear spring fed pond. Its water ran through the village as a creek, providing a habitat for garfish, turtles, iguanas and ducks. At the opposite end, another fenced-in spring-fed pond was home to a dozen of alligators and a few crocodiles. On its perimeters, half a dozen caged panthers roared every time someone walked by. The combined sound of all these animals gave the tourist a feeling of what the old days in Florida must have been like. The main attraction was the alligator wrestling shows.

It was under the guidance of my friend Duke and Skeet that I learned to properly wrestle and catch the prehistoric beast. The systematic technique made the procedure somewhat safe, unlike my younger days where Ulyses and I simply jumped on their backs only to be thrown off.

The term *wrestling* really implied to what took place. After choosing an alligator, you entered the shallow water of the spring. You then grabbed the alligator by its tail, and dragged it to dry land. It was during that phase that you really got a work out. The fight between gator and wrestler usually took anywhere between ten to thirty minutes, depending on the wrestler's experience and determination. A major factor working against the gator is a two-chambered heart. As a result, the prehistoric beast is not able to meet the oxygen demand required to continue fighting with the same intensity as a human can. Once fatigued, the gator's ability to fight starts to slow down. It is during this phase that the wrestler gets in front of the animal.

Siggy Second-Jumper wrestling alligators at the Native Village, Hollywood, FL, ca. 1997

A quick tap on the nose normally sends the gator into a defensive mode, which consists of a loud hissing sound and a full display of eighty teeth. Once the mouth is wide open, it prevents the gator from seeing the next move, which consists of placing a hand underneath the gator's lower jaw. The next step is the most dangerous in my opinion. Here, the wrestler raises the creature's head, resting it on his thigh. This forces the gator's jaw and the mandible to come together allowing the wrestler to grab them both.

Siggy Second-Jumper wrestling alligators at the Native Village, Hollywood, FL, ca. 1997

Once that is accomplished, the wrestler moves around and mounts the gator. This is not always successful; sometimes the gator regains or has enough energy to continue the fight which forces the wrestler to start all over again.

Siggy Second-Jumper wrestling alligators at the Native Village, Hollywood, FL, ca. 1997

These are the stages to successfully wrestle/catch an alligator and are by no means a teaching guide. Only after many years of practice will each wrestler develop his own feeling to accomplish this.

Traditionally, a special permission was needed from a member of the Alligator Clan prior to these dangerous activities. Because all Alligator Clan members moved to Oklahoma, one must go to its nearest relative, the Snake Clan, for permission. Sadly, on January 15, 2011, the Seminoles lost the last matriarch of the Snake Clan, Mrs. Betty May Jumper.

I should also mention that even with the Clan's permission and blessings, one stands a good chance of losing fingers or a hand, as seen with most veteran wrestlers. Today being a wiser man, I count my blessing for the wisdom to quit in early 1999, while I still could count with all my fingers all the close calls I had.

Finally, June of 1999 arrived. I flew into Albuquerque, New Mexico at the end of the month, spurred on by Carlos Enjady's invitation earlier that year. I rented a car and drove down to T or C where I met Jack Wood and his family. Jack informed me, that Carlos had already left to the Mescalero Apache reservation to make arrangements for his grandmother Katherine Kenoi and the rest of his family to meet with me.

Soon after arriving in T or C, Jack drove me around town. We passed many hotels that advertised their hot springs. A few minutes later, we arrived on the western side of the Rio Grande to visit one that was special. It was the largest spring in the area; measuring approximately one hundred by fifty feet. Around it, huge cotton and willow trees were seen swaying in the air. Surprisingly, the spring was not hot at all. Still it was lovely. Jack explained how a town's resident had discovered an old Apache camp there, next to the spring.

In early 1990's, Chiricahua Apaches from Mescalero where called to examine the site. I was told that it was determined by Geronimo's descendants that it was one of Geronimo's camp and the place where he married one of his wives. Once confirmed, the Chiricahua Crown Dancers from Mescalero blessed the site. As a result, the town's councilmen voted to have the place turned into a public park in order to preserve it. They built cement trails through and around it, to keep foot damage to a minimum. The site consisted of clusters of rocks, forming a ridge, perhaps twenty feet in height running along the western side of the spring. Along the small winding trail, many old grinding holes were seen on the rocks. Towards the rear of the camp, a natural indentation on a huge rock still showed old charcoal stains on its walls.

Chiricahua Apache Camp on the banks of the Rio Grande ****
Believed to be where Geronimo got married
Truth or Consequences, NM, ca. 1999

52

The most significant part of the camp to me was to see how much herbal medicine grew there. Never had I seen so many different medicinal plants in one place. After an exciting and interesting tour of the park, we went to a nearby restaurant for an early dinner. From there we called it a night

Early next morning, we began making preparations for our long awaited trip into Monticello Canyon. While Jack and I packed our tents and clothes, Jack's dad took care of the mechanical aspects. He checked fluid levels, gathered chains, shovels, and hydraulic jacks. About half an hour later, all items were neatly stacked in the bed of the faded yellow Dodge Power Wagon. The old truck was full of dents and scratches like an old war veteran. "*If only these dents and scratches could talk,*" I thought. Based on the preparations I knew, we were heading into rough country. My thrill-seeking spirit couldn't wait. Jack and I left T or C and began heading towards the Monticello/Cuchillo basin.

The drive was spectacular. Although I had driven it before with my family, it felt different. First I didn't have the tensions caused by my wife, and since I knew where we were going, I was able to relax and truly enjoy the ride. Because the windows were down I could smell the desert bloom, as my long and loose hair flew with the wind. Unlike the comforts from modern technology of the rental car, the rough suspension of the truck and the hot desert breeze made the ride feel more real to me.

As we drove deeper into the basin, I began to see the rolling hills and mountains deep in the distant horizon. Once we reached them, the ascending and descending turns began. Because of the rough suspension, they seemed sharper than before. Sometime later we reached the summit. From there, I saw the towns of Placitas and Monticello in the distant valley.

A while later we entered Placitas. Like before, things looked unkempt. In a blink of an eye, we passed the tiny hamlet and entered Monticello. As we drove deeper into the small village I got to see a very different side of town. Unlike the few remodeled homes with beautiful metal roofs at the entrance, I found many old adobe homes. Some of them were in very bad shape, with cracked walls and broken windows.

After driving through the village, we entered the rough and mysterious canyon of Monticello. At that moment, Jack got out of the truck and engaged the front differential, thus turning the vehicle into all wheel drive and ready for action.

As we drove in further, the landscape went from rolling hills to high canyon walls. At times, I had to crane my neck to see the tops of the sheer cliffs. Shortly after, we began to cross the creek beds that zigzag through the canyon's corridor. These were the waters of the Cañada Alamosa River. Its origin found more than twenty miles up the canyon and fed by different springs, including the sacred Ojo Caliente.

High up in some of the cliffs were partial stone walls still covering the entrances to what were once open caves. These walls were built long ago during the Pueblo Period (*A.D. 950-A.D.1450*). The people that inhabited the area were known as the Mimbres or Mogollon Culture.

Along the river's bank, beautiful cottonwood trees swayed back and forth, making the leaves dance in the wind like silver dollars tossed in the air. The rolling hills sprouted with pink and white flowers. Every now and then patches of Mexican sunflowers blossomed across the landscape. Pollen from Cattails and Cottonwood floated in the air, their fall happening in slow motion similar to falling snowflakes. As we continued our drive, the beauty seemed to intensify. Elk roamed everywhere as deer scattered throughout the canyon.

Cañada Alamosa River, Monticello Canyon, NM
Known to locals as Box Canyon
****

I couldn't help to wonder if this is what heaven looked like. Suddenly, it made sense why my ancestors fought so hard to keep such a place. I began to imagine what it must have been like, when my great-grandmother lived among all the beauty that surrounded me. Was she a happy and playful little girl or was she sad and forced into hiding? I was certain that the harshness of her life had robbed her of having the opportunity to enjoy it. The painful thought brought a lump to my throat and a feeling of sadness overwhelmed me. Luckily, Jack remained quiet and I was not forced to speak and show any weakness in my voice. As the drive continued, I knew I had to snap out my mood, after all, I was entering a new chapter in my life and I needed to be positive. I couldn't believe I was going to meet someone that was welcoming me. Because of that, I was not afraid to go through the gates that separated the private ranches found within the canyon. The slow drive made the trip seem endless. With each turn around the canyon walls, the Alamosa waters became deeper and the muddy ground softer.

About sixteen miles later, we came across some ranch homes. My anticipation grew stronger as I couldn't wait to meet the people that made the trip possible. After driving through two more gates and a deep creek, we were greeted by a pack of domestic dogs.

View of Monticello Box Ranch from Montoya's Butte
Monticello Canyon, NM
**

About two hundred yards from the creek was a two story wood cabin, where we were welcomed by Jack Noel to The Monticello Box Ranch. After conversing for a few minutes, he invited us in. Shortly after, we found ourselves on the second story balcony. The view was spectacular, as endless layers of mountains covered the horizon. Across from the cabin ran the Alamosa River. The sound of the running water was easily heard and soothing.

A while later, Jack Noel wanted to show us remnants of an old pueblo civilization. After driving for approximately two or three miles outside the property line, we came upon a series of rolling hills. On top of these mounds were old stone walls that once divided the many rooms that made up the ancient community.

Nearby, archeologists had made progress in excavating what appeared to be a one-room dwelling. The fully unearthed room revealed a square fire pit. That characteristic was typical of the Mogollon Culture. Unlike their Anasazi neighbors to the north, who made round fire pits.

Another characteristic that distinguished the two groups was the color of their ceramic ware. The Mogollon culture used gray ceramic instead of brown like their northern neighbors. Archeologist and historians have concluded that the Mogollon culture thrived in or around 950 A.D. Their reason for leaving the area five hundred years later remains a mystery today.

After the tour ended I felt a sense of ambivalence. *Was this a burial site that should have been left alone? Or did archeologists really belong there? Did the Pueblo Indians of New Mexico knew of such a project?* Regardless of my feelings, I kept opinions to myself as we drove back to the cabin.

"Montoya's Butte" Monticello, NM **

A few miles later, I noticed a very distinctive formation on a mountain top. I asked Jack Noel about it and learned it was called "Montoya's Butte." It was named after a pioneer Mexican family who lived in the canyon. Anyone traveling through the area could have easily seen the landmark from all directions. *"What a reference point,"* I thought. The butte stood high like an old lighthouse

Upon our return to the cabin, Jack Noel showed us a designated area to pitch our tents. The campsite was not far from his cabin. There, we found a series of wooden platforms that were raised about a foot from the ground. These high platforms not only gave us a level ground, but most importantly, it kept the snakes out. A shear, jagged canyon in the background gave me a sense of security. I sat on the platform and took a look at my surroundings.

The horizon seemed carved out of a postcard. Layers of mountains faded deep in the cloudless blue sky. In front of me was a pond which was partially covered by a curtain of cattails. About a hundred feet from the pond was the Alamosa River, whose banks were heavily forested with cotton trees. To my near left, an adobe house sat vacant, perhaps going through a renovation. To the far left, I noticed other houses. One was up on a mountain perch with big glass windows. It looked like a crystal palace to me. The other home was made with adobe and it had a metal roof.

After enjoying the beauty that surrounded us, Jack Wood and I dropped our camping gear off and drove out in search of Ojo Caliente Spring.

About four or five miles into our trip, I realized that we were driving inside the very narrow canyon walls that had impressed me so much a year earlier. It was the area that I had referred to as *"a Cathedral of Sacredness."* That part of the canyon was magical. The sharp turns and narrow path prevented us from seeing ahead. Up above, indirect sunlight filtered through the towering pinnacles, creating magical colors and shadows on the jagged canyon walls. The sound of running water along with that of our low gear and high revving engine echoed through, adding to the mirage.

"The Cathedral"
Alamosa River, Monticello Canyon, New Mexico**

A short time later, our wet and splashy drive came to the end. Ahead of us an open valley awaited. That area where the canyon greeted the valley was known to locals as "The Monticello Box." Once out in the open, we drove around a little bit, until we came up to the spot where I had parked the rental car with my family a year or so earlier. I felt I had to show Jack where his directions led me to. From there, we drove back towards the box. Once there, we proceeded to climb the hill that led to the mouth of the spring. Ironically, I had Jack follow me, as I wanted to show him the spot where my daughter and I had turned around. After that, Jack led the way, like a guiding hawk. We climbed higher and higher as we continued following the cascading water.

A few hundred yards later, we came across patches of sweet grass, whose pleasant smell rose in the soft breeze. We stopped to savor the sweet aroma and to rest. It was during that break that I noticed some grinding holes on the big flat stones along the water's edge. It was a moment that filled my mind with emotions and questions, as I thought of my ancestors. *"Did they play in this water? Was it here that they bathed? Were they happy? Did the children play and had fun along the cascading water? Who was Kukah's Mom? What did she look like? What were they grinding on those rocks?"* My deep thoughts came to an end when Jack asked *"Are you ready to go on?"* We continued our hike until the rocky trail came to an end, forcing us to cross over the cascading water. With each crossing, the power of the rushing water intensified. A few minutes later, we had reached the source of all that hydraulic power known as Ojo Caliente spring.

Siggy at Ojo Caliente, Homelands of the Warm Springs Apaches *
Monticello, NM, ca. 1999

The only word that may describe what I saw is "miraculous". At my feet was the genesis of all that cascading water, rising up from under the ground. The spring pool was approximately twenty by thirty feet and no more than one or two feet deep. *"What a perfect bathtub,"* I thought. Coming from Florida, I was accustomed to seeing all kinds of bodies of water, but I had never seen anything like that.

Instinctively, I sat on the edge of the spring, closed my eyes, and began to pray. I was thanking the Creator for allowing me to be there, when an unusual humming in my ear forced me to open my eyes. There, in front of me, were two hummingbirds hovering in the air. With a grin on my face, I closed my eyes and continued on. After finishing my prayer, I opened my eyes and realized that Jack had silently disappeared. I assumed that somehow he knew I needed time to be alone.

His intuition not only gave me the space I needed to reflect on my past, but it prevented him from seeing the tears of joy running down my face.

There I was, in the heart of my ancestors' homeland, more than a hundred years later. *"How can such an old event feel so recent and real to me?"* I wondered. Unable to come up with any answers, I took a pinch of tobacco from my pouch and offered it to the four directions. With my drum on hand, I sang a song titled *I Walk in Beauty*. This was a song I had learned from my Navajo friend, Ray. A few minutes later, Jack showed up and said. *"They probably haven't heard a song sang here in a hundred years. It is good that you bring life back to the canyon."*

After conversing for a while, we decided to climb the sacred mountain adjacent to the spring. There on its very top, stood a towering stone circle. It is believed to be the spot where Victorio, the last War Chief of the Warm Springs Apaches, gave his last speech before going on the warpath.

Siggy Second-Jumper kneeling down next to a rock ring, believed to be Victorio's last stand before going on the warpath. Monticello, NM, ca. 1999*

After spending some time admiring the overwhelming beauty that surrounded us, we decided to head on back to the ranch. Once back, we began setting our tents to settle down for the night. Food never tasted so good. With each passing hour the temperature dropped more and more, until it became so cold that I was forced to seek a thicker jacket. Above sparkled millions of stars, their glow like candles splashed across the clear sky. The two Jacks and I sat and exchange stories for hours until we decided it was time to go to sleep. One of the few things that took time to get used to was the drastic change in temperatures between day and night.

The next morning Jack Wood and I rose early and began to explore other parts of the canyon. We hiked many miles and discovered unbelievable hidden beauties. Just like the previous day, we had made the most out of every minute. Totally relaxed, three days of exploration and fun went by fast.

It was late afternoon on our third and final day, when we began to load our gear on to the truck. We were almost done, when I noticed a red pick truck heading in our direction. From the looks of it, it appeared to be a worker. I didn't make much of it, as there was some construction work being done to an adobe house next to us. The red truck pulled up behind Jack's Dodge Ram and out stepped a gentleman wearing blue jeans, a white T-shirt, and a straw hat. He came right up to me and said, *"You must be Siggy?"* *"Yes, sir,"* I responded. He shook my hand firmly and said, *"I am Denny O'Toole. Welcome home. I have heard a little bit about you and it is an honor to have you here."* *"The honor is mine, Sir."* I responded. *"I thank you very much for giving me the opportunity to come and stay here."* I told him what we had done during our stay and how meaningful it was for me. After conversing for a while, he took us over to the adobe house to meet his wife Trudy, who was working on a white pinewood floor. *"Hi Trudy, pleased to meet you,"* I said. I remembered feeling awkward. I wanted to say so much, but yet I said so little. Once again, I gave thanks and told them it was time for us to leave. Mr. O'Toole looked me straight in the eye, shook my hand firmly and said, *"You tell the Apaches they are welcome here any time."*

Right there and then, I knew that I had met someone very special. His firm handshake and the sincere look in his eyes gave me that feeling. I gave my farewells to my new friends and Jack and I drove out of the sacred canyon. It was hard to leave behind so much kindness and beauty, but I was satisfied and thankful. I only hoped I had made a good enough impression to be welcomed again.

A while later we drove past the town of Monticello and Placitas. Soon after, Jack showed me a distinctive formation on top of a distant mountain. As we got closer, I began to see clearly what resembled a turtle sitting on its top. The landmark named Turtle Mountain was located on the eastern side of Rio Grande and across from Jack's hometown of T or C.

"Turtle Mountain" Truth or Consequences, NM****

The next morning, Jack and I made plans to visit the Gila National Forest. The park was located about an hour north of Silver City, New Mexico. We left Truth or Consequences at 7:30am and arrived at the Gila Cliff Dwelling National Monument three hours later. At 11:00am, Jack and I eagerly joined a group of visitors like us on a tour led by a Park Ranger. After a short but strenuous incline hike, we reached the park's main attraction, the ancient Gila Cliff Dwellings of the Mogollon people.

Gila Cliff Dwelling
Ancient dwellings of the Mogollon People, Gila, NM
Built during the Pueblo Period (*A.D. 950-A.D.1450*).
****

It was indeed an impressive sight, the kind that leaves you breathless. Unlike the Monticello ruins, these were protected from the elements by a huge cave. A great part of the cave's opening was covered by adobe walls. Some of them were still supported by the original wooden logs. We proceeded to walk inside through a series of modern wood steps that led us to the center of the cave. The first thing I noticed was the cave's ceiling. It was covered with a thick layer of black soot; caused by hundreds of years of burning fires. Another amazing thing were the adobe walls that stood intact dividing the many rooms. As we made our way through the cave, we came upon a room on the edge of the precipice. Not only was the view spectacular but a pair of well preserved hieroglyphs caught our attention. They consisted of a snake and a bird, both painted red. The whole experience was amazing, a true testament of time and an in-depth look into the Native American way of life.

Just before the tour ended, Jack and I broke away from the crowd and made our way back to our vehicle. He wanted to show me some hot springs hidden deep in the Gila forest without having anyone following us.

Gila Cliff Dwelling, Gila, NM
Side view of the cave, showing various rooms
Built during the Pueblo Period (*A.D. 950-A.D.1450*).
****

A short time later, we reached a high ridge on the other side of the park's wilderness. Down below ran the Gila River. Jack led the hike into unknown territory. A posted sign warned us that we had just entered a Silver Back Wolf territory. Soon after, we began to follow a sandy trail that ran along the Gila River. During our first river crossing, the strong currents knocked the shoes off our feet. Suddenly, we found ourselves walking barefooted. A short distance later, Jack revealed to me that he was not able to go on. The blistering desert sand had taken a toll on his bare feet. *"Let's turn around and come back another day,"* I suggested.

After a few minutes of debate, he convinced me to go on by myself. I reluctantly agreed, but not before finding a shady spot for my pal to rest. Not knowing where I was going, I continued walking along the river's edge. About an eighth of a mile later, the sandy trail suddenly ended. A high mountain ridge obstructed my path, forcing me to cross the river again. After the crossing, I found myself path finding in the tall grass and unable to cover much distance. I continued on until I was past the mountain's ridge and able to cross back onto another trail. Crossing the river back and forth happened multiple times. With each crossing, the water felt warmer, encouraging me to go on. Despite not knowing how far to go, I continued my search.

While on the trail, I noticed a rocky mound about a hundred yards ahead of me. After climbing it, I discovered what I was looking for. There below me, were a series of pools being fed by a stream of steaming water that gushed from a mountain wall. The first pool, the one closest to the source, contained layers of a copper and purplish color algae floating on top of the steaming water.

It measured approximately three square feet. The second pool was twice as big, and the water was algae free. The third and last pool measured approximately seven square feet in diameter and half a foot deep. The two latter pools were cooled off by run offs from the Gila River. The combined water made that third pool feel very comfortable and inviting. Unable to resist, I proceeded to enter the third watering hole. I sat in the soft and paste bottom and gave my bare feet a well deserve rest. With the water level reaching my waist, I leaned back and submerged my head in the warm water.

There I began to pay attention to my surroundings. Above the cracked stone wall, where the gushing water protruded, was a small cave displaying similar signs to the cliff dwellings on the other side of the park. A partial stonewall still covered the entrance and its charcoal-stained ceiling indicated many years where contained fires warmed its inhabitants.

On the opposite side of the canyon a huge cave revealed its dark opening. It was so high that only an old time Apache or a modern rock climber would dare climb it. The top of that cave was decorated with towering pinnacles and protruding cliffs. There, a golden eagle perched. A few minutes later, it began to call out. Its loud screeching sound sent chills down my arms. The partly cloudy and blue sky along with the eagle's calling made me feel like I was in heaven.

Gila Hot Springs Cave, Gila, NM
****

A few seconds later, I closed my eyes and began to pray. *"Grandfather, hear me, I thank you for all your gifts. I humble myself in your presence and all your creations. I ask that you give me strength and guidance to meet the right people that will guide me into my family's arms."*

After my prayer and a good rubbing of my feet, I decided to head back and reunite with my friend Jack. Getting back was quick, as I already knew how the trail system worked. I ran most of the way back, trying to make up for the time spent at the spring. Upon my return, I found Jack patiently waiting at the same spot. I told him of my findings and although I tried to encourage him to take a look for himself, he declined. Later that afternoon we drove back to T or C where I spent the night.

The next morning, we drove north on I-25 as we headed to the Mescalero Apache reservation to meet Carlos Enjady and his grandmother Catherine Kenoi. About an hour later, we merged onto Highway 380, heading east. The intersection was called *Bosque Del Apache*, the words meaning Apache Forest, because of its extensive shrubbery and trees that surround it, creating an oasis in the otherwise barren solitude of the desert. The sanctuary probably served as a refuge to the Chiricahuas in their times of conflict with the U.S Government.

After leaving El Bosque behind, we entered a desert valley that spread like a blanket of sand from horizon to horizon. It was the type of terrain that made you look at your car's gauges twice. Being in the urban fire-rescue service, I couldn't help to think of the outcome of a head on collision and the time it would take for a rescue unit to reach the scene, not to mention a hospital.

About an hour later, we began to ascend in altitude. Just when I thought we were leaving behind the flat and barren desert valley, Jack smiled and said. *"Wait until you see what is coming up."* A short distance later, a sign read Valley of Fire. Once we reached the top of the mountain, a spectacular view lay beneath us, making the area behind timid and uninspiring. The scenery was really something. The huge valley floor below us gave the impression of a smoldering fire, just like the name suggested. A closer look revealed layers of black lava spreading as far as the eye could see. Certain sections appeared to be precisely cut into huge squares. Amazingly, the vegetation, mostly yucca and mesquite, thrived. Being there made me think of ancient days when dinosaurs roamed the earth. It looked like a place frozen in time.

About ten miles later we reached the village of Carrizozo. Driving through it I noted that it had a respectable Mexican/American population. We continued driving on the desert highway until we arrived at Alamogordo. That town was much bigger. Outside its perimeter was a military base. We chose to stay there because of its close proximity to the Mescalero Apache reservation.

The next morning we got up early and enjoyed a hot breakfast at a local restaurant. After that came the big moment I had prayed and waited for. I was finally going to meet face to face with Catherine Kenoi, a Chiricahua elder and former prisoner of war. Jack and I drove out of Alamogordo and prepared for the one-hour drive. Along the way, we passed two small towns, La Luz and Tularosa. These towns were located on the Tularosa Basin, a terrain where water flows in and none flows out. The unique ecosystem has created its own *playas* (*intermittent lakes*), such as Lake Lucero. The hydrological phenomenon provided rich moisture in the soil that made it ideal for farming. The most popular, or obvious, being Pistachio farms.

A while later, we got on Highway 70 heading east, the four lane highway cut through the heart of the Mescalero Apache Reservation. Some fifteen miles later, we reached the small town of Bent. By then, the barren desert terrain began to change. Signs of lush vegetation were seen everywhere, suggesting an abundance in moisture.

Shortly after, Jack pointed to a welcoming billboard that displayed a sacred Apache Crown Dancer. While staring at the billboard, I felt chills going down my spine. Not only had we crossed the Apache Reservation line, but I was about to enter a very special phase in my life. My nerves were on the edge.

I took a deep breath and composed myself. The time to meet Carlos and his family was getting closer, and honestly I was nervous. A couple of miles later, we made a right turn and entered what appeared to be the outskirts of a community. Modest looking homes were seen on both sides of the road.

After making a few turns through the neighborhood, we arrived at Carlos' house, where we were kindly welcomed by Carlos and his family. Carlos was about five feet four inches tall with a stocky built. His long black hair complimented his black eyes and olive skin. Immediately, they began treating me like I was an old friend. After a good and long conversation, Carlos asked if we were ready to head on out to the Feast Grounds, where the Maiden Ceremony - or Sunrise Feast - was to take place.

After driving five miles, we arrived on the outskirts of the Feast Grounds, which consisted of various flat levels carved out of a mountain. The lower levels were used as parking lots. We proceeded to climb to the camp grounds, an area of approximately twenty acres. The first thing I saw while walking around, were traditional Apache camps. Most were completely assembled, while a few were still under construction. *"What a sight!"* I thought. *"Like an old time Indian camp ground"*. All types of Apache dwellings decorated the landscape: all sorts of camps, from tepees to traditional wickiups (*traditional Apache dwelling made with wood branches usually in a dome shape*).

Apache Wickiup
The quick and easy-built dwelling provided shelter for Apaches on the move.
Feast Grounds, Mescalero, NM.
****

The most commonly seen dwellings were the square and rectangular-type arbors. These shelters were made using Oak branches approximately two or three inches in diameter. The freshly cut twigs were placed vertically and then covered with smaller diameter twigs placed horizontally. All branches were left with their leaves on, thus providing privacy. Most roofs were covered with plastic tarps, while a few were made with natural resources.

Traditional Apache Arbors from the previous year
Feast Grounds, Mescalero, NM,
****

After walking around the campgrounds, we reached the actual entrance to the Feast Grounds. The sacred area consisted of approximately three to four acres in size and was completely fenced in. After getting through the secured gated entrance, we came across dozens of vendors displaying and selling their Native American crafts. Not far from them, a handful of food vendors were ready to take care of our hunger needs. We continued walking through the grounds with no particular destination in mind.

A couple hundred feet in front of us, in the center of the Feast Grounds, stood the big ceremonial tepee, commonly referred to as the Big Tepee. Its entrance faced east. Carlos kindly explained that inside that Big Tepee, the maidens were going to be spending four nights of dancing and learning about the responsibilities associated with all stages of life.

To the right of the Big Tepee were four smaller ones. I asked Carlos if they had any significance. *"They represent the amount of maidens being honored"* he responded. *"This is no ordinary time, my friend,"* he added. *"We are in a time of great celebration.*

MESCALERO

Each year, on the 4th of July, the Maiden's Feast takes place. The four-day event is both a feast and a ceremony celebrating the passing of a young girl into womanhood," he said. The four lodges were set side by side. Each had a huge arbor in front of it. Each arbor had multiple cooking pits, which were attended by lots of people working together. All arbors were connected by a common corridor that ran in front of them. That passageway was approximately two hundred feet long and was built the old way, using oak branches, as described in Apache camps. Inside that corridor were multiple forty gallon cooking pots sitting on wood burning fires. The whole thing looked like an old working village. I had never seen greater amounts of food cooking in one place.

To the left of the Big Tepee were multiple sets of bleachers made to accommodate hundreds of spectators. Above the bleachers stood the announcer's tower booth, where I saw a few men setting up the P.A. system. It appeared that everyone inside the gated grounds had an assigned task to accomplish. Upon the conclusion of Carlos' informative tour, we sat on the bleachers and waited for the scheduled entertainment to start.

By 1:30pm hundreds of spectators had arrived. Strangely, just a few joined us, as the majority sat on lawn chairs forming two semi circles. Everyone was careful not to block neither the Big Tepee nor the eastern arena entrance. Their sitting arrangement left a huge opened area in the center that served as a dancing arena.

At 2:00pm the first scheduled show began. It consisted of a dance troop of Pueblo Indians from New Mexico performing their traditional dances. Their performance lasted about an hour. It was followed by a few other performing groups from other Indian Nations.

As the late afternoon approached, eight tables were set in front of the four tepees. Soon, they were filled with a variety of food. After waiting in line for about ten minutes, we reached the tables, where I was served beef stew, wild rice, potato salad, fruit, homemade chocolate cake, and a piece of fry bread. The last table contained plastic silverware, soft drinks and water. With our hands full, we took our plates to the bleachers and began to eat.

We were almost done when Carlos pointed out that his grandmother Catherine Kenoi had arrived from the nursing home where she resided. She was brought to the Feast Grounds by her family to meet up with me. Excited but nervous, I took a glance towards the V.I.P. area, where I saw members of Carlos' family pushing Catherine's wheel chair. The special section consisted mainly of elders. I took a deep breath and followed Carlos down the bleachers to meet the rest of his family. *Oh God*, I thought. *Give me strength.* Once there in front of his family, Carlos introduced me to everyone. *"This is Siggy; he is the one that came from Florida to meet Grandma. Siggy, this is my family and here is my grandma, Catherine Kenoi."* He said. *"Hello! It is an honor to be here. I want to thank you for bringing Catherine here to meet with me,"* I nervously said. *"Go ahead and sit next to her,"* a member of the family said, while pointing to an empty chair next to Catherine. Before sitting down, I reintroduced myself to Catherine and gave her a gentle hug. Her frail body was a true testament of human strength. The fact that she was born in captivity, had survived the hardships that annihilated most of her peers, was enough for me to know that I was about to sit next to someone very special. Even though Catherine was probably in her nineties, she sat straight up in her wheelchair and was sharply in tune with her surroundings. Shortly after, I began to speak to her. Her family told me she was hard of hearing and that I needed to speak louder.

MESCALERO

I told Catherine I had come from Florida and that I was a descendant of the Warm Springs Apaches P.O.Ws. that were taken there. Because I had to speak in a high tone voice, it caught the attention of other elders sitting nearby. As a result, they began to pay close attention to what I was saying. I told Catherine that my great-grandparents were taken from Fort Marion and shipped to Cuba. *"Oh my God, you are one of those, the lost ones. My family always wanted to know what happened to you guys,"* she said. I explained to her how they were forced into labor making rope until Cuba's independence from Spain, twelve years later. Once I finished with my explanation, she continued, *"My goodness! We made songs about you. We have been waiting for you. I am glad you're here. You are in the right place. Welcome home!"* Her words melted my heart and as a result, I became extremely emotional. From that moment on, I was unable to speak in full sentences without my voice breaking down. Trying to compose myself, I took a deep breath and attempted to ask her what she knew of those Apaches that were seen sailing away from Fort Marion in 1886. Half way through my question, the lump in my throat came back all over again. Luckily, Catherine came to my rescue when she took control of the scene and began asking questions of her own. *"What was your grandmother's name?"* she asked. *"Ku-kah,"* I responded. *"I don't know her,"* she said, followed by a pause. *"But it's ok, we are still related."* She never told me what she meant by that, and I never asked.

Among the elders sitting in the VIP section, were two ladies who became interested in my story and began asking questions of their own. Their names were Ruey and Kathleen. Ruey wanted me to visit her hometown of Apache, Oklahoma to meet some of her relatives and tell them my story. At the time, I had no idea who the two ladies were. Years later, I learned they were Kathleen Kanseah and Ruey Darrow.

Kathleen Kanseah, Chiricahua Apache
Photograph by Robert Ove

Kathleen was a revered Chiricahua elder from Mescalero. Ruey was the former Chairperson of the Fort Sill Chiricahua Warm Springs Apache Tribe of Oklahoma. Both ladies were descendants of the Chiricahua prisoners that were sent to Florida. After many questions and a long conversation with the VIP group, Kathleen asked if I knew an old classmate of hers by the name of Betty May Jumper. Kathleen had met Betty, *the first Seminole to graduate from high school,* while attending nursing school in Lawton, Oklahoma in the mid 1940's. *"Sure, I know Betty quite well. She lives about two or three miles from me,"* I responded. After graduating from nursing school, both classmates went their separate ways. Kathleen lost contact with Betty and was not aware of her many accomplishments.

I informed her that after graduating as a nurse, Betty became a traditional storyteller and a political representative of her people. She served from 1967 to 1971 as tribal Chair of the Florida Seminoles, the only Florida Seminole woman ever so elected. In 1984 she became the editor-in chief of the Seminole Tribe's newspaper known today as the Seminole Tribune. Betty was also the director of communications for the Seminole Tribe of Florida. In 1994, she received numerous honors, including a Florida Department of State Folk Life Heritage Award and a Doctorate of Humane Letters from Florida State University. In 1997, she received the first Lifetime Achievement Award ever presented by the Native American Journalist Association and was named Woman of the Year by the Florida Commission on the Status of Women. She wrote and co-authored many books including *"Legends of the Seminoles".*

Betty Mae Tiger Jumper (1924-2011)
The last surviving matriarch of the Seminole Snake Clan

MESCALERO

Kathleen was delighted to hear about Betty's achievements. We both expressed a sense of pride for knowing such a special person. In time, I became the messenger between the two old classmates. Our conversation was interrupted by the beginning of the Sunrise Puberty Feast ceremony. It all started with the lighting of the sacred fire. Shortly after, the Crown Dancers appeared. Although I had read about their power and sacredness to the Apache people, I had never seen them live. Kathleen was kind enough to explain in detail, each of the steps that were taking place.

A few hours later, Catherine Kenoi's family decided it was best to take Grandma back home. The temperature was dropping quickly and the cold wind had picked up considerably. I thanked the family for bringing her out to meet me and letting me share such an honorable time with all of them. I gave Catherine a big hug and watched as she was pushed away in her wheelchair. I remained seated with the Kathleen and Ruey for another hour or so.

At about10:00pm, I decided to reunite with my pal Jack. He wanted to know the outcome of the meeting and how I felt. Suddenly I found myself searching for words to answer his question. *"Well, Jack, to say that they made me feel welcomed and at home is too simple of a description for how I am feeling. In some strange way, it almost felt like God had allowed me to enter his kingdom."* I told him of Catherine's echoing words, *"We are related."* From that moment on, I saw Carlos as my own family. I called him The Gate Keeper, as I felt he was there at the gate waiting for my arrival. It was because of him that I was able to make contact with my people after more than a hundred years of separation and pain.

Later that evening, Jack and I returned to the hotel. That night I was not able to sleep. Among the many thoughts going through my mind, I remembered my wife's words after I expressed to her my desire to bring her and my children on the trip. *"You need to go by yourself on this trip,* "she said. She was right; I would not have been able to stay seated in the V.I.P section on a cold chilly night with my five year-old daughter and my two year-old son. The more I thought about what took place, the more welcomed I felt. I spent most of the night praying and giving thanks. If I got any sleep at all, it must have been in very short intervals.

The next morning, I couldn't wait to leave the hotel and head back to Mescalero. I was eager to see Carlos again. It didn't take long for Jack and me to get ready and away we went. We drove through the same small towns in a blink of an eye. Unlike the previous day, I did not pay much attention to all the small details along the way.

We arrived in Mescalero early that morning and found Carlos and his family still sleeping. We waited for Carlos to get ready and we drove to a restaurant in Ruidoso, a town of ten thousand residents adjacent to the Reservation. There, the three of us talked for hours. At 2:00pm, we headed to the Feast Grounds to enjoy the early afternoon show. Once there, we watched various groups of entertainers.

At about 4:00pm, local residents began to come in. The same semi-circle was formed around the arbor. Within the semi-circle, a section was left open for the elders. There, the group of ladies I had met the day before took their respective places. Again, an extra chair had been brought out for me. I sat among the same group of ladies and enjoyed the laughter and good times as on the previous night. Like a sponge, I was learning everything that was taught to me. With every minute that passed, I moved closer to the end of my dream. That night was going to be my last evening at Mescalero. I told everyone I was going back home the next day.

They all wanted to know if I was coming back the following year. *"I would love to come back,"* I replied. That evening I returned to my hotel with a feeling of sadness. I wanted to stay longer, but my family awaited back home. I was thankful to the Creator for everything that took place and I accepted that all things must come to an end.

The next morning, Jack and I headed to Carlos' house. After having breakfast, I thanked Carlos for the hospitality and everything else he had done for me. I also told him, *"You are like my gate keeper, because you were here at Mescalero awaiting my arrival."* I looked at Jack and told him, *"You are my Little Brother and the Guiding Hawk of my journey."* After a moment of silence, we gave each other a hug and I drove away towards Albuquerque for my afternoon flight.

I arrived in Florida eager to tell my family what had taken place. My Mom was delighted to learn that there were still Chiricahuas left alive. That evening, while laying in bed, I thought about all that had taken place, and realized what a major step I had taken in attempting to reconnect with my ancestral roots.

Back in Florida

Chapter Eleven

In the latter part of 1999 my life changed drastically. My ten-year marriage had ended in divorce. I found myself without a home and asking my parents for a place to stay. I focused on the positive things that came out of my marriage. I had two beautiful children and, most of all, they were healthy. Times were tough, and my spirit was often down. I was having a hard time adjusting to not seeing my children every day. Although I kept relatively busy during the aftermath of my divorce, time still moved slowly. I did some dancing at some local Pow Wows, but it was not enough.

In December of that year, I had a dream. In it, an Apache man by the name of Freddie was going to teach me how to sing old Apache songs. I wrote an e-mail to Jack and shared my dream with him. I asked him if he knew anyone named Freddie. He said no.

Within that same month I was contacted by my friend Skeet Johns of the Seminole Village. He was letting me know that in the neighboring town of Sunshine Ranches an equestrian women's club was looking for someone to break-in some horses. A few days later, I met with one of the ladies at the village who told me she had just purchased a couple of young and wild horses that needed to be broke. She said she had contacted the village for help and that I was highly recommended. I eagerly took the challenge in exchange for the privilege to ride the horses whenever I wanted. We shook hands and the challenge was on. Arrangements were made for me to start as soon as possible.

Siggy Second-Jumper
On a White Arabian Stallion, Sunshine Ranches, FL, ca. 2000

BACK IN FLORIDA

The next morning I showed up at a luxurious state of the art stable. There, I found more than a dozen women waiting to see the show. The two horses in question were a black Tennessee Walker and a white Arabian Stallion. I chose to start with the Stallion.

Among all the noise in the crowd, I heard one of the ladies saying, *"Here is the next victim! This is something we have to see!"* Her comment suggested to me that this had been attempted before. I immediately began to excuse myself. I told them it had been a long time since I had broken in a horse. I walked the Arabian to a soft sand filled round pen, and began to lunge him. Within minutes, a small crowd had gathered to watch the process evolve. Some of the ladies climbed up and sat on the round pen's horizontal wood beams, while others sat on the ground. I worked that horse until I had him sweating and tired. To my surprise, I was able to saddle him up and he willingly accepted the bit. I could tell he had been broke, but was simply very green (*not been ridden in a long time*). The minute I mounted him, he began to squeal like a pig. He took off bucking while I managed to hold on. Less than five minutes later, his rapid breathing and profuse sweating let me know he was done. Feeling satisfied and with a sense of accomplishment, I began galloping the horse in a clockwise manner around the ring. Not sure if he sensed my over-confidence or something spooked him, but without much of a warning, he put his head down and came to a complete stop. Within seconds I found myself on my back, and staring at a clear blue sky. I shook some of the sand off and got back on the horse. I worked him hard for the next twenty minutes until I was completely satisfied that the owner could ride him without getting hurt. Despite the embarrassing fall it all turned out in a positive way. As a result, I gained a lot of offers to work with different horses. I told the owner that I would be back soon to work with the Tennessee Walker.

After a few days of recovery, I went back to finish what I had started. I was told that the Arabian was doing great and would need very little work. I began to work with the Walker and I realized that he was also broke.
I got on him and rode away as if I had ridden him a hundred times before. After a few weeks of working with those horses, the owner said she was pleased with the outcome.

Overall I had gained a lot with minimal effort. Out of the two horses, I preferred riding the Arabian. His high spirit did wonders for mine. Soon after, I found myself riding him all over the neighborhood. About a month later, I began working with another horse that belonged to another club member. Working with those horses helped a lot and before I knew it, 1999 came to an end.

Even though my spirits were often down, I forced myself to train for the Seminole Tribal Fair and Pow Wow. The annual event was held on the second weekend of February at the Seminole Reservation in Hollywood, Florida. It was the biggest Pow Wow in Florida and one of my favorite events. It was also a time of laughter and a place where old friends gathered for a good time.

Before I knew it, I found myself registering at the booth, along with my friends William Cypress and Little William Osceola. William Cypress and I registered as Traditional Dancers, and little William as a Grass Dancer. On that particular year, hundreds of dancers along with sixty thousand spectators attended the event. The three days of laughter helped immensely in getting through the tough times created by my divorce. With each day that passed, my spirit felt stronger and stronger. I was amazed by the healing powers of prayers, dancing and singing.

Siggy Second-Jumper, Seminole Pow Wow, Hollywood, FL, ca. 2000

Just when I thought I was doing great, I learned that my Navajo friend Ray, our drum keeper/lead singer was moving back to Arizona. After his departure, William Cypress took over his spot. Although our drum group weakened, we managed to survive. A few months later, another one of our singers returned to his home in Minnesota. As a result, our drum ceased to exist. With no drum practice and most of my friends gone, I found myself alone and feeling down again. Seeing my children every other weekend was not enough. During my daily prayers, I asked for strength and courage. *"If only my Navajo friend could come back,"* I thought during my prayers. Singing was something that made me feel good and closer to God.

My friend Ray never came back, but the Creator did answer my prayers when shortly after, I was asked to join Cypress Prairie, a Seminole Drum, also of the Northern Style. The drum keeper/lead singer was a Seminole by the name of Thomas Storm, a member of the Otter Clan. Generally, drum groups are composed of family members who usually name their drums after something dear to them. Cypress Prairie was no exception; most singers belonged to the Storm family, such as Thomas Storm Jr. and the late Jeff Storm. The drum was named in honor of the Cypress Prairies found throughout the beautiful Homeland of the Seminoles, The Florida Everglades. William Cypress joined in every now and then. Cypress Prairie became popular in the southeastern Pow Wow circuit. Our glory lasted a few years.

Cypress Prairie
Seminole Drum
L to R: Thomas Storm (Otter Clan), lead singer and Siggy Second-Jumper
Orlando, FL, ca. 2000

Visit to the Southwest
Chapter Twelve

By the spring of 2000, life began to feel somewhat normal once again. The hardships of my divorce were fading away. Time moved on and with its passage, the wounds continued to heal. As a result, I felt strong enough to help others who were less fortunate.

My friend Patrick O'Neal had been taking care of his terminally ill mother for over a year. It was obvious that the difficulties associated with this role as caretaker had taken its toll. I noticed that he was becoming increasingly irritable, and in desperate need of a break. I felt that a trip to the canyons of Monticello would do Patrick (and me) much good. I e-mailed the owner of the ranch and asked if it was possible for some friends and me to visit the canyon again. Once I got the ok, I invited Patrick and another friend and co-worker, Gianni Morra, to come along. They both accepted the invitation with eagerness.

During the last week of April, Gianni and I flew to Albuquerque where we met up with Patrick who had driven his Jeep there. While in Albuquerque, we attended the famous Gathering of Nations Pow Wow in the company of Kathleen Kanseah. The annual event was held in The Pit, the biggest indoor facility in that city. Even the biggest arena appeared small once the Pow Wow got going. Not an empty seat could be found, long before the show started. As a result, dozens of people stood in the hallways to watch the grand entry. I had experienced that kind of magnitude before, in 1996-98, when I danced at the Schemitzum Pow Wow, in the state of Connecticut. Just like Schemitzum, The Pit was overflowing with Indians from just about every tribe in North America.

That particular year, Apache Crown Dancers from White Mountain, Arizona came to pay homage to one of their own. The honorable member was none other than Miss Indian World. She was a beautiful young woman, half Hawaiian, half White Mountain Apache. She wore a bright yellow-fringed dress, almost identical to those worn by the young maidens during their Sunrise Feast. With Crown Dancers performing behind her, she paraded around the arena waving at the crowd, who responded enthusiastically. Gianni and Patrick were speechless after seeing the Crown Dancers for the first time. Both my friends had heard and learned much about them through me, but to watch them dance and feel their power was an experience beyond any description.

After a couple of days of entertainment and shopping through the vendors, we decided to head out west. We wanted to visit Painted Desert-Petrified National Forest, located in eastern Arizona. Although I had visited the park in 1998 with my family, I still looked forward to the excursion and spectacular drive with enthusiasm.

A few hours later, we arrived at our destination. The first thing we did was to visit the Painted Desert, an area of more than 5200 acres covered with bright colored rolling hills found within the National Park. The beauty of the place could only have been sculpted by the Creator himself. Although these colored mounds were next to each other, they seemed to retain their individual pureness. The most prominent colors were yellows, oranges and reds. It was no surprise that this marvelous place was named the Painted Desert. Along the perimeter, a paved road circumnavigated the park. After driving for a few miles, we came upon a rest area, where visitors were allowed to go for hikes on marked trails. After a few short hikes and taking some memorable pictures, we headed towards the Petrified Forest.

Siggy with daughter Emily
Petrified Forest National Park, AZ, ca. 1998

That section of the park was bigger and much more interesting. On our way in, we stopped at the visitor center, where we found a small scale replica showing what the once rainforest looked like in its hey days. It was hard to believe that the once thriving woodland had turned into a flat barren desert. From the visitor's center we drove deeper into the park, to see what millions of years of evolution had accomplished.

Upon our arrival, we found enormous pieces of petrified tree trunks laying on the ground at different angles. The broken logs looked like marble sculptures. Their age-inner rings had turned into a variety of florescent colors; similar to a striped lollipop. Some were turquoise blue, while others were pink, green, gray, and white. The combinations were so wonderful and so diverse that even modern technology would have found it difficult to replicate. Along the way, we found many hiking trails, which allowed us to explore much of the real beauty the park had to offer. After an enjoyable day filled with fun and laughter, we headed back east towards Truth or Consequences, New Mexico.

Once there, we met up with Jack Wood. The next morning we packed Patrick's Jeep and the four of us headed out towards Monticello Canyon. On that particular trip, heavy winds and dust storms made the trip unusually slower than normal. Our visibility was limited, preventing us from enjoying the serenity of the desert. We entered the canyon through the town of Monticello. Once inside the gorge, its massive rocky walls blocked the strong winds, thus allowing us to see the beauty that surrounded us. Although I had traveled that path before, I was still stunned by the overwhelming splendor.

VISIT TO THE SOUTHWEST

A few hours later, we reached the Monticello Box Ranch without any delays or incidents. There we met with the owners who welcomed us with open arms. After a short conversation, the owner asked if there was any specific place that I preferred to camp. *"In the same spot as the previous year would be great,"* I replied. *"That would be fine,"* he said. We unloaded our camping gear and proceeded to set up our tents on the wooden platforms. Then we began stripping the jeep of its canvas-top and doors.

A short time later, I found myself driving towards the spring. Patrick rode shotgun and Jack and Gianni rode in the back. What a special feeling it was to drive through the canyon with the top down. It allowed us to see in all directions, but the most spectacular view was looking up, at the upper crest of the canyon underneath the cloudless blue sky. It also allowed us to feel the cool breeze running between the narrow canyon walls. By the time we reached the dry open valley, Gianni and Jack were soaking wet from all the water splashing.

I proceeded to park in the valley underneath Ojo Caliente. We hiked up to the spring where we sat and enjoyed the moment. After a good rest, we went for a hike on a well-marked trail. I could tell my friends were having a good time by the way they carried on, but it didn't take long for us Floridians to be gasping for air at such high altitudes where the air was thin. Jack, on the other hand, appeared to be barely warming up. The elevation throughout the canyon was approximately five thousand plus feet above sea level, something Jack was used to after living in T or C for many years. Patrick, Gianni and I on the other hand, were totally exhausted after a few miles of a moderate level hike. After stopping for a much needed rest, the three of us unanimously voted to head back to camp. The cool breeze and water splashing on the way back was greatly appreciated by all of us.

Upon reaching our campsite, we began making preparations for our evening meal. At nighttime we sat on the wooden platform and told stories. We were all amazed at the clarity of the sky and the millions of stars that decorated it. It was during that time that we noticed some unusual activities taking place in the distant horizon. It consisted of half a dozen or so beams of lights flying in very bizarre patterns. Some flew in a zigzag fashion; while others flew in a straight line at lightning speed. Their stops and take offs were sudden. They all seemed to stay within the same area. The silent laser show went on for so long, that eventually we lost interest. We all concluded that it was probably coming from the nearby White Sands Military Base.

The next morning we sat on the wooden platform drinking coffee and enjoying our surroundings. About two hundred feet in front of us was a pond that attracted all kinds of wild life. Among them were elk and deer. Both came by the dozens. After spending a couple of days in the marvelous and majestic canyon, a sad feeling came over me, when the time came to leave. We shook hands with the owners and drove away. With each mile driven, I felt that a piece of my essence was getting torn from me. We arrived in Truth or Consequences late that afternoon.

In the early morning hours of the following day, we made plans to go to the Gila Cliff Dwelling, located north of Silver City, New Mexico. The four hour-drive went by quickly as Jack told stories of our many excursions together. One in particular, took place at the same park a year earlier, when we both lost our shoes during the initial crossing of the Gila River. He explained how the strong river currents had ripped the shoes right off our feet and how the hot desert sand had caused his feet to blister. As a result of that injury, he never made it to the hot springs found in the park.

To prevent the incident from happening again, Jack wore hiking boots. He also expressed how eager he was to make it to the springs with all of us.

We arrived at the Gila Wilderness Park close to 1:00pm, where we learned that the next tour was about to start. Soon after, a Park Ranger addressed a fairly large group, which included us and a dozen other visitors. After a brief history of the park, we proceeded to climb an old ancient trail that led to the main attraction, the famous Cliff Dwellings. Although Jack and I had already visited the site, we found that particular park ranger to be a lot more knowledgeable and informative than the previous guide. As a result, the tour was a lot more pleasant and captivating. Upon its conclusion, we left the area and headed to the opposite side of the park in search of the hot springs.

Once there, we began our hike on a well-marked trail that led us to the Gila River. To everyone's surprise the previously described deep and dangerous water, was shallow and calm. After the first crossing, we preceded our hike on another well marked trail that ran along the river's edge. A short time later, Jack spotted the area where he had patiently waited for me nine months earlier. From that point on, I led the way crossing the river at specific areas. After a number of crossings, I was able to see the mound that blocked the spring. It was the landmark I was looking for. Soon after, we found ourselves soaking in the hot pools and enjoying the beauty around us. It was great to see my friends having a good time. It also felt good helping Patrick get through that difficult period in his life. A few hours later, we decided it was time to call it a day. We returned to the car and began our journey back to T or C.

The following morning, we gave our farewell to Jack and his family and the three Floridians headed back home. Within a short time I found myself making plans to return to Mescalero again.

Singing and dancing in Mescalero
Chapter Thirteen

In late May of 2000, I was contacted by Carlos Enjady, the grandson of Catherine Kenoi. He wanted to know if I was interested in dancing in Mescalero during the July feast. I told him I would be honored. The next day, I contacted my Navajo friend Ray, who was living in Arizona. I asked him if he was interested in joining me on a hike through Monticello Canyon followed by singing and dancing at the Mescalero Apache Reservation. He eagerly accepted my invitation and on June 30th, we met in Truth or Consequences, New Mexico.

The town of T or C was part of the sacred homelands of the Warm Springs Apaches. It is an area filled with hot springs where the Apaches came to soak and heal their wounds. After showing Ray a few of the hot springs found throughout the small town, I took him to see the one that meant the most to me. It was located along the Rio Grande in down town T or C. As we drove there, I told Ray the same thing that Jack Wood had told me a year earlier. *"It is believed that this was an old Chiricahua encampment and the place where Geronimo married one of his wives."*

Upon our arrival, Ray and I ascended through the narrow cement covered path that cut through a rock fortification that stood next to the spring. Acting as a tour guide, I pointed out all the different grinding holes found alongside the cement trail. Once we got to the back of the refuge, I showed him the botanical garden that thrived under the hot desert sun. He was just as impressed with it, as I was a year earlier when Jack showed it to me. How could he not be! After all, Ray was a descended from a long line of Medicine Men, and as a result, was quick to recognize the medicinal value in most of the plants found there. Half way through the tour, we reached a large indentation found on the walls of a boulder. Although the hole was not big enough to hide a human, it was deep enough to conceal a small fire - a conclusion based on the faded charcoal stains found on the boulder's inner wall. It was there that Ray and I sat down and began to pray. Our prayers were interrupted by a high pitch screaming noise coming from above. We were surprised to find out that the commotion was coming from none other than a spotted tail Golden Eagle, which hovered in circles perhaps fifty feet above our heads. We both looked at each other and smiled. It was a clear sign that we were in a good place and that our prayers would be carried to higher above. (*It is a common belief among many Native Americans that all living things are born with a role to play. The Eagle's role is to carry our prayers to higher above.*) Within a few minutes, the young bird of prey was gone. We proceeded to come down the ridge to the huge spring below us. Surprisingly, the water was cold to the touch, unlike others in the area.

In order to avoid the hot summer sun, we took cover under a huge willow tree, which branches rested on the spring's water. It was there that Ray and I decided to cut a piece of a branch and make ourselves a pair of drumsticks. The twig was soft and pliable, allowing us to bend the end into a hoop. As the sun began to set, we decided to call it a day.

The next morning Ray and I met up with Jack Wood at a local restaurant. Our agenda for that day was to go hiking at Monticello Canyon. An hour later, we had reached the southern part of the canyon. We spent many hours driving, hiking, climbing, and looking for caves, hieroglyphs and petroglyphs.

By day's end we had almost reached the north and final part of the canyon, when I noticed what appeared to be an entrance to a hidden corridor. After entering the ravine, we discovered what appeared to be an old Indian campsite. *"What a perfect place to hide,"* I thought. Once inside, I found a series of tunnels (some narrow; some not), that disappeared through the massive canyon walls. In the middle of that fortress, we found a high and dry area approximately twenty feet square. Tired from the long hike, we sat on flat rocks, our positions forming a semi circle. Within minutes, I began to smell a strong aroma coming from various plants in the area. After gathering some of the leaves, I determined that they were medicine by their mint smell and taste, which was refreshing.

Not far from where we sat, I noticed what looked like an unfinished hand carved statue approximately fifteen feet in height that sat at ground level. It appeared to be a human head wearing a medicine cap, similar to those worn by Apaches. On top of the cap sat a bird, perhaps a hawk. High above our heads, we noticed another rock carving that also resembled a human head. From our point of view, the three of us agreed that it looked like the profile of Geronimo. Once rested, we began praying to God and our ancestors.

It was during our prayer that we heard a familiar screech. Upon the conclusion of our prayer, we noticed a Spotted Tail Eagle flying above the narrow canyon walls. Ray and I looked at each other and realized it was the same bird that had come to us at the sacred spring back in Truth or Consequences. Like an old friend, it had come to say hello. Its aerial display, which consisted of gliding in circles above the canyon walls, went on for a couple of minutes. The incident was so ironic, that I had to explain it to Jack. I was glad that something so special had taken place in the presence of my friends. Needless to say we celebrated the occasion with an honor song.

Once done, Jack said, *"Siggy, I hope you are ready for the next place."* I just nodded, still enthralled by such an astounding incident involving the eagle. *"What did it all mean?"* I wondered. I told Jack that I was not sure if I could handle another surprise. *"Yes you can,"* he replied.

We got in the vehicle and we drove away. Many miles later, we stepped out of Jack's truck and began a long walk through dry arroyo beds. About an hour into our hike the scenery began to change, after entering a very distinct canyon. Its walls were reddish in color unlike any others in the area. As we penetrated deeper and deeper, the scenery continued to transform. The sharp and jagged canyon walls were beginning to convert into beautiful rolling hills, with multiple bright colors. Some of them where white as snow, while others were bright red, like blood. Even the trees were different, as tall pines decorated the landscape. Their unusual presence in an otherwise barren desert-like terrain was something that the three of us talked about. Underneath those pines, on the dry arroyo floor, laid small circles of a blue powder-like substance, approximately five inches in diameter. The small but beautiful mounds looked like ant piles. Needless to say, we did not disturb them at all. As we hiked deeper into the painted canyon, we came across dozens of boulders sitting on top of a red earth mound. Although they varied in size, most appeared to be between four to five feet square. As we got closer, we observed a very strange phenomenon on some of the rocks. It consisted of what appeared to be splashes of a bright yellow paint scattered across them. The color was so bright, that it looked like cattail pollen. Tired and out of breath, we decided to sit and take a well-deserved break, while admiring God's creation. By the grin on Jack's face, I could tell that he was up to something. Our quiet moment was interrupted when Jack asked.

SINGING AND DANCING IN MESCALERO

Siggy Second-Jumper at Red Paint Canyon
One of the most sacred places of the Warm springs Chiricahua Apaches
Monticello, NM circa. 2000 *

"Do you know where we are?" It was at that moment that I realized where Jack had taken me. *"I am almost afraid to say it."* I responded. *"Well my friend, this is Red Paint Canyon."* His words not only confirmed my suspicions, but they sent chills down my spine. I couldn't believe it; I was stunned to know that I was sitting on the grounds that defined my ancestors. It was the place that gave genesis to a bloodline known as the Chienne, meaning Red Paint People.

The remote and beautiful sanctuary appeared untouched since its creation. For the first time, after four generations, I sat on what could possibly be the most sacred spot on earth to a Warm Springs Apache. The mere essence of the *Chienne* lay there in front of me. Suddenly, it all made sense. All the fighting, all the bloodshed that my ancestors endured were over the oasis that surrounded us. I thought about how lucky I was to be there with friends in times of peace. *"Why me? What did it all mean? How many other descendants knew of this place? Why was I there more than a century later?"* I wondered. I stopped torturing myself, when I realized that some questions simply didn't have answers.

Touched by so much beauty and power, I began to pray. *"Oh Grandfather, for some reason you have guided me here, give me the wisdom to see the things you want to show me. Lead the way and I will follow. I humble myself in front of you, I ask for nothing. I am thankful for your gifts...."* When my prayers were done, I found myself on my hands and knees. Upon opening my eyes, I realized that my friends were gone. I also noticed that a small amount of the red dirt had clung to the palm of my sweaty hand. After making a fist, I brought the sacred powder close to my heart. With that red earth clutched in my hand, I began to pray again. *"Oh Grandfather, I thank you for this sacred gift. It is so much more than just dirt; it symbolizes the blood of my people, their tears and the essence of their spirit. I will cherish it, and promise to defend it as long as blood runs through me."*

After my prayer, I remained in place and took one good look at my surroundings. Not knowing if I would ever return to see it again, I decided to keep the precious gift in my hand. With a sense of euphoria, I walked away in search of my friends, whom I found waiting by Jack's truck. The three of us remained quiet as driving away from such a place was not easy. I consoled myself by knowing that I had lived to witness something as old as the beginning of earth. Furthermore I had taken a trace of it as a reminder of the place my ancestors loved and called home. I treasured that red clay like white man treasures gold.

Our silence was interrupted, when Jack said, *"Are you guys ready for some good Mexican food?"* He suggested having dinner at the Old Cuchillo Restaurant, which was located many miles away in the town of Cuchillo. Jack kindly explained that Cuchillo Cafe was not your typical restaurant. Instead, it was the home of a Mexican family, who converted their living room into a small public Diner on certain days of the week.

About an hour later, we arrived at Cuchillo Negro Café, with some sunlight to spare. From the looks of the outside, one could have been easily fooled. The faded business sign complimented the cracks on the adobe wall. Not wanting to judge the book by its cover, I withheld my opinion, as we proceeded to enter through an old wooden screened door.

Cuchillo Negro Café
A family-owned diner in the heart of Apache Country
Cuchillo, NM, ca. 2005
****

Once inside the house, we found a small living room containing a few tables. Soon after sitting, we were welcomed by a middle-aged woman, who handed us a menu. As we looked through it, we were served water and blue corn chips. We knew that it would take some time for our food to be cooked and served.

Based on its remote location, I am sure that many days went by without a single customer coming in. On the other hand, it was awesome, just the three of us enjoying ourselves in a unique setting.

The walls were decorated with old framed newspaper articles/stories. Through them, I learned a lot about the town's history and the origin of its name. I was pleased to learn that it was named in honor of Cuchillo Negro (*Spanish for Black Knife*). He was a Warm Springs Apache Chief, who lived, fought and died there.

About half an hour later, our food was served. I was glad I had not judged the restaurant by its look. Jack was right, the food was delicious. I had some of the best carne con papa and green Chile ever. The sopapilla bread was soft and sweet. After feasting like kings, we headed back to T or C and got some much needed rest.

The next morning, Jack, his twin brother Richard, Ray, and I headed to Mescalero. The three-hour drive went by quick, as it was filled with stories and laughter. We arrived in Mescalero in the early afternoon. After picking up Carlos Enjady, the five of us drove to the Feast Grounds. It was the first day of the four day feast. We walked around and enjoyed looking at the various items being sold by a handful of vendors. After that, I took Ray to meet some of the people I knew, including Kathleen Kanseah and Ruey Darrow, the two ladies I had met during my previous visit. We told them that we had brought our regalia and that we were looking forward to a good dance.

At about 1:00pm, the Master of Ceremony made an announcement, *"All Pow Wow drums start making your way into the arena."* Within a few minutes three drums began setting up on the northwestern corner of the Feast Grounds, next to the Big Tepee. One of the drums was from the Zuni Nation, the other one was from California. Both were of the northern style.

Jack Wood, Siggy Second-Jumper
Mescalero Apache Reservation, NM, ca. 2000
Photographed by Richard Wood

85

The third drum was a well-known southern style World Champions, 'Cozad'. Ray and I introduced ourselves to the California drum and asked if we could sit and sing with them in-between dances. This is commonly done among singers. We were warmly welcomed to join in. I felt great, not only was I going to sing and dance with my old time friend again, but I was going to do it in front of my people. Although the temperature exceeded one hundred degrees and the elevation was at around six thousand feet above sea level, it didn't matter, my adrenalin was pumping and I was ready for it.

At 2:00pm, the Cozad Drum ignited the energy in the air with its first drumbeat, followed by the sound of jingles and bells coming from the dancers. The grand entry was a lot smaller than Ray and I were used to, but the energy in the air exceeded anything we had ever experienced. After the opening prayer and the flag song, the Pow Wow got started.

The first song was a Hunter/Scout song, which is usually played in the style called 'Sneak Up'. Like all songs in this manner, it began with very fast, irregular drumbeats. During this phase, the dancer kneels down and mimics looking for tracks of either game or enemy.

Siggy Second-Jumper
Northern Traditional Dancer in full Regalia
Mescalero Apache Reservation, NM, ca. 2000 *

SINGING AND DANCING IN MESCALERO

When the beating of the drum changes to a slow and regular rhythm, the dancer stands up and proceeds to dance, only to be tricked by sudden stops of the drumbeat. If the dancer does not stop on time with the drum (*referred to as 'over stepping'*) he is disqualified. This style of song is common in competition dancing and is usually referred to as a 'Trick Song'. They originated as a teasing that goes on between singers and dancers. It is common for drum groups to make mistakes. Most of the time these errors go on unnoticed by the crowds, but the dancers pick up on it immediately. This prompted the dancers to start teasing the singers. In return, the drum groups came up with trick songs to tease the dancers back and to make them over step. These songs are usually crowd-pleasers and are a lot of fun for all.

The second song was a 'Crow Hop', which mimics the bird hopping from place to place. It is believed that this style song originated out west in Crow Country. After that came regular 'Straight Songs'. These melodies are sung without any tricks or specialties.

Regardless of how many songs they played, I danced like each one was my last. What a feeling it was to be performing in front of my people. I remembered Jack and Carlos staring at me in awe. Not only was I dancing on Apache's most sacred grounds, but I was doing it in front of elders and ex prisoners of war. Every spot, every inch of that ground was special. Next to me, dancing just as hard, was my old time pal Ray. Dancing with him again felt good and brought back lots of pleasant memories. In between special songs we sat and sang with the California Drum.

When the Pow Wow was over, we changed into our regular clothes and headed back to the group of ladies, who so eagerly watched us dance. *"Your dancing is beautiful and so is your outfit, but your regalia needs to say who you are. You need to work on your colors."* Kathleen Kanseah said. My colors were red, white and blue, far from the Chiricahua traditional colors of black, white, yellow, and green. I told her I would work on that and in time I did, adopting the traditional Apache colors to a new dancing outfit.

At about 4:00pm, Ray's wife arrived from Arizona to pick him up. We spend the next few hours shopping, eating and having a good time. That evening we all sat on the bleachers and enjoyed watching the Crown Dancers perform. It was my pleasure to explain to Ray's wife, a Florida Seminole, what was taking place in the dance arena.

The next morning after breakfast, I watched my old time pal Ray and his wife as they drove out west. At 2:00pm Jack, Richard, Carlos and I drove to the Feast Grounds. Once there, we waited for the scheduled entertainment to begin. We soon learned that the M.C. and his sound system had not arrived. As a result, the schedule programs were running a little late.

After a while, a man wearing glasses and a pony tail stood in the center of the arena and addressed the crowd. Without a microphone, he found himself yelling out loud. *"Everyone! Bear with us, the MC is not here so we are going to step things up. We are going to be singing some songs for you until he gets here."* The man headed to a wooden bench where a handful of Apaches awaited with their water drums on hand. A few minutes later, they started singing Apache War Songs. The pleasant entertainment was interrupted with the arrival of the M.C and his sound system, half an hour later.

It was during that break, that an overwhelming feeling came over me. I told my friends that I was going to ask the gentleman with the pony tail if I could sing with them. I ran down the bleachers and approached him. *"Hello Sir, my name is Siggy Jumper; I am a Warm Springs Apache descendant from Florida. I was wondering if I could sing along with you guy?"*

87

He looked at me from head to toe, and said, *"These are very hard songs to learn, what makes you think you can learn them?"* he asked. *"I have a very strong desire to learn the old ways,"* I stated. *"Do you have a drum?"* he asked. *"Yes, sir,"* I responded. He paused for a few seconds and said, *"Very well, come tomorrow and sit at the end of the bench."* *"Thank you very much, sir."* I replied with a grin on my face. I shook his hand and ran back to the bleacher where Jack, Richard and Carlos awaited. *"What was that all about? What did he say?"* they asked. I told them what took place and how thrilled I was to be granted permission to sing with them. We remained seated and watched all the scheduled groups of entertainers perform. After that, we stood in one of the four lines that were serving food made by the maiden's family. I took my portion and headed over to sit with Kathleen Kanseah and Ruey Darrow.

Because it was cold, Catherine Kenoi's family decided to take grandma home. Her presence was missed, especially by me. Once the sun set, the sacred fire was lit, marking the beginning of that evening's ceremony. Shortly after, the Crown Dancers made their grand entry into the sacred arbor. I felt extremely privileged sitting in such a special place surrounded by elders as they explained to me what was taking place. Through their teachings, I learned about the sacredness of the Crown Dancer (sometimes referred to as Horn Dance, Fire Dance, Mountain Spirit Dance) and how all Apaches should respectfully bow their heads in their presence. *"They represent the mountain spirits and no one knows their human identities, expect the medicine people,"* I was told by the elders. At about 10:00pm, the ladies decided it was time to go home. Once they were gone, I returned to my buddies and sat with them until midnight when we decided to head on out as well.

The next morning I woke up fully energized. That was a big day for me. I was going to sing with my people for the first time. Although I had sang for many years with other groups, it felt different, I felt nervous. I drove up to Mescalero, where I picked up Carlos. From there we picked up Jack and his brother Richard. The four of us, headed for a warm meal in Ruidoso, the nearest town to the Reservation.

At about 2:00pm, we arrived at the Feast Grounds. Jack, Rich, and Carlos wanted to shop through the vendors. I, on the other hand, decided not to join them because I didn't want to draw unwanted attention by walking around with a drum on hand. Instead, I looked for a place to sit and stay low key. Luckily, I spotted an empty space at one of the food vendor's bench. I ordered a cheeseburger and a coke, thus giving me the right to take up the only available spot. Rather than sitting normal facing the table, I sat sideways. The straddling position allowed me to conceal my drum in-between my thighs. To top it off, I leaned over, further covering the drum with my Seminole patchwork jacket. I was still waiting for my order, when a young man came over and sat next to me. *"What's up? What is your name?"* he asked. *"Siggy Jumper,"* I replied. *"Where are you from?"* he continued. *"Florida"* I replied. *"Are you a Seminole?"* he asked. *"No, Warm Springs Apache"* I replied. *"My name is Cyrus Simmons. I am a Chiricahua myself. I am also the grandson of Chief Chihuahua."* Cyrus demeanor was pleasant, and he seemed very interested in learning about me and my family history. I told him of my family trip, and how I had traced my ancestor's journey, starting in Fort Marion and ending in Ojo Caliente. He began telling me of a similar trip he took along with other tribal members into Northern Mexico, which included a visit to Tres Castillos and Casas Grandes, two significant places in Apache history. After a few minutes into our conversation, Cyrus' curiosity got the best of him, when he asked me what I was hiding under my jacket.

"Oh it's my drum; I am going to be singing with the War Singers." I explained to him how I had been granted permission the day before from a gentleman with a ponytail. *"It must have been Freddie,"* Cyrus said. His reply sent chills down my spine, as I thought about the dream I had on the previous year, where a man by the name of Freddie was going to teach me to sing old Apache songs. *"Could this be for real?"* I thought. I remained calm as I tried really hard not to over react to what I had just heard.

A short time later, Jack walked by me and said, *"Hey Siggy, you know the guy you asked permission to sing, his name is Freddie."* The fact that he kept walking seemed strange to me. Immediately I thought it was a joke, and Cyrus was in on it. Set ups like that I was very used to. Fifteen plus years as a fireman had exposed me to all kinds of locker room jokes. A few minutes after the incident, my order was ready. I continued talking to Cyrus while I ate the juicy burger.

Shortly thereafter, we were interrupted by an announcement over the PA. *"All War Singers and dancers, start making your way into the arena."* I stood up and shook hands with Cyrus and proceeded to walk towards the big ceremonial tepee, which was approximately two hundred feet away.

I stood next to the lodge and waited for other singers to arrive. Once all of them were sitting down, I proceeded to sit at the right end of the bench as previously told. That sitting arrangement created a four to five foot space between the singers and me. While waiting for a few missing dancers, I was approached by the gentleman sitting to my left. He was stocky built, with dark complexion and short black hair. *"Hey, Handsome! Why are you sitting so far away?"* he asked. *"I was told to sit at the end of the bench, sir,"* I responded. *"Who told you that?"* he went on. *"The gentleman with the ponytail,"* I responded, as I pointed with my nose to the man sitting at the center of the bench. *"Who are you referring to, Freddie?"* he asked. *"Yes."* I responded. It was at that moment that I realized that his name was really Freddie. *"Move over here next to me. You are not going to learn the songs sitting way out there,"* the gentleman said.

Suddenly, I found myself caught in between not doing what I was told and not wanting to be disrespectful to the gentleman next to me, so I moved over half way and sat closer to him. *"What is your name?"* he continued. *"My name is Siggy Jumper. I am a Warm Springs descendant from Florida. I flew here for the ceremonies."* The gentleman introduced himself as Carson Carrillo, also of Chiricahua blood like me. For a moment I thought, how strange, it seemed that everyone I was meeting was a Chiricahua, and yet I was at the Mescalero Reservation. *"Will I ever meet a Mescalero?"* I wondered. Shortly after, he began asking me questions about my family history, which I proceeded to tell as I had done earlier with Cyrus.

Years later, I was to find out that this was no coincidence. The Chiricahuas were intentionally approaching me to see if indeed I was who I said I was. However at that time, I did not realize that and I soon forgot my concerns when Freddie began singing the first war song. His powerful voice sounded like echoes of thunder across a canyon. The rest of the singers followed right along. Within a short time, I caught on to the words and began singing my heart out. Somehow I picked up on the lyrics as if I had sung them many times before. When the song ended, I felt happy and proud to have finished it without any major mistakes, which is very easy to do when singing a new song. Soon after, Freddie began singing other songs. By the third or fourth song, I started to relax and began paying attention to the Apache War Dancers. The coed group of performers numbering perhaps twenty consisted of Apaches of various backgrounds.

L to R: Freddie Kaydahzinne, Rachel Tortilla, Bo Kaydahzinne, Thurman Sago,
Wayle Eagle Claw, Nelson Kaydahzinne, Matt Summa, Kristen Kaydahzinne
Photo taken and provided by Edith Kaydahzinne

Bo Kaydahzinne *(G-Great Grandson)* *Of* *(Cochise and Chatto)*	*Thurman Sago* *(Descendant)* *Of* *(Fatty)*	*Wayle Eagle Claw* *(Descendant)* *Of* *(Kinzhuma)*
Nelson Kaydahzinne *(G-Great Grandson)* *Of* *(Cochise)*	*Matt Summa* *(G-Great Grandson)* *Of* *(Cochise and Chatto)*	*Kristen Kaydahzinne* *(G-Granddaughter)* *Of* *(Cochise and Chatto)*

*Kaydahzinne = Standing Moccasin in Apache *Kinzhuma = Pretty Moccasin in Apache

Those of Chiricahua descent were easily identifiable by a white stripe painted across their faces (males only) and their toe-guarded moccasins, their trademark.
The male dancers wore long breechcloth, tied at their waistline by thick leather belts. The majority wore long sleeve shirts, while a few were shirtless with just a vest covering their upper bodies. On their hands, they either held a lance or a rifle. Some of them wore medicine caps on their heads, decorated with eagle and turkey feathers. Others tied bandanas around their heads, which kept their long hair out of their faces. The females wore long dresses; some made from solid bright colors while others made theirs from a multi-dotted calico material. Around their waist, thick leather belts held a sheath for their sharp knives. The majority of them danced with their knives on hand, which they moved up and down in rhythm with the beats of our drums. All of them wore their long hair loose.

SINGING AND DANCING IN MESCALERO

It was a spectacular sight indeed, especially from where I sat, so close that I could hear their heavy breathing. For the most part, a break followed each song, allowing the dancers to catch their breath. During a break Carson jokingly said to me, *"Man, you are good! How did you pick up the songs so quickly?"* Not sure if he was serious or not, I responded by saying, *"I don't know. I must confess, that I found some easy to follow while others were very hard to understand, but I am glad that you think I sang well."* Carson asked me to sit closer so he could help me with the words. I moved closer and waited for Freddie to begin singing the next song, which he did a minute later. Carson slightly turned over my way and was careful to pronounce the words of the lyrics until he was satisfied that I was pronouncing them correctly. The songs were sung over and over in verses. By the second or third time around, I could sing along comfortably. During breaks, Carson was kind enough to translate the songs and explain their meanings and origins. With each passing break, Carson's friendliness increased. My new friend was opening up more and more, and I began to feel cautiously comfortable. After singing for over an hour, Freddie addressed the audience and prepared for the last song.

Once done, all singers got up and shook hands. I thanked Freddie and everyone for the opportunity to join them. I was about to walk away when Carson asked *"Siggy what are you doing later?"* *"Nothing, I am here for the evening."* I responded. *"Well, don't go far; the Medicine Man wants to talk to you."* Carson said. *"Yes sir."* I responded. We shook hands and Carson walked away.

Shortly after, I was joined by Carlos, Richard and Jack. I told them that I wanted to go to the car to put my drum away. Upon our return, we joined hundreds of spectators who left the comfort of their seats to either use the restrooms, or walked throughout the common grounds enjoying the many items on display by the vendors. Standing in the middle of the crowd was Carson, who appeared either anxious or lost. I walked over to him, tapped him on the shoulder and asked if everything was ok. His restless demeanor quickly changed to one of relief. *"Where have you been? I have been looking for you all over! Come with me, the Medicine Man is waiting for you!"* he said. I quickly realized that he meant business. I looked at Carlos and Jack as if saying *"please, don't let me go!"*

I began to follow Carson without saying much, but deep inside I was full of questions and anxiety. *"Who is the Medicine Man? Why does he want to talk to me? How does he know who I am?"* Unable to come up with any answers to relieve my stress, I followed Carson with apprehension as we walked towards the cooking arbors. Once inside, I found myself surrounded by more than a dozen people who were busy cooking and attending various fire pits.

Among them was Carol, Carson's wife, whom he introduced me to, along with everyone else working there. What impressed me the most was seeing such enormous amounts of food cooking in one place at the same time. Within a matter of minutes, Carson and I found ourselves with two plates full of food which Carol had generously prepared. Carson and I sat at a homemade picnic table to enjoy the delicious meal. Outside, dozens of Apaches were beginning to assemble in line for their complimentary dinner, a courtesy fulfilled with pride and pleasure by the maiden's family. Before I took my first bite, I expressed my concerns about eating before so many tribal members who waited patiently in line. *"You are our guest so you eat first. This is the way we do it here, relax,"* Carson said. *"Well, I am honored,"* I humbly responded. *"Let's eat fast, we've got to get going,"* Carson said. Eating fast was something I had mastered after fifteen years of working for various fire departments.

Within minutes we were done and ready to go. Where we were going, I did not know, but I was ready and anxious. I thanked Carol for the food and expressed my pleasure in meeting everyone there.

Chiricahua Camp
Chapter Fourteen

Minutes later, we found ourselves walking away from the Feast Grounds. We headed towards the parking lot and soon came upon a dirt road from which sprang many narrow trails. We merged onto one of those paths and marched for a while towards the outskirts of the campgrounds. As we did so, I began to feel nervous. *"Who is this medicine man I am going to meet? Why are we going so far? Should I even trust this Carson guy?"* After all, I just met him! My thoughts along with the long and silent walk ended when Carson stopped and turned around. *"Do you see that camp over there?"* He asked, as he pointed with his nose towards a small brush arbor located in the southwestern corner of the campgrounds. *"Yes, I do"* I replied. *"That is where we are going. It is the camp of the Chiricahuas."* he said, as he started to walk again in front of me.

The arbor was approximately 15' x 10' and perhaps seven feet in height. As we got closer, I saw a group of people in it, carrying on as usual. Some of the adults sat on portable chairs conversing with each other, while others sat eating at a picnic table. The children, on the other hand, ran in and out of the arbor as they played. Once inside, Carson introduced me to everyone. *"This is Siggy; he is a Warm Springs Apache from Florida. He has an interesting story - his family was left behind when our ancestors left Florida. He will tell you more about it."* There must have been close to ten adults in the camp. Before I was able to say anything, I was being served a plate of food. Although I was still full from Carol's treat, I was unable to say no. In some way, I was going to have to accommodate a little more. How I was going to get it to my stomach was a different story. My nervousness had caused a lump in my throat that prevented me from swallowing. Somehow by the grace of God I was able to put a dent on it. The laughter and carefree nature of the young ones helped break the self-imposed tension. Once I composed myself, I was able to tell them about my ancestor's fateful mishaps; how they were taken to Cuba, their hardships, the making of ropes, and their times of shame and their relentless endurance throughout that difficult period. I concluded my story with the arrival of my family in Florida and my desire to find my long lost relatives. Everyone kept asking questions, as I answered to the best of my ability.

It was there that I took the time to share with Carson the dream I had six months earlier, where a man by the name of Freddie was going to teach me to sing old Apache songs. I was about to tell him how I felt when I found out that Freddie was the one who gave me permission to sing along with the group, when I noticed the laughter of the children and the whispering from the elders coming to an abrupt end. It didn't take me long to realize that the Medicine Man had walked in.

There, standing in front of me, stood a young looking individual, perhaps thirty years old. He was dressed in a dark blue long sleeve shirt covered by a black leather vest, black jeans and boots. His dark olive complexion complimented his black eyes and long black hair, which reached below his shoulders. Although his presence was commanding, to my surprise, his demeanor was gentle and pleasant. He introduced himself as James Kunestsis; a name meaning "Puts the Fire Out". He began asking questions about my ancestors and present family. The cordial interrogation went on for quite some time.

Once done, James spoke of his side of the family, which included Roger Toclanny from his mother's side and Jasper Kanseah from his father's side.

Roger was a Warm Springs Chiricahua Apache Scout, and Old man Jasper Kanseah was Geronimo's nephew and the youngest warrior in his band. Jasper was thirteen years old when they surrendered at Cañon de los Embudos, Mexico, in 1886.

About half an hour later, James spoke some words in Apache to Carson and walked out. Soon after, Carson said *"Let's go, Siggy,"* as he walked out of the arbor. Instinctively, I began following Carson, only to realize I had left without saying thanks. I turned around and acknowledged the group of Chiricahuas for their kindness and hospitality.

By the time I caught up with Carson, he was knocking on a tepee's door.
The lodge was white with four morning stars, painted in the Chiricahua traditional colors of black, white, yellow and green. It stood all alone on the southwestern side of the campgrounds. A few seconds later, the flap that served as a door opened and Carson walked in. Immediately, the door closed behind him. Not knowing what to do, I stood there in silence. I am sure what seemed forever was just a few minutes in time. Suddenly, the door was opened and I was invited to come in.

Once inside, I found myself surrounded by four Crown Dancers in full regalia. Their faces fully covered with black leather masks and on top of their heads they wore huge wooden crowns (sometimes referred to as horns) measuring about two feet in height. In each hand they held long wands, resembling sharp pointed swords. Their naked upper bodies were covered with paint. From the waist down. they were dressed in a long yellow-fringed skirt decorated with hundreds of tiny metal jingles, their feet covered by toe-guarded moccasins.

Chiricahua Crown Dancers, ca 2007 ****

They danced around me in a clockwise manner making chilling whooping sounds. Feeling nervous and apprehensive, I stayed motionless until they were finished. Immediately after that, Carson introduced me to the men who sat on wooden benches with their water drums on hand. After meeting all of them, I sat at the end of bench, leaving plenty of room between the singers and me. My heart, in full tachycardia, was dying for a break. I sat on that bench and took a deep breath in hopes to adjust to such an overwhelming experience. It felt like I had entered a time machine traveling back hundreds of years. *"Is this real or am I dreaming? Who am I? How did I get here?"* I asked myself. It was a deep spiritual awareness unlike anything I had ever experienced. Honestly I felt scared and helpless. Even though no one was physically holding me down, I was unable to move or leave the tepee even if I wanted to. It was all mental, as if someone or something had disabled my abilities to physically function in my new surroundings. There I was, a big husky guy who could easily defend himself, in fear of the unknown. For the first time in my life, I had entered something so spiritual and powerful that it made me feel small and powerless. Not knowing what else to do, I began to pray. *"Grandfather, please hear me. You have guided me here, I am at your mercy, have pity on me, give me strength, show me the way and I will follow...."* Shortly after my prayer, the Tepee's door opened and James walked in. He was accompanied by a clown, a young boy painted in white, wearing raggedy jean shorts and a white mask over his head.

A few minutes later, James stood in front of me; he then called the lead dancer over. As both of them stood there, I felt paralyzed. Not knowing what to say, I stayed quiet while looking at the ground, as I dared not gaze upon them. The brief silence was interrupted when James spoke to me. As I looked up, he began telling me the origin of his group and how it had been passed down to from generation to generation. Pointing to the dancer's regalia, he began describing in details what each item meant. He started with the toe-guarded moccasins, a trademark of the Chiricahuas. He continued his way up to the long fringed yellow skirt that covered the dancer from the waist down. It was decorated with black designs in the shape of pyramids that represented the four sacred mountains of the Chiricahuas. The skirt was adorned with hundreds of hand-rolled metal jingles. James continued working his way up the dancer's white painted upper body, as he explained the meaning of the black painted lightning that ran from the hands to the shoulders. Upon reaching the torso, James pointed to a black painted star that partially covered the dancer's chest and abdomen. *"This is the Morning Star which I painted on him,"* he said. *"You are like the Morning Star; you come from the East to bring knowledge to us. We know who you are and we had been waiting for you. You are welcome in our camp."* After that he asked the dancer to take his mask off. I was shocked to see the dancer's face, as I had been told by the elders that no one was allowed to know who they were. Their true identity was forbidden. Only those of the medicine way were allowed that privilege. Most Apaches bowed their heads (out of respect) in their presence to avoid recognizing the person behind the traditional outfit. The dancer is meant to signify the mountain spirits and as such, it is important that everyone while in their presence acknowledge this tribal custom. These were among the Apache traditions I had learned a year earlier while sitting with the group of Chiricahua elders and ex-prisoners of war.

To my surprise, the dancer was someone I had met previously. When James was done, the dancer donned his mask with horns and returned to his lead position. James proceeded to sit down in the middle of the bench between the other singers.

He grabbed a medal pot, a piece of deer hide, along with a strip of rubber band, and began to assemble a drum. Once done, he passed it down to me along with a drumstick.

A few seconds later, he began beating his drum at an unusually fast rate while reciting prayers in the Apache language. I bowed my head and began to pray in my own way. I thanked the Creator, as I knew He had placed me in a very special and sacred place. After the opening prayer, James began to sing. The rest of the singers followed, while the dancers danced around the fire in the center of the tepee. Their unnerving whoops were soothed by the sound of their jingles.

After a few verses, I found myself singing my heart out. Some of the singers looked at me in amazement, probably wondering how a stranger had captured such sacred songs so quickly. It was really incredible, song after song, I found myself singing right along. I didn't know how I was doing it and I was too busy to try to figure it out. Strangely, it felt as if a spirit had taken over me and I was letting it. At times, I caught myself singing way too loud. *"Be humble, Siggy,"* I told myself, as I lowered my voice in sync with the others. I often wonder what came over me that day. The prayers, singing, and dancing went on for a while.

When James was done, he walked out of the tepee followed by the clown and the four Crown Dancers. Since I was sitting at the end of the bench and we moved in a clockwise manner, I was signaled to follow them out. The rest of the singers followed, as I exited the lodge.

Once outside, I found a group of young mothers carrying their newborn babies. All of them had patiently waited to have their babies blessed by James Kunestsis, the medicine man. Prior to the blessings, the dancers formed a single file row and the singers stood perpendicular to them. I was surprised when asked to join the singers for the occasion. I took my position at the end of the line and asked the individual next to me for guidance. *"You are doing fine,"* he responded.

Berle Kanseah
Photographed by Robert Ove, ca. 1991

CHIRICAHUA CAMP

He was an older gentleman, perhaps sixty years-old, about five-foot, six inches tall, stocky, with short spiky gray hair and dark complexion. His name was Berle Kanseah, (Geronimo's great grand nephew) James Kunestsis' dad. Berle kindly explained what was going on, as James blessed the mothers and their offsprings with the sacred pollen.

Soon after, we began singing, as the dancers performed in accordance with the newborn blessing ritual. Berle turned his head to face me in hopes that I would catch up with the lyrics. When all the blessings were finished, the young mothers gave us baskets filled with fruits and household goods.

Once the gifts were put away, we began to walk uphill towards the Feast Grounds to join three other Crown Dancer groups. James led the way and the dancers followed in a single file row. At their tail end, the young clown purposely stepped out of line every now and then, as if trying to break the seriousness of it all. Not far behind, the singers followed in pairs. My partner Berle began telling me the importance of the language. *"You need to learn the language. Without it, all of this will cease to exist."* *"Yes, Sir. I am very interested in learning it,"* I replied. I found Berle to be kind and encouraging, but most importantly, I felt protected by him. Just before entering the Feast Grounds, Berle explained how we were to behave and what was expected of us. His guiding words gave me strength as I stepped into an unknown world.

By the time we arrived at the Feast Grounds; the sun had set and with it came a chill carried lightly on the evening breeze. We stood at the eastern side of the arbor (sometimes referred to as the arena, the sacred area where the dancers perform), and waited for the sacred fire to be lit. Our group was the first to perform that night. As we walked through the arbor, I noticed that the bleachers were full of people. On the ground, hundreds of spectators, mostly families sat on lawn chairs on both sides of the arbor forming two half-moon circles.

In front of us stood the Big Tepee, the sacred lodge where the young Maidens were to dance for four nights. It is through holy songs sung by medicine men and the guidance of their female sponsors (medicine women) that the Maidens will learn how to properly carry on through the stages of their adult life.

In front of the Big Tepee were four wooden benches awaiting our arrival. Out of the corner of my eye, I spied the group of V.I.P. ladies that had welcomed me a year earlier. Sitting on the bleachers behind them were Carlos, Richard and Jack. How ironic I though, just a few hours earlier Carson had swept me away like a Florida hurricane. I felt nervous and scared as I followed him into the unknown and away from the comfort zone of my friends. Even more ironic was the way I felt as I walked through the arena. In some strange way, it felt as if I was protected by an invisible shield.

Upon reaching our destination, we sat and waited for the Crown Dancers to bless the fire, a ritual done in a synchronized manner as they follow their leader. Once the fire was blessed from all four cardinal directions, James led the way, as he began to sing. Within minutes, the fire had grown into a bonfire and the dancers began to perform in a free style manner, allowing themselves to show their individuality and personal moves.

As the night grew darker, the fire grew brighter, creating mystical ghostly figures out of the dancers as they moved in and out of the light, posturing and making strange noises. Every so often, the dancers came so close to us, that I could hear their breathing. Their radiant energy was powerful and contagious and within minutes I had succumbed to it. The euphoric experience was like something I had never felt before. To top it off, I had a drum in my hand that connected me to them.

At that moment, I realized how blessed and privileged I was, and how the Creator had guided me back to my people and their customs. In a strange way, I sensed my ancestors smiling at me and saying, *"This is where you belong. You finally made it home. We are proud of you. We can now rest in peace knowing that our broken family hoop has finally mended."* That evening, I felt proud and more Apache than ever before in my life. The feeling was overwhelming. There I was sitting among other Chiricahua descendants singing for the Chiricahua Crown Dancers. My limited knowledge did not prevent me from realizing that I was in a very special and sacred position. Not knowing if it was a one-time opportunity, I sang my heart out. Overwhelmed by the power of the songs and my surroundings, I became dazed and ecstatic, as if I had fallen into a trance. As a result, I heard myself singing along with the group, and yet inside I was praying to God. It was a spiritual transition I had never experienced before. Not only was I participating in one of the most sacred Apache ceremonies, but I was also communicating with the Creator. Through my prayers, I had entered His Kingdom; there, all was simple and beautiful. I can only compare that moment as equivalent to the birth of my children.

Occupied by singing and praying, the nigh moved on. About thirty minutes into the ceremony, I began to feel normal again and in tune with my surroundings. I looked to the sky and I saw millions of stars and a bright moon. Because of the moonlight and the reflection from the sacred fire, I was able to see the glowing silhouette of my three friends. I wondered what was going through their minds. It had been hours since they last saw me. *"What are they thinking? Can they see me? Do they realize that it's me sitting here?"* I kept asking myself.

As I began to relax, my singing became even stronger. Again I found some of the songs easy to follow, while others extremely hard. Every so often, the dancers would come right up to us and make their whooping sounds, sending chills down my spine. During small pauses when James did his sets (a period when the singers stay quiet and the lead singer recites words out loud), I prayed and thanked the Creator for allowing me to be part of such sacred moments. At last, my journey had come full circle.

When our group was done singing, I felt as if I had awakened from a dream. A singer, by the name of Lynn Hank, said to me, *"Well it is over for us tonight. Are you going to sing with us again tomorrow?"* he asked. *"Yes Sir, I would love to, if I am allowed,"* I replied. *"Of course, you are!"* he said. What felt like a dream was becoming a reality. I had been invited to sing again! As the other group of singers approached the bench, we shook hands with them. I believe it was around 10:30pm in the evening, when we were officially done. I thanked everyone in the group and began to walk out. I stopped to say hello to the group of ladies when Kathleen Kanseah said to me, *"You know, Siggy, you must go now. Do not mingle with the people in the crowd, you must go home."* *"Yes Ma'am,"* I said, puzzled by her words and their meaning. Instinctively I understood how solemn the experience had been and that sharing would only cause me to lose the power of the moment.

In time, I learned that the Crown Dancers also known as the Mountain Gods represented a spirit and like all supernatural things they must not interact with humans. As a result, most dancers and singers do not return to the site where the sacred dance was performed. Observing the unspoken rule adds to the essence and mystery associated with the dance of the Mountain Gods. After hearing Kathleen's advice, I caught up with James and thanked him for the opportunity. *"We are going to do it all over again tomorrow evening, hope you join us"* he said. *"Yes, of course."* I replied.

I thanked the rest of the singers and told Carson and Berle that I would see them the next day.

As I walked towards the exit, I heard my friends calling out my name. *"How did you do that?"* Carlos asked. *"We looked for you for hours and next thing we know you are walking through the Feast Grounds with James' group,"* Jack stated. *"It's a long story and in many ways, it all happened because of you guys,"* I replied and humbly thanked them both, as we continued walking towards the parking lot. Once there, I gave Carlos the basket full of goodies that I had received from the mothers of the newborns blessed by James.

Soon after, I drove down to my hotel where I showered and laid down to rest. Although I was totally exhausted, I was unable to sleep that night. So many thoughts and emotions kept running through my mind, and yet I had no one to express them to. I kept asking myself: *"Was the experience real? Did it really happen? Did they really say to come back tomorrow?"* I remembered looking at the clock over and over and wondering if I should call my family back home. I wanted to share my experience with them, but decided not to, when I realized it was 2:00am in Florida.

Despite having slept very little, I woke up the next morning fully energized. The first thing I did was to call home. I told them of my experiences and how I was invited to return. My family's reassuring words made me feel at ease and gave me strength. Later that morning, I drove to Mescalero where I met up with my friends. After a meal, the four of us headed to the Feast Grounds.

Early that afternoon, I ran into Freddie who gave me permission to sing with them again. A short time later, the M.C., (Master of Ceremony) made the announcement, *"All war dancers and singers! Start making your way into the arena."* Within a few minutes, all participants were ready to go. I took my outer position on the bench with Carson by my side. It was at that moment that Carson noticed my drumstick. Although it was hooped at the end, it simply did not look like everyone else's. *"Who made your drumstick?"* he asked. *"I made it myself while visiting T or C with my Navajo friend. We sat under a willow tree next to a spring; cut a couple of green branches and made two, one for each of us,"* I replied. *"We make ours from oak and a little smaller at the hoop end,"* he said while pointing to his drumstick. Although mine worked just as good, it simply did not look right when compared to Carson's and those belonging to the other Apache singers. To my surprise, Carson said *"I am going to make you one for next year when you return."*

Our conversation was suddenly interrupted when Freddie's powerful voice came through the speakers like echoes of thunder. Not only did it send chills down my arms, but it jumped-started the dancers into motion. What a sight! What an incredible feeling, as I felt my arms covered with goose bumps. I was almost living the dancers' story with each of their steps. In between small breaks some of the dancers adjusted their outfits while others drank water. I, on the other hand, kept thinking about Carson's words, as they echoed in my mind. *"I am going to make you a drum stick for next year."* Once again, I was being invited to return. We continued singing and the dancers stayed in rhythm with the beat of our drums. Our performance ended at around 5:00pm. I shook hands with everyone and followed Carson into the same cooking pit as the day before.

Once there, I was eagerly welcomed by everyone. Feeling somewhat comfortable, I offered a helping hand. My offer was accepted and within minutes Carson and I found ourselves carrying fire wood and heavy pots of boiling water.

CHIRICAHUA CAMP

Once fed by Carson's wife, we headed down the mountain to the Chiricahuas' camp. Surprisingly we found the encampment empty. It was clear that we had arrived way too early. We then headed to the Crown Dancers' tepee and found it empty as well. Carson and I walked in and sat down to talk. Even though I had just met him a few days earlier, it felt as if I had known him my entire life. I was able to converse with him freely and ask questions.

A short time later, other group members began to arrive. The atmosphere was pleasant and full of joy, good humor and laughter filled the air, thus making me feel like I was at home. By 6:00pm, all singers and dancers had arrived. Simultaneously and in a systematic way, all dancers got dressed. After donning their moccasins and skirts, paint was applied to their naked upper bodies. The color of the paint never, or rarely, changed. It always followed the traditional Chiricahua colors. On the first day, the dancers' upper bodies were painted black with white designs. On the second day, they were painted white with black designs. The third day, it was yellow with green designs and vice versa on the fourth and last day. The clown was always painted white. Once all dancers were dressed and painted, the clown was sent to bless the path leading to the Feast Ground. Upon his return, the ceremony began with James' rapid beating of his drum along with prayers and singing. The ritual appeared to be similar or identical as previously observed. When preparations ended, James, the clown and the rest of us walked out of the tepee.

Once outside, I expected to see the mothers with their newborns waiting for blessings, but they were not there. Instead, Berle asked me to bless his son, James. The honorable request left me staggering. There I was, just beginning to relax and thinking I knew what was next, when in a split second, I was put on the spot. I could almost hear the Creator laughing out loud.

In order to accomplish such task, Lynn Hank stepped in to show me the way. He escorted me to the lead Crown Dancer and told me to take a pinch of pollen from his medicine pouch. With a nip of powder in between my fingers and a shaking hand, Lynn and I walked over to James, who sat waiting a short distance away. There I began to do as told. After honoring all four cardinal directions with the pollen, I was ready to bless the medicine man.

The blessing consisted of making crosses on his body in a clockwise manner. Using my index finger and my thumb, I drew the first yellow cross on James' right foot. I proceeded to do his right shoulder, forehead, followed by his left shoulder and foot. The blessing ritual ended by me turning in a full circle. After that I was asked to bless all the dancers in the same manner. The only difference was that the dancers stood as I did the blessings. Once done, I returned back to my spot among the singers. *"You did well... But there is a lot more for you to learn,"* Berle said. A few minutes later, we began walking towards the Feast Grounds. During our walk, Berle started telling me about the many hardships endured by the Chiricahuas since their surrender in 1886. He finished by saying, *"It's all good. We are still here. You are with the right group, now you have to learn the language."*

Once inside the sacred grounds, we waited at the eastern entrance for the fire to be lit. While waiting, the Master of Ceremony, narrated over the P.A. the sacredness of the feast and the story of how the Mescalero Apaches opened their doors to the Chiricahuas and the Lipans in their times of need. As a result, the Mescalero Apache Tribe is composed of all three groups. The M.C. also emphasized on the zero tolerance of taking pictures inside the Feast Grounds.

He also warned people about the danger of fireworks associated with the extreme dry weather conditions that existed. Despite his requests not to light the incendiary device, the skies glowed with multi colors and the sound of big bangs. After all it was the Fourth of July weekend! Once the fire was lit, we walked across the arena and proceeded to sit on the wooden benches in front of the Big Tepee. By then, I had learned the singers' names. In no particular order they were: James Kunestsis lead singer, Lynn Hank, Leroy Coonie, Carl and Pete Kazhe, Carson Carrillo, Jerry Rice, Berle Kanseah and Vernon Simmons.

That night, I sat between Berle and Lynn. In the beginning of each song, Lynn sang into my ear, in hopes I catch up on the song's lyrics. I found his voice to be clear and easy to follow. Lynn quickly became my teacher and mentor. Having him next to me gave me strength and confidence. *"You are doing well!"* he said. *"Thank you, but honestly, I am overwhelmed. It is hard to sing these songs without knowing the language,"* I replied. *"Don't worry. In time everything will fall in place. Feel free to ask questions, that is what we are here for. We want you to learn the ways of the Chiricahuas,"* he said. His words of encouragement made me feel like I was part of the group. An overwhelming feeling of belonging came over me. I wanted to say so much, but the lump in my throat barely allowed me to say thanks.

Throughout the evening, I prayed and thanked the Creator for such acceptance and all his gifts. Many times during those prayers, I felt my spirit rise. Never before had I experienced anything like it. It felt great to be among the Chiricahuas and accepted as one. With that acceptance came a strong desire to learn more about the power that drives all traditional Chiricahua Apaches, their Crown Dancers.

In between songs I asked Berle to tell me about that power. *"It is power with a big P. Our Crown Dancers represent the good mountain spirits that protect the Apache people. They have the ability to drive away evil spirits, but most importantly, their sacred blessings have kept the people close to their God, Unsen. Most Apaches have experienced that power one way or another, and you are no exception. Amazingly, what connects you to that power is your drum. In some mystical way it is the main source of energy that keeps those mountain spirits moving."* Berle's explanation made me realize that I was in a very honorable positions and one of great responsibility. As my mind wondered with questions and emotions, I thought about Ray, my Navajo friend and my Seminole friends. It was them who taught me to sing and play the instrument that was allowing me to learn about my ancestor's ways of life and beliefs. I felt proud and tall. Caught in deep thoughts, I continued singing until our session ended late that evening. After shaking hands with the singers, I was invited to join them again the next day. With a grin on my face, I walked up to the group of ladies and said goodnight. From there, my three friends, and I walked down to the parking lot. After chatting for a few minutes, we decided to call it a night.

The next day I headed up to Mescalero to reunite with my friends. At about 3:00pm, we arrived at the Feast Grounds. It was my third day of participation, but the fourth and last day of the feast. I asked Freddie if I could sing with them again. Although I already knew the answer, I still asked out of respect. I didn't want to take anything for granted. I had no problem being humble in his presence. A short time later, the announcement for singers and dancers to make their way into the arena was made.

I sat at the end of the bench with Carson by my side. Shortly thereafter, Freddie's powerful voice broke the silence when he began to sing. The dancers seemed to dance harder than ever; ignoring the fact that it was 3:00pm in July at six thousand feet above sea level. At times, I felt bad for them as no breaks were given in-between songs. Their way of dancing truly showed their warrior spirits. Their battle stories told with each of their dancing steps. As time passed, I began to understand why Chiricahuas were considered different even among other Apaches. When the singing was over, I shook hands with all the singers and dancers and personally thanked Freddie for everything.

With drum on hand, I followed Carson into the cooking arbor. While eating there, I took one good look at all that was going on. The amount of food, workers and love that went into making the feast a reality made me think about the privilege bestowed upon me as a singer. Sitting next to me was the person that helped guide me through three of the most meaningful days in my life. I thanked Carson for everything he had done for me. *"You are very welcome, but it's not over yet,"* he replied. Once done eating, I thanked everyone for everything they had shared with me. With regret, I gave them my farewell.

Soon after, Carson and I headed down to James's camp, where we found the dancers donning on their gear. While sitting inside the tepee, my mind began to drift. I thought about all that had taken place. With a sense of sorrow, I began to pray. *"Grandfather, I thank you for allowing me to share these powerful moments and all your gifts. I have asked you to help me find my family and nothing more than that. You have fulfilled my desires and then some. Being accepted by the Chiricahuas is more than I expected. I thank you again. Grandfather, I ask that you look after and bless the Mescalero People who so kindly open their doors to my Ancestors in their times of need. As long as they are here, they will have a home. Although I will like to stay here among them, I know I must return to my family. Give me strength to fight my weaknesses. Show me the light and I will follow...."* My prayers ended when I heard a sound coming from a drum. I opened my eyes and realized that my blessings were not over. I still had one more night to rejoice. James' rapid beating of his drum signaled the beginning of the ceremony.

After the conclusion of our preparations, we headed to the Feast Grounds, just like we did on the previous nights. Once James's voice pierced through the silence of the night, the ceremony began. Our dancers came from the east, looking like thoroughbreds out of their gates. The air was filled with energy and their power felt stronger than ever. While watching them, my mind drifted into deep thoughts. *"Indeed, the Mexican and U.S. governments' barbaric acts against the Apaches accomplished many of their objectives, but it was obvious that they had failed to succeed in breaking their spirit."* There, dancing in front of me to the rhythm of my drum beat was my bloodline. The tigers of the human race were alive and well. To see them dance made me feel proud and unconquered. During singing pauses when James did the prayer, I found myself asking the same questions: *"Where do I stand? Is this a onetime experience? Will I ever be allowed to sing again?"* I reminded myself to be humble and thankful. *"One day at a time, Siggy. Enjoy it, it's not over yet!"* I told myself. Suddenly, Lynn spoke to me and snapped me out of my deep trance. *"Did you have a good time?"* he asked. *"Of course, this experience has been indescribable,"* I responded. *"Well now, you have a reason to come back next year and do it all over again."* I couldn't believe what I was hearing! It was a lot more than I could digest. I stayed sitting on the bench wanting to pinch myself, only to realize that our session had really come to an end. I stood up and shook hands with the singers from the next group of Crown Dancers.

By then, my group had gained some distance on me. After catching up to them, we shook hands and with it came the conclusion of one of the most powerful experiences of my life. I gave my farewell to everyone, including all the ladies in the V.I. P. section. They were eager to know how I felt about sharing such special moments with them.

The lump in my throat barely allowed me to say, *"It was beyond anything that words could express or describe."* They all wanted to know if they would see me again the following year. *"Yes, I will do my best to be here!"* I replied. Those ladies meant so much to me. To walk away from their kind love was not easy.

Soon after, Jack, Richard and Carlos showed up. After walking down to the parking lot, I shook hands and gave them a big hug. Expressing my gratitude was hard to do, as the lump in my throat reappeared and prevented me from expressing how much they truly meant to me. Driving away from Mescalero was difficult to say the least. To think that I had to wait a whole year to see everyone again was hard to accept.

During the long and lonely drive to Alamogordo, I began to look for answers to my earlier questions such as *"How come everyone I met in Mescalero was a Chiricahua? How did the Medicine Man know who I was? Why was I allowed to enter such sacredness?"* Suddenly, I realized that the entire Chiricahua community had been watching and following every move I made. *Why not?* After all, I was an unknown, a total stranger asking for permission to enter into their private world. Certainly they must have been suspicious of me in the beginning and rightfully so. I guess at some level I must have passed the test, which prompted the Chiricahua Crown Dancer group to take me in as one of their own. *"Which test could I have possibly passed, that made them welcome me into their group? How come they did that for me? Is that something they commonly do for their guest?"* I asked myself. I remembered the elder's comments about the fact that only medicine people were allowed to know the Crown Dancers true identity. *"Well, now I know who they are,"* I told myself. *"Why me? Who am I?"* I wondered. Unaware of my bloodline's past tribal history, I began to pray. *"Grandfather, I am thankful for learning and experiencing my ancestor's ways of life, but I am puzzled. I only want to come back and do this if it will bring me closer to you. If this is your wish, Grandfather, please show me the way and I will follow."* It was at that moment that an overwhelming peaceful feeling came over me. In some mystical way, I could hear the Creator saying, *"Relax, Son. In time everything will fall in place."* I consoled myself, with my old saying. *"Be humble Siggy, and most of all, be thankful for all your gifts and do not question the holiness that you experienced."* A while later, I arrived at the hotel. That night, while laying in bed, I realized that a person doesn't have to be dead to enter God's Kingdom. Sometimes, we can enter through the power of dance and song and the acceptance of traditions and rituals as old as time itself. At least that was how I felt that night.

The next morning, I drove to Albuquerque to catch my flight back home. Once up in the air, I remembered looking out the plane's window at the quickly fading desert mountains. I didn't want to return to Florida. I felt like a big piece of me was staying behind.

At home, I felt a sense of lightness and relief that I had never experienced before. My soul and spirit were fully charged. I began to tell my story to my family. My Mom was in total shock. She would only nod her head in agreement, but I could tell it was too much for her to comprehend all that had taken place. The rest of the year flew by, not only was I happy to know that there were still Chiricahuas left alive, but that the culture was far from being dead, as I always thought.

Honor Song
Chapter Fifteen

In 2001, I return to Mescalero during the 4th of July Feast. The first person I visited was Carson Carrillo and his family. To my surprise, Carson had finished making the drumstick he had promised me a year earlier. It didn't take long for me to make good use of it, as the next day I had the pleasure of using it during a special gathering. The ceremony consisted of honoring a former Chiricahua prisoner of war, Katherine Kenoi and her family, the same people that welcomed me with warmth and love when I first arrived in Mescalero. Unfortunately Katherine's grandson, Carlos Enjady was out of town during the occasion. His presence was greatly missed.

The event took place at the Feast Grounds; it consisted of Honor Songs and sacred dances performed by the War Singers and Dancers. *"What a perfect way to say thanks,"* I thought. Filled with pride, I sat next to Freddie Kaydahzinne, Carson and other singers and sang for Katherine with enthusiasm and confidence, spurred on by my acceptance among the Chiricahuas.

Later that afternoon, Carson and I reported to James Kunestsis' camp to prepare for the evening's Crown Dance. Not surprisingly, I was welcomed by the group and treated as one of their own. It was great to see them all again, especially Berle Kanseah and Lynn Hank, my teachers and mentors. A year had gone by and we had a lot of catching up to do. As we sat to talk, we were joined by another group member, Vernon Simmons, the adopted grandson of Eugene Chihuahua. I found Vernon to be kind hearted and eager to teach. That evening, as we sang for the Crown Dancers, I sat next to Vernon and learned in depth the purpose of the Crown Dance and the history of our group. *"Since long ago, our group has performed the dance of the mountain Gods. The purpose is to call upon the winds and the rain and to bring health and fortune to the Apache people. With the brandishing of their wands against unseen enemies, they drive away sickness and evil. It was our dancers who gave strength and blessings to the Chiricahuas during years of peace, hostility and imprisonment. After their release from Fort Sill, Oklahoma, our group was led by the Fatty family. In the 1940's it was passed down to my grandfather Eugene Chihuahua,"* Vernon said. Learning the history of our group made the experience that much more meaningful. Upon the conclusion of our session, I felt a great sense of honor for the privilege of being accepted into something so powerful and traditional.

The next morning I decided to explore and learn more about locations of interest pertaining to the Chiricahuas and their history. One significant place was White Sands National Monument, which was adjacent to the Mescalero Apache Reservation. This national treasure measures approximately twenty miles long by ten or fifteen miles wide. It is covered with pure white sands that resemble powdered sugar.

After stopping at the visitor center to study the road map, I drove into the park. Once deep in it and away from other visitors, I got out of the car and began to walk along a series of sand dunes that flanked the desert road. It didn't take long to realize this was a dangerous place. It was easy to see and feel that walking on such terrain was exhausting. As a result, I remained close to my vehicle and climbed some of the nearby hills. It was fun to run and jump off them, but I was only able to do it a few times before I became totally exhausted. Once rested, I went on a hike and found some to the most amazing hideouts. According to the elders and as told by James Kaywaykla, a member of Victorio's band, it was in those dunes that the Warm Springs Apaches successfully evaded the enemy.

White Sands, New Mexico
Photographed by Laure Marmontel

Mr. Kaywaykla, a Chiricahua-Warm Springs Apache, was among the ex prisoners of war who decided to reveal old Chiricahua stories to a respected writer by the name of Eve Ball. His memoirs can be found in The Days of Victorio, one of her many books. According to Mr. Kaywaykla, the magical white sands served as a buffer between the Apaches and their enemies as they hid deep in the surrounding mountains such as the Sacramento Mountains, and Dog Canyon. The white painted desert not only made the U.S. soldiers visible but it slowed them down, thus giving the Apaches plenty of time to plan their ambush.

After spending half a day enjoying the beauty of the White Sands range, I drove up to the Feast Grounds to sing for the War Dancers. Upon conclusion, I headed to James' camp where I joined my group for the second evening of the Maiden Ceremony. The four day feast ended two days later when four young Apache girls took on their new endeavors as young adults and keepers of their people's traditions. I was honored to have taken part in such sacred event and looked forward to the following year's feast. On the final day of my visit, I spent a lot of time visiting friends and giving thanks to the Creator for all his gifts.

Once home, reality set in when I reported to work the next day at my firehouse. My energy level was such that not even a four-alarm fire was going to slow me down. On my time off, I continued singing and dancing along my Seminole friends. By January of 2002, I had danced at most of the southeastern Pow Wows from North Carolina to South Florida.

HONOR SONG

On the second weekend of February I was ready to dance at my favorite Pow, The Seminole Tribal Fair and Rodeo. The annual gathering was held at the Seminole Reservation in Hollywood, Florida. On that particular year close to fifty thousand spectators attended the three day event. William Cypress and I registered to dance as Northern Traditional. We were both eager to play with the big boys, as singers and dancers came from as far as Montana and Canada. It all translated to great competition and lots of fun. Too bad it ended so soon. That concluded my dancing for the season. Somehow winter had come and gone.

In the spring of 2002, my sister Sonia and I planned a surprised visit to see our parents who were still living in the City of Hialeah. The small battalion consisted of my sister, her husband and their son Jake Frew along with me and my children Emily and Lance. After knocking on the front door with no response, my brother-in-law and I decided to go around the house to see if my parents were in the backyard. Instead of finding them we came upon a very significant discovery. It consisted of Prickly Pear leaves hanging on a clothe-line, going through different stages of sun-drying. My brother-in law jokingly asked, *"What kind of voodoo they got going on here Sig?"* *"I have no idea,"* I responded. By the time we reached the back-door, the whole gang was in the house. The first thing I did was ask my Mom about the Prickly Pear experiment found in her backyard. *"I am making soles for my shoes,"* she whispered as if she didn't want anyone else to hear it. *"Mom, these are the things you need to tell me about. Can you please tell me how you make them?"* I asked. *"I will tell you another day, let's enjoy the gathering,"* she responded in a low tone voice. *"No, I need to know now. Tell me how you make them,"* I asked. After insisting multiple times, she began to describe the process. *"You take a pair of Prickly Pear leaves, take out the thorns, step on them and cut it to your foot's pattern. Shave the skin and hang the gooey soles for four days or until they dry out completely,"* she said. I asked where she had learned such a thing. *"I don't even know, it goes way back,"* she said, as she quickly walked away to join the rest of the family. I decided to leave the issue alone, as I didn't want her to start crying, a common occurrence every time I bring up her past. In the end, it all worked out, as everyone enjoyed themselves and I learned something new.

In late spring of 2002, I received a phone call from an Apache friend asking for help in the breaking-in process of a horse belonging to a Seminole. Without hesitation, I took advantage of the opportunity, as working with horses has always been my passion. Arrangements were made to meet the individual at one of the Seminole Reservations know as Big Cypress, aka (B.C.).

A week later my friend and I arrived in Big Cypress, where I met Sam Frank, a Seminole from the Panther Clan. Sam was a cattleman and in his pasture was the horse that needed to be broke. This was not a foreign concept to Sam, but for personal reasons he was not able to do it himself. Little did I know that the gentleman asking for help was what is known today as a horse whisperer.

Sam Frank
Seminole, Panther Clan.ca. 1996

The horse in question was a three-year-old Arabian. After spending some time studying the animal's behavior, I decided it was time to get down to business and start the break-in process. A slight problem existed; there were no round pens in Sam's pasture. The only thing available was a cattle-holding pen approximately four hundred feet square. As a result, we were not able to tire out the animal. This forced us to go to the next step, which consisted of saddling the horse. Once the saddle was on, came the part that I loved most, which meant get on and hold on for dear life. For about thirty minutes, my friend and I took turns getting beat up. It didn't take long before the smart Arabian realized he was not going to win. Within a couple of hours we rode him out of the pen. Luckily everything went easy and no one got hurt.

From that day on Sam and I conceived a friendship that continues to this day. The lucky break-in gave me a positive reputation among other Seminole tribal members, who hired me for various equestrian related activities. Within less than a year, I had broken in a hand full of their horses.

In order to continue working with Sam's horse, he gave me the key to his pasture's gate. His lot consisted of more than two thousand acres, half of which flooded in the summer months. The muddy heaven created all sorts of four wheeling activities which my children and I enjoyed. At times the challenges were too great to overcome even for my Ford F-150, a V-8, 4 x 4, with a 5" lift and Mickey Thomson mud tires. Getting stuck and dirty was part of the fun. Just like me, my children were growing up in the swamps of the Everglades.

That winter, I began to work with Sam's cattle. Within a short period of time I had learned a lot about the business, from driving cattle, to branding, purchase, and sales. It was during those times that I learned a lot about the struggles endured by Sam's family and other Florida Seminoles. The following stories were written as told to me by Sam himself.

Back in the early 1930's, the U.S. Government attempted to remove all Seminoles living in scattered villages throughout South Florida into a reservation called Brighton, located near Lake Okeechobee, Florida. Sam's family was among those who accepted relocation. Soon after their arrival, Brighton was fenced in, and the Government introduced a cattle program in an attempt to help the Seminoles prosper in their new way of life.

The Seminoles welcomed the idea; after all they had a long history of owning cattle for over three centuries. "Early Europeans recorded in their journals how some Seminoles took pride in their herds. One in particular was a Seminole known as Cow Keeper. He lived north of Ocala in an area known as Paynes Prairie, where he owned over ten thousand head of cattle.[7]" Regardless of that history, these were indeed times of change and adaptation for the Seminoles.

In 1934 the first herd of cattle arrived at Brighton from Arizona. Sam's father, Phillip Sam Frank (Otter Clan) took advantage of the program along with J. Osceola, the late Jack Matlow and J. Tucker. These Seminoles were among the first cattlemen in Brighton.

Phillip who spoke Miccosukee was married to Maude Johns (Panther Clan), who spoke Creek. Once Maude learned to speak Miccosukee, it became the only language spoken by the family. During the first few years, the men worked together for the good of the community.

As the program grew, a foreman was needed to oversee the entire operation. Soon after, ear marking and branding became necessary. In time, individuals began to fence in their own pastures.

By the late 1930's, cattle business became a way of life for the Seminole people. As the venture gained strength, so did their political views and ideas. By early 1950's, the Seminoles were ready to join main stream America as an organized contender in the political arena.

In March of 1954, the famous medicine man, Josie Billie, along with Henry Cypress, Toby Johns, Billy Osceola, Larry Mike Osceola, Laura Mae Osceola, and Sam Tommie went to Washington to express their desire to become federally recognized as a tribe. Soon after, a board of directors was created. Bill Osceola became the Chairman and Laura Mae Osceola, Secretary. On March 26, 1957 a constitutional committee was selected to write a constitution and corporate charter. The Constitutional Committee members were: Billy Osceola, John Henry Gopher (Brighton), Bill Osceola, Jack Willie (Dania), Jimmie O. Osceola and Frank J. Billie (Big Cypress), and Larry Mike Osceola (Trail). Bill Osceola of Dania was elected Chairman of the Committee. Once the documents were completed, Laura Mae Osceola translated on all three reservations. Finally, after three years of hard work, the Seminoles Tribe of Florida became federally recognized. Under the leadership of their first elected chairman, Billy Osceola they ratified their Constitution and Bylaws and took control of their own destiny and sovereignty[5].

Sam was about four years old, when the monumental accomplishment took place. Soon after, his family abandoned their traditional Chickees and moved from Brighton to the Hollywood/Dania Reservation. While living in Hollywood, Sam's family sold arts and crafts.

Sam Frank, Seminole, Panther Clan.
Standing in front of what is left of his childhoods sleeping Chickee
Brighton Seminole Reservation, ca. 1996

To supplement their income, Phillip wrestled alligators for the amusement of the tourists. Even though Sam's family had officially moved to Hollywood, they migrated back and forth between Reservations according to farming seasons. During their annual migration to Brighton, the men always left ahead of the women and children. Sam remembers his Mom's stories of how she hitched a ride to Brighton in a Ford Model T.

Once there, the families lived in clusters of Chickees. In the middle of the village were the cooking and eating Chickees surrounded by the members' private sleeping quarters. These structures were made from Cypress and Sabal Palm fronds. All ends were tied with green vines. During wind storms loose items were moved up into the Chickees' rafters, including the people themselves. During severe storms, such as Hurricanes, the people stayed on the ground and tied themselves to trees using vines or ropes.

After graduating from high school, Sam moved to Lawrence, Kansas, to attended Haskell Jr. College, an all Indian school. By the age of 21 he was back in Hollywood, where he moved in with his great-grandmother Suzie Billie, who lived close to Sterling Road and 64 Avenue, four blocks north of Sam's present home.

In 1975 Phillip sold his cattle business. Seven years later, Sam continued the family tradition when he bought seventy-five head of cattle from the late Albert Billie. Sam started his business out of Big Cypress Reservation, where it is still found today.

Along with the cattle came the horses, Sam quickly noticed that although bigger and stronger, the horses seemed to fear him. Any eye contact or sudden movement of an opened hand spooked the animals, sending them on a wild run, thus making the break in process, tedious and time consuming. Because the horses were a vital part of the business, Sam began to experiment different ways in which to speed up the taming process.

Sam Frank, Seminole, Panther Clan.
Training horses at Big Cypress Seminole Reservation, FL, circa. 1996

In time, Sam noticed that by looking at the horses' hindquarters and moving his hands slowly, he produced a positive change in the animals' behavior. Instead of being spooked, the horses followed him around the pasture. It didn't take long for me to realize that Sam was a humble horse whisperer. His approach was very different than mine.

Under Sam's guidance, I was able to produce the same effect on the other horses that roamed his pasture. In time I learned to combine the two styles. It was a winning situation. The results were great, not only was I breaking-in horses, but I was doing it without breaking their spirit and most of all with less risk of getting myself or the animals injured.

Spending time with Sam was great. He loved to reminisce about the old days, as much I loved listening to him. One particular story I remembered was how Sam loved playing in the woods west of 64th Avenue with other Hollywood Seminole kids. Through him, I learned what Hollywood looked like in the early 1960's.

Unlike today, it was densely wooded and very dusty. Anything west of state road 441 was considered the Everglades. Other things Sam spoke about were the two irrigation wells that provided the community with their utility and daily needs. One was located on what is today 33 Street and 64 Avenue. The other one was under a canopy of Oak trees, north of Sterling Road and just east of the Florida Turnpike, where the First Baptist Church presently sits. In particular, Sam remembered when the Government provided green canvases for tribal members to bathe with privacy. Another location of great significance was Council Oak Tree. That particular tree can still be found, south of Sterling Road, just west of Highway 441. It was chosen for its convenient location and cool shade. Council Oak became the common place for tribal leaders to meet and conduct their business, especially during those years of negotiating with the U.S. Government for federal recognition.

In order to understand how Seminoles based their decisions one must understand the roles of their clans. They are Panther, Big Town, Bird, Deer, Wind, Otter, Bear, Snake and Alligator. All Alligator clan members moved to Oklahoma.

Origin of the Seminole clans

"When the earth was ready to be occupied, the Creator put all animal in a shell. He set it along the backbone of the earth and told the animals when the timing was right, the shell will open and you will crawl out. Go on and take your respective place. The Creator gave the Panther special powers and therefore favored the Panther to come out first. As the shell began to crack the wind circled around until the crack was made big enough for all animals to egress. The wind remembered that the Creator wished for the Panther to come out first. Honoring the Creator's wish, the wind reached down and helped the Panther out. The Panther thanked the wind for its noble and humble action. Next out, were the birds, followed by the Bear, Deer, Snake, and Otter along with all other animals. When all was done the Creator decided to name the animals and put them in clans. He rewarded the Panther with Patience, strength, knowledge of herbs and the power to heal. For the noble and humble action he told the Wind: You will serve all living things so they may breathe, without you all will die. You will be brother to the Panther. When the Panther is making medicine you will be there next to him. The Bird, for being able to take flight, will be ruler of earth. He told them: You will carry the messages, and will make sure that all things are put in their proper place.[2]"

The roles of the Seminole Clans, as told by Sam Frank:

"Birds are known for talking, if an individual wants to communicate with a Medicine Man he must use this messenger. A Panther member must use a Bird to relay their messages. In 2006 there were less than a handful of the Deer Clan members. When a clan is about to become extinct, the Medicine Man can assign other Clan members to join in, or he can assign non-Clan members. Non-Clan members are individuals who have a Clan father but lack a Clan because their mother is not a Seminole. Big Towns are the Judges, most of them were killed by other tribal members perhaps for unjust judgment. Because of it, very few are left, forcing them to combine with Otters. Each Clan has their own Medicine Man."

As previously mentioned, all Alligator clan members were relocated to Oklahoma along with other Florida Seminoles. The removal came as a result of the Payne's Landing Treaty of 1832. That treaty not only took away all Florida land claims from the Seminoles but demanded their relocation to Indian Territory. Seminole opposition led to the Great Seminole War. As tribal leaders surrendered, their followers were sent to Oklahoma under military escort. The first arrivals were led by Chief Holahti Emathla in the summer of 1836. The war lasted almost seven years ending in 1842 with an agreement that some Seminoles could remain in Florida. Their descendants are the Seminole and Miccosukees participants found in this book.

Among the Seminoles and their kin, The Miccosukees, are small groups of Individuals who call themselves Independents. These individuals not only have refused Government aid but have also chosen to waive their rights to any dividends coming from Casino profits. Some of them can be found throughout the Big Cypress Preserve, but the majority live in traditional Seminole villages on the western part of Tamiami Trail.

Seminole Camp with Totem Pole, Miccosukee Camp, Big Cypress, FL

Victor Billie (Bird Clan) ****
Independent Seminole, Big Cypress Seminole Reservation, ca. 2006

Many years ago, I had the pleasure of meeting one of those Independents. His name was Victor Billie, a proud keeper of his culture's traditions. Victor earned a living by teaching his Native language and the art of carving canoes and totem poles at the Immokalee Cultural Center, not far from his home village. He was proud to survive on the ways of his grandfather, Josie Billie. Josie and his brother Ingraham Billie (Panther Clan) were the two most famous traditional medicine men of the twentieth century. The two brothers kept and protected the Seminole medicine bundle for more than 80 years. According to Victor and tribal elders, Ingraham was one hundred and twenty years old when he passed away.

In April of 2002, I invited Gianni Morra to join me again on my annual trip to New Mexico. After arriving in Truth or Consequences, New Mexico, we were greeted by Jack Wood and his twin brother Richard. That evening, we ordered pizza and rented a movie called BUFFALO SOLDIER, starring Danny Glover. The film pertained to the struggles encountered in the late 1800's by the all-black U.S. Calvary Troop H, as they pursuit Chief Victorio and his band of Warm Springs-Chiricahua Apaches. After watching the movie, we made plans to go to the Guadalupe Mountains the next day. The sacred mountain range was one Victorio's favorite hideouts.

Early next morning Jack, Gianni, and I loaded up the vehicle and headed east across country. Unfortunately Richard was unable to come along. After driving east through endless deserted country, we entered the towns of Artesia and Whites City, where we stopped to stretch and eat. Once energized, we continued our drive through the flat barren desert.

Many miles later we began to see the Guadalupe Mountain range in the distant horizon. Half way there, we noticed a sign that read historical marker up ahead. These markers are common throughout New Mexico and we assumed it pertained to the Guadalupe Mountains. Once we got to it, we found ourselves totally amazed by its contents. The sign read, *'Rattle Snake Springs.'* Coincidently, it contained a brief history of the Buffalo Soldiers and their encounter with Victorio's Apaches in 1880. While watching the movie on the previous night, we learned that it was at Rattle Snake Springs, that the Buffalo Soldiers captured Victorio and his band of Warm Springs Chiricahua Apaches. After a unanimous agreement, the independent unit of the U.S. Calvary decided to let Victorio and his band go. And so they did, allowing their escape into Mexico.

As much as we wanted to go on and see the high peaks of the Guadalupe Mountains, the unexpected opportunity was not one to be passed up. Without hesitation, the three of us decided to check it out. And so we drove west along a gravel road. To our left, an enormous ridge ran in a southern direction. About mid-way along the horizon the ridge was broken by a gap that allowed passage to the west. It was easy to see why settlers moving west, risked cutting through there rather than riding hundreds of miles around it. As a result many travelers felt victim to Apache attacks, and the gap earned its name as Slaughter Canyon.

We stayed on the gravel road and continued on a westerly direction. Shortly after, we came across a small, abandoned cemetery with tombstones dating back to the early 1800's. We all wondered if the people buried there, were Buffalo Soldiers. As we drove deeper into the canyon, I saw a magical forest emerging from one of the most deserted and infertile stretch of land I had ever traveled on.

Minutes later, we arrived at a floral oasis canopied by hundreds of cotton trees, some larger than I had ever seen before. We parked our car and proceeded to walk around the park grounds. The air was filled with pollen, like snowflakes falling in summer. As a result the ground was partially covered with thick clusters of cotton balls.

While sitting on a log, we admired and commented on the incredible beauty that surrounded us. Coming from above was the continuous loud sound of joyous birds chirping away.

VICTORIO AND RATTLE SNAKE SPRING

For a moment I thought I was in a tropical forest instead of a little oasis surrounded by hundreds of miles of dry, barren desert. Enthralled by all the natural beauty, we decided to explore further. Within a couple hundred feet, we discovered patches of spring grass sprouting from a wet ground. As we continued to walk around the park, we found clusters of willow trees in the near distance. The forested area, reminded me of the hammocks throughout the Florida Everglades, except this one rose above the desert instead of a swamp, or so I thought.

It was easy to see why Victorio had chosen the area as a hideout for his people. The peace and tranquility I felt there was like nothing I had ever experienced before. It was amazing to think that such a place existed. Totally satisfied with our experience, we decided to head back to our vehicle and on with our trip. On our way out, we were undecided whether to make a left and follow a sign that read, *'One Way,'* or make a right and go the wrong way, but much shorter way out. After all, there was no one else around that cared if we traversed the roadway in the opposite direction. For some reason we made a left and drove on a road that appeared to loop around the park. A short distance later we came upon a cross road with a sign that read, *'Rattle Snake Springs, 0.8 miles.'*

It was at that moment that we realized we had not been at the famous spring after all. Ironically that road cut across a marsh. To our left a slew of willow trees covered the wetland. Strangely to our right, the ground was high and dry. Then, to our amazement, we saw many wild turkeys plucking the ground. As we drove deeper, their numbers increased. Soon dozens of them were seen on the ground as well as on the limbs of pear and apple trees. Scattered throughout were hundreds of their molted feathers. As we drove further, the sound of running water caught our attention. Soon we discovered a man-made cement channel that ran deep into the woods and seemed to have no ending. A stream of water, crystal and clear rushed through it. We were tempted to drink it, but it was polluted with fresh turkey droppings. After taking some pictures and collecting some feathers, we got back in the car and drove further down the road. Soon we came upon a house. It belonged to the park ranger, but no one was home. A few hundred feet away, was Rattle Snake Spring.

Rattle Snakes Spring, where Victorio's band encountered the Buffalo Soldiers in1880 Guadalupe Mountains, NM. ****

It was perhaps a hundred feet in diameter and about six feet in depth. The water was crystal clear with an algae covered bottom. The first thing I noticed was the influence of man. The once free running spring water was sadly controlled by two manmade floodgates. One of the gates allowed the water to flow towards the ranger's property through the previously mentioned cement channel. The other one allowed water to flow into the marshland that ran along the dirt road and ultimately ending at the entrance of the park, where the cotton trees were found.

While standing along the edge of the spring, I began to see the entire area in a totally different perspective. The oasis, hidden deep in the middle of a desert, was also an incredible fortress. Concealed by a high ridge, it protected the area from anyone coming from the west. Hundreds of miles of desert to its north, east, and south, discouraged anyone unfamiliar with Apache land to make pursuit.

When most army generals thought and reported that the hostile Apaches were homeless, on the run, starving and eating cactus, groups of Chiricahuas found refuge and met all their needs, in such oases. After studying the place and its logistics, it all made sense how the Buffalo Soldiers got the upper hand. A natural fortress like that one does not discriminate. Who ever got there first was simply going to win. According to the movie, the soldiers got there first, hid in the ridge and waited for Victorio's band to arrive. As the Apaches bathed in the spring, they were taken by surprise. After a short speech by Victorio and a long debate by the soldiers, the Apaches were released.

Chief Victorio
of the Chihenne Apache
The only photographed ever taken of Victorio
Courtesy of St. Augustine Historical Library

VICTORIO AND RATTLE SNAKE SPRING

Victorio and his followers headed south into Mexico. Under similar circumstances as Rattle Snake Springs, they reached a watering hole at Twin Buttes, (Tres Castillos), located about sixty miles inside Mexico. There, they were surprised by 350 Mexican soldiers led my Joaquin Terrazas and his second-in command, Juan Mata Ortiz. Unfortunately, the outcome from that encounter turned deadly.

On October 14, 1880, sixty year old Victorio lost his life defending his people. Among the dead, were his three sons and most of his warriors. The prisoners, mostly women and children, were taken to Chihuahua City, where they were imprisoned for several years and some sold as slaves.

Victorio was survived by a daughter Dilth-cley-ih and a son Charles Istee. It is not known how Dilth-cley-ih, who was thirty-four years old at the time survived the battle. Eight year old Charles Istee was in San Carlos, Arizona with Chief Loco (Jlin-tay-i-tith), when the massacre occurred.

Dilth-cley-ih, married Carl Mangus (1846-1901) son of Chief Mangas Coloradas (1790-1863). Their marriage produced two daughters – Cora Mangus (1874-?) and Lillian Mangus (1894-1936). Dilth-cley-ih also had a daughter by a previous marriage Elsie Vance Chestven. Victorio's granddaughter, Lillian Mangus, married George Martine (1890-?) son of Old Martine (1858-?) and his wife Kah-gah-ahshy.

While I sat on the edge of Rattle Snake Springs, I realized that I was experiencing at first hand a very significant and historical piece of American history. Once satisfied with our discovery, we decided to head out to the main highway in search of the Guadalupes Mountains.

As we drove south, a ridge to our right prevented us from seeing towards the west. To our left, nothing but flat barren desert met the horizon. Although we had not seen a sign, per say, it was clear that we had entered the Guadalupe's Mountain Range. While driving on the highway, we noticed a huge cave hidden deep in a mountain cliff. I couldn't help to think, if it was there that the dance of the Mountain Gods was born.

Each group of Crown Dancers has their own story as to how they received their instructions to perform the sacred dance. "Legend has it that long ago a band of our Apache people were passing through their territory moving rather quickly. Within this band were two young men, one was blind and the other one crippled. So as not to slow down their trek and for the good of the band, it was decided that these two men be left behind with enough provisions to carry them over until their return. The two handicapped braves were left in a dark lonely cave. Many days and nights passed as they waited for their tribesmen to return. Their provisions ran low and their bodies grew gaunt. They began to fear that they had been abandoned and that they might soon die. One night as they huddled together in the darkness, they heard strange frightening noises coming from the back of the cave. The sounds became louder and louder. Finally, into the cave stalked five strange frightening figures, four of them painted black with white symbols and with strange mystical headgear. The last one painted all white. Suddenly a mysterious light illuminated the cave silhouetting the strange figures. The luminous rays somehow became a bonfire. The ghostly figures danced around the fire, posturing, making strange noises and chanting, calling upon the winds and the rain, brandishing their staves against unseen enemies. The two men cowered against the side of the cave certain that the ghosts had come to take them. How wrong they were, these beings were powerful Gods who would drive away the evil that handicapped them. The mountain Gods led the two men to the back of the cave where the white painted God struck a gigantic rock with the feather he carried, dividing the rock and creating a new passageway out. As the two men went through this new opening, the blind man could see and the crippled man was no longer lame. Each man was clothed in the finest buckskin clothing and each carried the finest bows and arrows. The mountain Gods were gone and in the far distance the men could see their tribesmen who returned to get them. As they met with their people, they related their experiences. They performed the dance just as the mountain Gods had done. Since that time for many generations hence, the Apaches have performed the dance of the mountain Gods to drive away sickness and evil and bring health and fortune to the Apache people.[4]"

As we traveled south, the high rocky ridge to our right seemed to transform into beautiful jagged mountains with towering pinnacles. A short time later, we arrived at the Guadalupe Mountains visitor center. There we learned that we did not have enough time to start any kind of productive climb. We satisfied ourselves by hiking some very short trails just to get a feeling for the place.

One particular pathway let us to a beautiful gorge. Once in it, we noticed a series of corridors that seemed to disappear into the heart of the Mountains. We chose to go into the narrowest one, and after a few hundred feet of strenuous climbing, we decided to stop and rest. We sat on a boulder and looked at the corridor below us. It was at that moment that we realized that we were in a unique place, a natural rocky fortress.

Such fortified places provided refuge for Victorio's people against the U.S. and Mexican armies. Apaches knew instinctively what took most military leaders years to comprehend. While sitting on that rock, we saw other corridors and crevices leading to various hideaways. Amid such harsh environment the simple and efficient fighting machine called Apaches was able to thrive. The Chiricahuas ability to survive where others perished, earned them the name given by a U.S. Major General, George Crook, as the "Tigers of the Human Race". It was easy to see and understand why finding an Apache was an impossible mission. After our break, we decided to climb just a little further, reaching a small plateau that allowed us a view of the western horizon. There I began to imagine what a young Apache assigned on look-out must have felt like.

It was awesome knowing that in those mountains Victorio found refuge and planned his attacks. His guerilla warfare tactics were so effective that his strategies are taught today at West Point Military Academy. After a couple of hours we headed back to our car. It was unfortunate that we were not able to see and experience the many other hidden treasures that these sacred mountains had to offer.

Once back in our vehicle, we continued our southerly drive. The mountain ridge we had followed was coming to an end. As the highway curved to the west and around the ridge, we got to see the grand old Cathedral Peak of the Guadalupe Mountains. It consisted of beautiful jagged pinnacles that reminded me of certain sections of Monticello Canyon. In front of us was a beautiful sun setting, its reflection created shadows and magical colors on the southwestern mountain walls.

Soon after, we found ourselves driving on a high plateau, hundreds if not thousands of feet below us lay an immense valley. On both sides of the road, a white desert floor glittered with magical crystals, revealing what was once the bottom of an ocean. Little did we know, we were about to enter the salt flats. I wondered if the rich mineral was used in trade by the Apaches. If it wasn't, at least it was readily available to preserve and cure their daily goods. With each mile driven, we penetrated deeper and deeper into no man's land. That was another of the many roads in New Mexico that kept me looking at the water temperature and fuel gauges.

Like always I carried a blanket, plenty of drinking water and enough beef jerky to last me four days. Fortunately, we survived the journey without any incidents.

We arrived in El Paso, Texas in the early evening hours. Needless to say, we were tired and hungry. We stopped at a restaurant to rest and eat a hot meal. By 9:00pm we were on I-25 heading north towards Truth or Consequences, where Jack lived. Even though it was late, and we were tired, we found time to reminisce on all that had taken place.

The next day we decided to take it easy. I headed to downtown T or C in search of a much needed soak at one of the many hot mineral springs found along the Rio Grande. Not knowing much about the appropriate length of time a person should soak, I booked myself for an hour at one hundred and ten degrees. After paying and receiving a towel, I was directed to a cabana. Once inside a series of steps led me down to a small manmade square pool. I descended into it and learned real quickly what one hundred and ten degrees meant. Never mind the hour, in less than ten minutes I began to feel light headed and weak. I came out and headed back to the desk where they were not surprised to see me at all. After a good laugh by all, they asked if I wanted to try cooler one. I found the cooler soak much more relaxing and enjoyable.

Feeling good and relaxed, I drove around the small, sleepy town looking for something to do. A short time later I noticed a sign that pointed to Elephant Butte. Intrigued, I followed the sign and drove upon a huge lake. Protruding from the lake was a huge rock formation resembling an elephant. After spending some time admiring God's creation, I decided to head back to Jack's house where I met up with my friends.

The next morning, before heading home, Gianni and I left T or C and headed north to Old Town Albuquerque and Santa Fe. Both towns resembled each other, with plenty of Spanish and southwest adobe style homes and businesses. Both towns had a plaza where Natives people were found selling their crafts. Some of the Mexican restaurants around the plazas were owned by the same families for centuries. Needless to say the food and the selection of Native American crafts were excellent.

Freddie Kaydahzinne
Photographed by Vincent Kaydahzinne

Spring of 2002 flew by quickly. Three months later, I found myself back in Mescalero for the 4th of July Maiden's Feast. Mescalero was becoming like a second home and my circle of friends had grown greatly. Everyone treated me like family. It was that addictive dose of warmth and love that kept me going back for more. It became common practice for me to visit the Land of Enchantment at least twice a year. Singing for the Crown Dancers and Freddie's group was the icing on the cake. On that particular year, I sang and participated in all four days of the feast. During that visit, I learned that Freddie Kaydahzinne was a Chiricahua, and the composer of many of the songs that I had learned.

After spending a week in Mescalero, I returned to Florida and realized how blessed I was. I remember humbling myself to the Creator and thanking Him for what had become a routine. I wanted to let Him know that I was not taking anything for granted. On my daily prayers I included all those Chiricahua families who had opened their homes and hearts to me.

I prayed for their protection and prosperity and for all the Mescaleros who gave so much to the Chiricahuas and Lipans in their times of need. I was thankful for their acceptance and my role as a singer with the Crown Dancers, which is considered by traditional Apaches as a very sacred thing.

As I learned more about the maiden's puberty ceremony and how the four-day feast reflected throughout their adult life, made me realize how much trust had been bestowed upon me. The old questions of how and why I had entered or been allowed to enter into the sacred circle were no longer in my mind. It was God's will and I simply accepted the responsibility with honor. Out of the many Crown Dancing Groups in Mescalero, I belonged to the Chiricahua group led by James Kunestsis. Our group had been passed down from generation to generation. Its origin told to me by James himself.

Back home in Florida my family and friends noticed a big change in me, they said I had become more balanced and patient. In time, I began to see and believe that the Creator really has a specific journey for each and every one of us. At times I felt out of place living in Florida. I wanted to live in New Mexico so badly, I could taste it. With each year that went by my desires grew stronger but I knew I couldn't leave my family behind. My parents and young children needed me. I consoled myself with the old saying, *"Be happy with what you have and be careful what you wish for."* There must be a reason why things were that way, after all the Creator knows best. I had always followed my intuition and my prayers had always guided me right. *"Be thankful, and enjoy both worlds,"* I told myself.

When home, I enjoyed spending time with my family and teaching my children the value of friendship and love. Just like me, I was raising them to respect and love their surroundings, that being the Florida Everglades. After all, I knew no other place. Not only did the Everglades were my playground while growing up, but in many ways it served as my teacher. It was there, that I learned about balance, harmony and the precincts that existed among all creatures and myself. Respecting those boundaries and applying the discipline learned from martial arts contributed to the foundation of my character and influenced my behavior throughout my life.

Even today, despite all the urban growth around it, the Everglades remain as beautiful and wild as they have always been. This wilderness has been ranked by experts as one of the most hostile environments in the world. With no defined trails or reference point, it will take an outsider just a blink of the eye to get disoriented and lost.

The following story is a good example of that. An old friend of mine by the name of Jim, whom I met while going to EMT-Paramedic school, introduced me to a different area of the everglades. The section was known as Stair-Step, off Loop Road, located east of Turner River and south of Tamiami Trail, in the southern part of the Big Cypress Preserve.

In 1984, during one of our many excursions, he and I headed out early one morning on a deer hunt. After parking his truck on loop road, we entered the murky swamp water in the early morning darkness. After walking for about an hour with water up to our waist, we reached a hammock *(dry/wooded islands, rising above the marsh)*. It was there that we planned to set our hunting tree chairs *(a backless chair with a strap, that is place high in a tree)* and wait for dawn when most animals are up and about.

Once he found a spot he liked, he told me to move on to another area, where I would set up for the early morning ambush. I walked away in search of that perfect spot.

Siggy, Emily and Lance playing in the murky, waters of the Everglades.
Loop Road, Big Cypress, FL, ca. 2000

Sometime later, I came upon a huge oak tree next to an animal trail. I set my tree chair and waited. A while later I began to doze off and soon fell asleep. It was early morning when the rays from the rising sun woke me up. It didn't take me long, to realize that it was not going to be a fruitful day, so I decided to look for hunting partner. After spending more than an hour searching for him, I realized I was lost. Not knowing what to do, I fired my rifle in hopes of finding my friend. Within seconds, I heard another shot in response to mine. Once reunited, I learned that he had also been looking for me for hours. The mutual search had distracted both of us enough to the point, where we became completely disoriented. Together, we searched for the path that led us to the hammock, but each time, we found ourselves unable to go on, as water rose up to our chins. As a result, we were forced to retreat and search for a shallower alternative route. It didn't take long before we became totally exhausted. Our minds quickly began to play tricks on us. Before we knew it, we had run out of options and had no choice but to spend the night in the hammock.

Siggy with son Lance.
Mitchell's Landing, Loop Road, Big Cypress, FL, ca. 2006

The next morning, somewhat rested, we reentered the swamp looking for any means of egress. My friend remembered reading in a hunters' magazine that most people when lost tend to go in circles to the right. We began to purposely walk towards our left and hoped for the best. Little did he know that reading that article would save his life one day. It was that experience that made me realize how easy and dangerous it was to get lost in the swamps. Needless to say, he and I never went out again without a compass.

Although the Everglades is known as an inhospitable land, it is also a place of beauty and wonders, where one can find some of the most unique species of plants and animals in the world. Cutting through that splendor is the Turner River, a narrow and shallow waterway located in the southwestern section of the Everglades.

In the winter of 2005, my children and I launched our canoe at the Tamiami Trail boat ramp. The first thing we noticed was that the water level was very low. A short distance later, we found ourselves digging our paddles into the river's muddy bottom in order to propel ourselves. The unusual low water level caused by a severe drought, made the first few miles of the seven mile trip extremely dangerous. Little did we know that our voyage would almost turn deadly. It didn't take long to see that lots of alligators had made their way into the river after leaving the high and dry grounds. The prehistoric beasts camouflaged perfectly in the seaweed like grass that covered most of the mucky bottom. About an eight of a mile into our trip, we came upon a section of the river where the water level was just inches deep. There we found ourselves completely stuck in the muck and surrounded by alligators. With no other choice but to step out of the canoe, I began fighting dozens of gators by slapping them with my paddle. It was during that commotion that I stepped on one of them.

Siggy, deep in the heart of the Everglades, at Turner River
Everglades City, FL, ca. 2005

The reptile quickly turned back and attempted to bite me. Luckily it bit the paddle, and not my hand. Even though, I was encouraged by my children to turn back, I decided to continue on. My decision paid off, as shortly thereafter, the water became deeper. With no gators in sight, the tensions eased and we began to enjoy the beauty that surrounded us. Among the most memorable sights encountered, were sections of the river that appeared prehistoric. There were hundreds of turtles resting on logs and basking in the sunlight along the water's edge. The banks were dotted with all sorts of fish hunting birds who stood motionless waiting for their next meal. All that beauty was enhanced by clusters of willow branches dangling over the water. As we slowly made our way through them, we came across a beautiful canopy of trees filled with flocks of spoonbills that began squawking in response to our arrival.

About half way down the river, we encountered an area completely covered by mangroves. Ironically an ancient passageway, cut through it. After navigating through the tunnel-like corridor, we reached an area called Ten Thousand Islands.

The region was once home to the Caloosa Indians. Their recorded history as told by Spaniards began in 1513 when they compelled the Spanish Conquistadors led by Ponce de Leon to withdraw, after an all-day fight. Spaniards stated that in 1763, during the transfer of Florida from Spain to England, the last remnants of the tribe, numbering approximately 350, were sent to Havana, Cuba.

Among the Ten Thousand Islands, there is one in particular named Chokoloskee Island or Shell Island. As the name implies, it was built out of shells by the Caloosa people. As we traveled and explored other islands, we found that a few were full of broken pottery pieces from the Caloosa era. Most of the islands we visited were covered with native trees and pristine shores. The brackish water that ran between them was crystal clear with a deep blue and a green turquoise contrast.

The immensity of the area was such that we never saw another human being during our trip. After a long day of fun in the sun, we set camp on an island with beautiful sandy shores. That evening we sat by the warmth of a small fire, while I told stories under a canopy of a clear sky filled with millions of glittering stars. Next day, we were awakened by the sun's new-born morning radiance and the sound of splashing water. To our surprise, it was made by none other than two playful dolphins. While that was going on, we had the pleasure of observing another beautiful sight. It consisted of a flock of pink flamingos that landed on a distant marsh. Shortly thereafter, a pair of bald eagles flew in for the kill. Descending at a high rate of speed, they made their hits. Instead of landing to gorge, they continued their flight only to return quickly and repeat the hits all over again. Within minutes all the flamingos began making screeching sounds as they flew off. When all were gone, the bald eagles returned to feast on their fruitful hunt.

Even though, I was tempted to further explore the region, I held back in fear of getting lost. As a result, we stayed in the same area enjoying the beauty that surrounded us. After spending one and a half days in paradise, we decided to head on back home. What was almost a canceled trip, turned out to be one of the most beautiful and memorable expeditions ever.

The following weekend, my children were ready to go camping again. Ironically, my thrill seeking children wanted to go back to the Ten Thousand Islands. Not wanting to push my luck, I convinced them to go to my Everglade's cabin which was located off Jane's Scenic Drive. The eleven-mile scenic drive, cut through the heart of the Fakahatchee Strand Preserve, located just northwest of Ten Thousand Islands. It is one of the most protected areas of the Everglades. Its beauty consists of unique species, such as the world's only Bald Cypress-Royal Palm forest. The exclusive habitat is also home to more than forty-five types of Orchids and fourteen types of Bromeliads. The variety of animals found there, range from Otters, Alligators, Black Bears, Deer, Snake, White Peacock, Bald Eagles, Hawks, bobcats and panthers. Among the blooms of the gardens of flowers are the butterflies flittering from flower to flower.

In the middle of that oasis sat a former hunting cottage that belonged to a Miami Firefighter, by the name of Craig. For almost two decades, I have called his rustic cabin, my own. I met Craig, shortly after getting hired by the City of Miami Fire Department. He was looking for someone to help him built bridges in order to drive his swamp buggy to what he described as a rustic cabin in the middle of the swamps.

MESCALERO, NEW MEXICO - EVERGLADES, FLORIDA

Not knowing what I was getting into, I quickly volunteered along with other Firefighters. Soon after, we learned that the lodge, which sat on an old levee, was impossible to get to because the swamp water had busted through certain sections of the man-made barrier. In order to make the cabin reachable and enjoyable seven bridges needed to be built by using rail road tie beams. The heavy timber was to be laid over the creeks to allow passage onto the cottage located two and a half miles from Jane's Scenic road. The owner described the tin cabin as big enough to sleep seven. Its front porch sat on a levee while the rear was suspended on stilts which kept the structure above the swamp water. Also mentioned was a boardwalk that needed to be redone. That footpath was also suspended in the air by wooden stilts. It originated at the cabin's front porch, and it stretched back seventy-five feet into a lake, the size of a football field. The story sounded like something out of movie set, which I found fascinating.

About a month later, on a hot spring morning, I drove two and a half hours to the Fakahatchee Preserve where I met with my newly-found friend, Craig. *"Wow, I can't believe you are here. Out of all the people that promised to help, you are the only one that came through on your word,"* he said. *"It is my pleasure to help you."* I replied. The heat, humidity and mosquitoes made the job unbearable; as a result it took six month to finish the excruciating task.. Upon conclusion of the project, my new friend made me an offer. *"From now on, this will be your cabin as long as I am not using it,"* he said.

In the winter of 1988, I stayed in the cabin and enjoyed the benefits of my hard earned labor. It was there, that I truly began to observe and learn what the Everglades had to offer. While driving with my children on Jane's Scenic road, on our way to the cabin, I began to think of the days long ago when I questioned my sanity for volunteering to help a total stranger. Little did I know, that a quarter century later, it would serve as the teaching grounds to my children.

Big Cypress
Chapter Nineteen

The year 2002 quickly came to an end, but my blessings were far from over. A friend of mine, who worked for the Seminole Tribe, was given the ok to start a program that consisted of horseback riding and camping for the tourists. Seven tepees were going to be set up deep in the swamps for the overnight stays. My friend asked if I could help with the break-in and selection of the horses needed for the adventurous excursion. I eagerly accepted the offer.

By late January of 2003, most of the fleet of horses had arrived at the Big Cypress Seminole Reservation. Among the cowboys involved in the process were my friends, Duke, an Apache, and William Cypress, a Seminole. Our job was to select which of the horses had the right temperament needed for the job. The first group we rode consisted of half a dozen horses or so. Among the ones that did not make it, was a young mare that appeared to be perfect until the time came to cross a creek. She was terrified of water and had made her mind not to get her feet wet. After pressuring her to cross a creek, she leaped over, making me hold on for dear life. Any water crossing after that, she simply flew across. Other horses simply did not stop once they got excited. Out of dozens of animals, only a few of them made it to the safe-ride list. Needless to say months went by and the proposed plan never materialized.

Just when I thought the fun was over, my Lieutenant at the fire department, S. Landa asked me if I was interested in a free horse. He said that a gentleman who attended his church was looking to get rid of an expensive but crazy horse. The animal was known to bite and kick, thus causing problems for the manager of the ranch. To prove his point, he opened up his shirt and showed me a perfect set of teeth branded on his chest by the horse in question. He described the beast as a beautiful Black gelded Arabian with a temper of a stubborn mule. After thinking about it for a few seconds, I eagerly accepted the offer. I did it, not so much because it was a free horse, but because it sounded like a challenge. Arrangements were made for me to go and see the horse.

A few days later, I arrived at an exclusive gated ranch located a few miles from my home. The ranch consisted of about five acres, with many round pens and about twenty stalls. Next to the horse facility, was a landing strip. Across from it stood the owner's two-story house, which was attached to a hanger for his two single engine airplanes.

Upon my arrival I found the ranch manager conversing on the phone. While waiting for her to finish, I noticed a beautiful, long mane Liver Chestnut Arabian tied up with two chains to its halter. I did not think much of it; after all, most of the horses there were Arabians. I walked around the barn looking for the black one, but I was not able to find him.

A few minutes later, the manager was off the phone and said, *"You must be Saggy? Well, there he is, his name is Iben,"* as she pointed to the one tied up in chains. She asked me if I wanted a Western or an English saddle. *"Bareback will be ok,"* I replied. I was not trying to be arrogant, but since the horse had a bad reputation, I felt it was in my best interest to ride him bareback in case I needed to jump off quickly. *"Very well,"* she said as we both walked Iben, to a fancy round pen/obstacle course. Once there she lunged him for about fifteen minutes. Soon after mounting him, my Lieutenant showed up. I continued riding until the manager felt satisfied that I could handle the beast.

Once on the ground, the manager asked me to make the horse walk backwards, which I did, but not to her satisfaction. She walked over to me, took the lead rope from my hand and said, *"Like this,"* as she kicked the horse in the chest while yanking on the rope furiously. The horse's eyes revealed his state of panic. She concluded by telling my Lieutenant *"Your friend can definitely ride. I will let the owner know and he will decide."*

That evening I met with the owner, who stated, *"The horse is yours as long as I approve of his new home."* I informed him that Iben was going to be boarding at the Junior Cypress Stables and Rodeo Arena. It was located in the Big Cypress Seminole Reservation and named in honor of the late Junior Cypress, one of the first Seminole Cowboys/Cattle owners.

The following weekend Iben was transported and delivered to his new home. Upon arrival, the owner was very impressed with the state of the art facility. The forty two-stall barn was spotless and all the horses looked healthy. To top it off, it had it had a round pen, hot and cold water for bathing the animals and thousands of acres of fenced in pastures. Needless to say, we were both happy. He had found a good home for his troubled horse, and I was the proud owner of a beautiful full-blooded registered Arabian.

On that particular weekend my children and I spent some time working with our new buddy. Both of them agreed to name him Spirit, for his restless manner and proud gate. A few hours later, I took him to the round pen to work with him. Once there, he charged at me and attempted to bite me. A quick jerk on the lead rope and he realized I was in command. After an hour of training, we cautiously bathed and groomed him. The weekend passed without any incidents.

"Spirit"
Siggy's favorite Arabian horse ****
Junior Cypress, Big Cypress, Seminole Reservation, ca. 2003

I returned a few days later. Feeling somewhat confident, I saddled him up without lunging him. To my surprise I experience the first of many accidents to come. As soon as my left foot slipped into the stirrup he took off, dragging me on the rough asphalt pavement. The incident left me with ripped jeans and some road rash. On my next attempt, I stood him against a building in order to prevent him from repeating the same stunt again. Once on him, I said, *"Let's see what you're made out of."* I rode him to an open pasture and loosened up the reigns. I had never been in such a fast horse in my life. Just when I thought he had reached top speed, he seemed to find a higher gear. Immediately I knew I had something special, a very fast horse. Within weeks he was eating carrots out of my hands and following me around the rodeo arena. Naively, I began to relax and felt comfortable riding him, not knowing that my next accident was around the corner.

Early one morning while riding at full gallop through the reservation, Spirit came to a complete stop after spotting a huge bull laying under an oak tree. From his reaction, it was obvious he had never seen cattle before. The sudden stop sent me flying over his head. He ran back to the stall leaving me somewhat hurt in an open pasture with an eighteen hundred pound bull staring at me. Luckily the bull remained calm and showed no signs of aggression. The walk back was long and embarrassing. When I arrived at the rodeo grounds, the workers were wondering what happened to me. The horse was back in his stall, still wearing the saddle. I didn't even get mad at him; instead, I found excuses to justify his behavior. The ranch manager and workers on the other hand were telling me to get rid of him. They were old time cowboys who loved their quarter horses and had no sympathy for the notoriously spooky and nervous Arabians. Against their advice I decided to keep him. A few weeks later I questioned my decision.

The next incident took place while riding on the shoulders of the reservation's main highway, where he panicked over an old tire laying on the side of the road. Again, he turned and stopped on a dime. I didn't go over his head that time; instead I slipped sideways, forcing me to dismount. That time he did not take off, instead he stood by me almost like saying, *I am sorry I didn't mean to hurt you.* A few miles later he repeated the same thing with a huge black garbage bag. Luckily I did not fall. Little by little we got used to each other and our rides became enjoyable. Within a short period of time, I started going to neighboring ranches with groups of cowboys. On the way back from those excursions, members of the groups, most of them riding quarter horses, would challenge me and the Arabian into racing back to our camp. During the initial part of those races, I would hold back on the reigns and listen for the quarter horses' labored breathing. Once I felt they had given their best, I loosen up on the reigns and pull away from the group like they were standing still. In time, I became known as the Indian with the crazy, but fast Arabian.

Back at the Big Cypress I enjoyed riding through endless prairies and wooded hammocks. One of my favorite rides was from the rodeo arena to Billie Swamp Restaurant. The Diner was located next to Billie Swamp Safari, a fenced in area originally designed as a hunting camp for the rich and famous. It was home to thousands of imported game animals from all over the world. The safari was later converted into an animal refuge and a tourist attraction.

The first few miles of the seven-mile ride cut through a small community town, where most of the tribal members lived. Once past the town limits, open fields allowed me to fly with my Arabian. One day, after leaving the restaurant, and about to enter the outskirts of town, I heard a very loud noise coming from behind.

The strange sound, not only scared me, but spooked the horse into an uncontrollable run. With every second that went by, the sound intensified until its origin was revealed. To my surprise the noise was generated by a huge Seminole Leer Jet.

As soon as Spirit saw the plane he turned and stopped. As a result, the saddle slipped and I found myself looking at his belly. Luckily I was able to hold on to one of the reigns, as my feet remained dangerously stuck in the stirrups. Perhaps sensing that I was in trouble, he stood motionless and waited for me to unstrap my feet. That incident proved to me that we had bonded and fully trusted each other. Once back at the stalls, I learned that the plane was due for landing at the B.C. airport, which happened to be less than a mile from where the incident took place.

Spirit grew to love my children as well, in time they had him barrel racing in the rodeo arena. Amazingly, the same horse that was forced to be given away for kicking and biting never showed any signs of aggression towards us. On the contrary, he was gentle and extremely loyal to us.

Emily and Lance at the Junior Cypress Rodeo Arena ****
Big Cypress Seminole Reservation, ca. 2004

A few months later, I called the previous owner with a progress report. He confessed that the problem was his ranch manager, and it had come down to letting one of them go. Whatever the circumstances were, it did not matter, I was happy with my horse and he was content with the outcome.

Things kept getting better for me at Junior Cypress in B.C. A few stalls down from Spirit was another beautiful seven year old Arabian Stallion who appeared to be somewhat neglected. I spoke to the ranch manager who told me the horse belonged to a Seminole from the Hollywood Reservation. A few days later I called the horse owner and introduced myself. Ironically, he knew who I was. *"I have heard your name mentioned by my brother Sam Frank. You broke-in some of his horses a while back,"* he said. I told him I had started boarding my horse at the Junior Cypress arena and I was interested in working with his horse.

"That would be great! I am very busy and don't have the spare time that a stalled horse requires and deserves," he said, as he eagerly agreed.

I began working with the horse immediately. The first thing I noticed was how appreciative and smart he was, almost like saying thank you for giving me some attention. I took the young stallion to the round pen and worked him for about half an hour. After a sweaty workout, I attempted to saddle him, only to find out he was more than green *(broken, but not ridden in a while)* and far from broke as previously told.

A few days later I took him back to the round pen to continue with the break-in process. On that particular day, the place was packed with cowboys, mostly tribal members. With their help, I was able to saddle him and put a bit in his mouth. From there, I took him to the rodeo arena, and half an hour later, I rode him out the gate. Using a combination of Sam's break-in techniques and mine, the whole process took less than three hours and it stands today as my record to break-in a horse. To top it off, I had done it with an extraordinary horse, a seven-year-old Arabian Stallion with a chest and neck of a quarter horse.

In time I called the horse my own. I named him Geronimo, for his power and stamina. Suddenly, I found myself taking care of two Arabians. The never-ending adventures of my new buddies kept time moving on. April and May had gone by and I missed going to Monticello Canyon in New Mexico.

Siggy training Geronimo, an Arabian Stallion
Big Cypress Seminole Reservation, ca. 2003
Photographed by Elaine Schmid

Ojo Caliente - Red Paint Canyon

Chapter Twenty

In the summer of 2003, I made plans to visit New Mexico again. The difference that time was that my children were going with me. Prior to our trip, I made my daughter a pair of toe guarded moccasins and my Mom made her a dancing shawl for the much anticipated trip. I called the owner of the Monticello Box Ranch and asked if my family and I could stay and camp in the canyon. Besides being welcomed, I was told that the Maytag cabin was ready and available for us to use. The Maytag was the cabin going through renovation during my first visit to the Monticello Box Ranch. Although my children were used to camping in tents, it was nice to know we had a house to sleep in, especially on those cold desert nights. The three of us arrived in New Mexico in late June. It was Emily's second visit and Lance's first.

After flying into Albuquerque, we drove down to Cliff, New Mexico. The long drive through the desert was beautiful, especially between the towns of Datil and Reserve. During that stretch we came across many creeks. Among them were Old Horse Spring, Apache Creek, and Mangus Creek. I explained to my children that we had entered the ancestral homelands of Chief Mangas Coloradas, (1790-1863, Spanish for Red Sleeves) the last leader of the Mimbreño Apaches. His territory included Silver City-Santa Rita region of southern New Mexico. In the 1850's Chief Mangas merged with the more numerous, the Warm Springs Apaches where he became principal chief. Mangas was feared by those who settled in his territory, especially miners. He was a relentless fighter against mining.

An hour and a half after leaving Reserve, we arrived at our final destination, the small town of Cliff. After hiking some small trails in that area, we return to our cabin and spent the rest of the afternoon resting and enjoying the beauty that surrounded us.

On the second day we drove to the Cliff Dwellings National Monument located in the Gila Wilderness. There we enjoyed a guided tour offered by a park ranger. After leaving the monument's site we headed out in search of the hot springs on the other side of the park. Once there, we began to hike along the Gila River. On that particular year, the river was deep, and the water was cold. As a result, I found myself carrying my children on my back to get them safely across the strong running current. After a few crossings, we arrived at the hot springs, where we found ourselves all alone. While submerged in the warm spring's water, I proceeded to teach them about their heritage and their ancestor's homelands. After a long and exciting day, we returned to Cliff, where we relaxed and camped for the night.

The next morning we drove west on Highway I-10 towards southern Arizona to visit a powerful and inspiring landscape, known as the Grand Canyon. During the long drive, I began to teach my children about the canyon and the indigenous people who helped shape its history. Among them are the Southern Paiutes, who called the canyon *"Mountain lying down"*. They ventured into the canyon in the 1300's, along with the Cerbat Tribe. Today, Cerbat descendants , the Hualapai and Havasupai people occupy reservations in the western part of the canyon.

Most importantly, I told them that the last Indigenous Tribe to arrive was our ancestors, the Dine or Navajo people. Their migration from the Northwest took place at approximately 1400 A.D. They settled in the eastern part of the canyon, where they are still found today. Surprisingly my children had the same question I once asked. How are Apaches and Navajos related?

OJO CALIENTE – RED PAINT CANYON

The following story was given to me by a Navajo-Apache medicine man: "The Dine people lived in harmony upon their arrival. They settled in a huge portion of land known today as the states of Arizona and New Mexico. In the mid 1500's they witnessed the arrival of the Spaniards. Not only were the newcomers different but they had something never before seen, armory and a beast called horse. As a result of what they perceived to be a threat to their existence, they decided to subdivide in order to survive the inevitable clash of cultures. As groups began their migration, they were told that they would reunite one day when the time was right. Furthermore, they were told that they will always know each other by their language and songs. As these groups began to settle throughout different regions, they became known by various names given to them by other Indian Tribes. Apachu or Apache, meaning "Enemy" or "Fighting Men" was the name that came to defined them. Regardless how others referred to them, they called themselves Dine, or Inde. Today Apaches, refer to themselves as Inde, and Navajos as Dine, both words meaning "The People."

By the time I finished the story, we had reached the outskirts of the canyon. The first thing we did was rent a helicopter, in my opinion, the only way to really appreciate the canyon's beauty. The fact that my children had never flown in one, added to the much anticipated excitement. The slow ride allowed us to see the hidden beauties of the magical canyon, including some adobe dwellings tucked deep in some remote caves. Some of these structures dated back thousands of years.

The next day, we visited the Petrified Forest-Painted Desert. The park was just as impressive as the Grand Canyon. Although not as grandiose, they were still way up there in the scale of God's greatest creations. Two days later, we headed back east towards Monticello, New Mexico. Our trip was long but beautiful.

We arrived at Monticello, New Mexico with some daylight to spare. After driving through town, we entered the canyon of Monticello. The soft and bumpy terrain forced me to switch into four-wheel drive mode. The rough conditions added to the thrill, almost making it feel like a ride at an amusement park. The splashing of water and mud soon made our silver Jeep look like a Camouflage war tank. Every now and then I stopped to show my children remnants of the Mogollon civilization. They consisted of partial adobe walls found throughout the canyon, some protruding from the ground, while others covered the openings of some scattered caves.

About an hour and a half later, we reached the Monticello Box Ranch. We were quickly greeted by the ranch manager who escorted us to the Maytag Cabin. Upon entering it, we were overwhelmed by its beauty and simplicity, not to mention a strong but pleasant smell coming from the fresh pine wood floor. The living/dining room was decorated with two country sofas and a beautiful wood table. A fireplace stood next to the front door. In the front of the house, comfortable chairs sat under a wood covered porch. Across from the porch was a beautiful pond full of cattails that provided refuge to wild ducks and a source of drinking water for the owner's horses. In the far distance, endless layers of mountains seemed to blend with the horizon.

What a treat it was to be there with my children in the land of our ancestors. After unloading our luggage, we stood outside facing the pond and the beautiful layers of mountains, as they faded in the darkness of the night. There I began to give thanks in a thought type prayer. *"Grandfather, here we are, the bloodline of the Red Paint Canyon has made it home. I thank you for all you gifts. Please guide us and keep us safe...."* It was during those prayers, that I pictured my ancestors and the entire Chiricahua Tribe smiling at me.

Upon the conclusion of my prayers, I wanted to tell my children about my Ancestor's vision, but instead, I found myself choking with emotions. As tears ran down my face, I walked away to prevent them from seeing a grown man cry. *"How odd,"* I thought. How could something that happened so long ago, felt so real to me? *"How did other descendants felt about it,"* I wondered. With no answer in sight, I continued to pray and accepted that some things in life are meant to be left unknown. I console myself with the fact that we were really there and I was to make the best out of the opportunity. As the evening progressed, the three of us called it a night.

The next morning I was awakened by my son Lance. *"Dad, Dad, Wake up, let's go for a hunt, there are lots of deer out there,"* he whispered in my ear. I opened my eyes only to find his little face in front of mine. His black eyes shone like stars and the grin on his face was one I couldn't say no to. *"Ok, give me a minute,"* I said. *"Let's go before Emily wakes up,"* he insisted as he pulled me by the hand.

I got up and walked out with him. Indeed my son was right, less than a hundred yards away, dozens of elk rejoiced themselves on the shores of the pond. Using my index finger across my lips, I signaled to him to stay quiet. To make the approach more real, I bent over and began to mimic my dance, as if I was on a hunt. Our silent approach was made possible by the heavy morning dew that covered the scarcely dry grass. We did this for some time. The closer we got, the lower I crawled. We finally made it to a natural curtain of cattails. Once there, I glanced at my son's face and saw the purest form of innocence. The little hunter loved every minute of it. *"You are going to be a good hunter one day,"* I said. By then Emily had woken up. She stood on the porch and began calling us. Once in the cabin, Lance began teasing his sister by telling her that we had gone hunting without her. As I winked at her, she understood the reality of it.

After having breakfast, we drove out towards the spring. My daughter was eager to get there. She still remembered bits and pieces from her first visit. The five mile drive to the spring consisted of driving through the shallow water of the Alamosa River. The river's bank was landscaped with all sorts of blooming flowers and fish eating birds. A great section of the canyon was shaded by huge cotton trees. About fifteen minutes into our trip, Lance noticed a Spotted Tail Eagle eating on the ground next to the water's edge. I stopped immediately to enjoy the rare sight. To my surprise the Eagle did not leave. It remained dancing *(flapping of the wings)* while attempting to control its prey. I couldn't help to wonder if it was the same Spotted Eagle I had seen a couple years earlier while visiting the canyon with Jack Wood and Ray, my Navajo friend.

A few minutes later, after gorging on its kill, the Eagle left. As it flew away, I told my children to say a prayer. Afterwards, I explained to them how the Creator made everything with a purpose and gave all living things a job to do. Most Native Americans believe that the Creator chose the Eagle to carry our prayer to his Kingdom. This is the reason why the Eagle flies higher than any other bird.

As we continued our drive towards the spring, I told them that I wanted to show them a special place that I have used for praying since the first time I saw it. Five miles later, we reached that special place which I named *"The Cathedral."* Upon entering it, my children had the same reaction I had when I first discovered it. *"Wow Dad, this place is incredible,"* they both said.

We stepped out of the vehicle and proceeded to walk into it. There the canyon walls were narrow and curvy and water ran about a foot deep. Once in The Cathedral, it felt like the only opening was to the sky. It is a place that has always made me feel small and humble.

As I bowed my head, I asked my children to join me in a short prayer. *"Grandfather, please hear us, we have come here in a good way to learn and experience the ways of our ancestors. We ask that you protect us from harm and show us your way so that we can follow it. We are thankful for all your gifts...."* Once finished, I told them that our prayers would rise through the opening and straight to heaven. After spending some time taking pictures, we got back in our Jeep and drove out of the canyon and onto an immense valley. A short distance later, we reached the same spot where four years earlier I had parked the rental car. Although we had come from a different direction, my daughter was still able to remember it. Once out of the vehicle, she began telling her brother how scared she was during her first visit. *"Dad how come we didn't come this way the first time? It sure felt a lot easier,"* she asked. *"Well, it felt easier because this time we had a four wheel drive vehicle,"* I responded.

Siggy with Lance in front of the "Monticello Box"
Monticello, NM, ca. 2003

While enjoying the beauty and serenity of the valley, we began to climb in search of the headwaters of the spring. On our way up, my daughter pointed out the spot that she and I reached before turning around four years earlier. *"Here, this is where we turned around. Do you remember Dad?"* *"Of course I do, how can I forget something like that,"* I responded. From that point on, she and her brother acted like typical kids on a discovery trip. They couldn't wait to see what was around the next bend. We stayed on the trail and continued our climb, crossing the water at every turn. When we finally reached Ojo Caliente spring, I felt a sense of accomplishment. Not so much for enduring the hike but for bringing my children to such sacredness.

After sitting on the banks of the spring, I began to tell them that it was from there that the Warm Springs Apaches got their name from.

I told them that most likely our ancestors played there as kids, hiked those trails and drank that water, just as we were about to do that day. I pointed out how the water simply came out of the earth. Like me, they had both grown up seen many different bodies of water, but never seen anything like that. After drinking it, my son asked if he could go for a swim. Soon after, my daughter followed. Next to the spring, laying on the ground was an old willow tree. Its trunk was smooth and polished like a piece of petrified wood. I sat on it and watched my children as they played and enjoyed themselves. A few minutes later, I reached into my backpack and pulled out my Mom's old cooking pot. Next I pulled out a piece of buckskin I had brain tanned myself, followed by a strip of rubber cut from the inner tube from my daughter's old bike. I poured some spring water into the pot and I proceeded to assemble my water drum. In my hand I held Carson's handmade drumstick. How much more essence could someone ask for. I felt I had a piece of all that was dear to me. I began to pray and gave thanks to the Creator for the many blessings bestowed upon me and my family. After the prayer I sang an honor song. I wanted to pay homage to all the beauty that surrounded us and to our ancestors for giving us life.

Siggy singing at Ojo Caliente, Monticello, NM

After singing a few songs, I walked into the crystal water and joined my children. Without any agenda in mind, I let them played until they had enough; we then headed down the old trail and got in our Jeep.

While driving back through the canyon we came across a herd of wild horses. The stallion stood ahead of his harem flaring his nostrils and letting me know who was in charge. The first thing I noticed was his small frame. His hooves were tiny and in bad shape, but overall he looked healthy. I told my children to stay in the vehicle while I played a game with him. Once out in the open, I extended my arm out and began to walk towards him, only to turn around and walk a couple of steps away. I did that a couple of times, to spark his curiosity. Within minutes, I had his undivided attention.

About fifteen minutes into the game, I picked up some grass and extended my arm again. Within minutes I had him eating out of my hand. Soon after, the rest of herd began closing in. I could tell they were wild but it appeared they had been exposed to humans. Perhaps some of the canyon residents were hand feeding them. Ten minutes later, I found myself completely surrounded by them. The level of trust had grown to where the stallion was allowing me to touch his neck. As a result, I began to mentally psych myself for my next move. With a quick sudden move I grabbed his mane and jumped on him. A few seconds later, I found myself on my back staring at the blue sky.

The incident spooked the herd into a wild run up the canyon. I returned to the vehicle and spent the next ten minutes recovering from the pain. I started telling my children how stupid my actions were and that I would never attempt a stunt like that again. My daughter looked at me and said, *"Dad who are you kidding! You would do it all over again in a heartbeat."* It was obvious they knew me well.

We continued our drive towards the cabin. After dinner, we sat on the porch and listen to all the night critters come alive. My children were fascinated with the sound of crickets and bullfrogs. We all enjoyed the endless amount of bright stars lighting up the clear skies. That was something we were not used to. Back home in the city, the stars are no longer seen. For the most part people will never notice if the sun rose from the west and set in the east. No one pays attention to the moon and stars anymore.

The next morning I got up early and saw the name *'Horse Canyon'* on a wall posted map. After studying it for a while, I realized that it was the same place where we had encountered the herd of horses. Next, I began to make coffee and breakfast while the little ones slept. The noise from all the commotion woke them up. No one wanted anything to eat, they just wanted to go for a morning hunt. Within minutes, the three of us were doing the same thing that Lance and I had done the previous morning. Once done, we returned to the cabin and got ready for another day of hiking and adventure. Instead of heading towards the spring, we drove down stream. I quickly pointed out to a very distinctive rock formation on top of a mountain. I told them, it was known as *'Montoya's Butte'*. Not far away, ancient cliff dwellings were perched above the walls of a beautiful canyon. After driving a few miles, we came across an ascending rocky trail that led us to a partial stone wall that covered the entrance of a small cave. Inside we found three hieroglyphics. They consisted of a faded red Crown Dancer, a boy and a panther.

On our way back from that discovery, Lance lost his footing and began to roll down a slope filled with Cholla and Prickly Pear Cactus. When he finally came to a stop, he found himself covered with thorns all over his back and legs. As a result, my boy panicked as he suffered in pain. His writhing prevented me from evaluating the extent of his injury. Once I got him to calm down, I realized that there were too many thorns for me to remove. A rather funny story today surely was not one back on that day! Less than a hundred yards away ran the crystal clear water coming from the spring. The river provided me with the only answer I could come up with at that particular time. *"Son, take your clothes off and run to the water from the sacred spring,"* I said. I had never seen him run so fast. Within seconds the pain had ceased. His face lit up with relief. *"Dad it's gone, the pain is gone,"* he kept on saying. To this day, he still believes that those are healing waters. Wrapped in a towel, we returned to the cabin where we spent the next few hours removing thorns. After having lunch, I proposed to head on out again. Lance had one request. He didn't want to go down stream again; instead, he wanted to go back up to Ojo Caliente Spring. *"That would be fine,"* I said.

OJO CALIENTE – RED PAINT CANYON

We drove out of the box canyon and continued our drive through the valley. After a long drive, I parked the vehicle and told them to follow me. *"I have a surprise for you guys,"* I said. *"Where are we going, Dad?"* They asked. *"You will soon find out,"* I replied. Full of anticipation, they hiked a long distance without complaint. After entering a secluded canyon the terrain began to change. Mysteriously, light shades of yellow and orange emerged throughout the landscape, making the walls of the canyon look like a golden cathedral. As we hiked deeper into the gorge, the colors not only changed but got brighter and more intense. The light yellow colors turned brighter and the orange changed into a deep red. Those rich colors were backed by a light blue sky and big white clouds, which made them, look even brighter.

About thirty minutes into our hike, we reached an area made up of painted rolling hills. They contained a variety of different colors such as red, yellow, and various shades of white, and gray. As we continued walking deeper into the magical canyon, their eyes glowed more and more with each step they took. After a forty minute hike, we had reached our destination. It was a section of the canyon where the pines grew tall and the colors of the earth and rocks were bright red. Stunned by the surrounding beauty, my son asked. *"Dad where are we? Who made this?"* *"This is Red Paint Canyon. It was made by God,"* I replied.

Emily and Lance standing on the most Sacred Grounds of the Warm Springs Apaches "Red Paint Canyon" Monticello, NM ****

It was obvious they were having a hard time believing it was natural and not manmade. *"I have brought you here last, since this is the most sacred of all places. It is from here that our bloodline comes from,"* I said. *"This red clay,"* as I grabbed a handful, *"represents the blood of our ancestors."*

After enjoying the surrounding beauty, we sat under the shade of the pine tree to enjoy our lunch. During that break, I took the time to teach them about the history and sacredness of the place. I also expressed to them my personal believe in regards to the origin or birth of the Chiennes and their Crown Dance. Based on the stories I was told, I concluded that a group of Dines migrated south and settled around Ojo Caliente. Soon after their arrival, they discovered the magical place of Red Paint Canyon, which they came to associate with. Thus the name Chienne *(Red Paint People)* was born. Years later, as they began their raids and or migrations into Mexico, they came upon a mountain range located south of present day Deming, New Mexico. There the spirits of the mountain Gods gifted the Crown Dance to a Chienne lady for the good of her people, thus giving birth to the Chiricahua Crown Dance. I explained to my children with great emphasis that the story I had just told them was something I had thought about over and over, thus leading me to that personal conclusion.

Red Paint Cave
Sacred Homelands of the Warm Springs Apaches
Sierra County, NM
****

139

Once rested and energized, we push on to our next site. It consisted of a hidden cave. This was no ordinary cave; this was the most sacred of all. Although rather small, when compared to others in the area, it contained the most valuable cache. Once we got to it, we proceeded to look into its belly where we found its hidden treasure, pure red clay. Its richness was best described by my children as homemade tomato sauce. It was from that cave that the medicine man collected the sacred clay. He would then mix it with water, turning it into a form of paste or paint. The muddy concoction was applied to the warrior's face before a raid or battle. It not only produced a psychological power that made the warriors fearless, but it also offered protection and a safe return.

After visiting the cave, we walked a short distance to see another place of interest. It consisted of side by side pure white clay hills. *"This is sacred white clay. It is also mixed in water, and used for various applications, such as face and body painting. Facial paintings consist of a stripe across the warrior's face. Body painting is done during the sacred Crown Dance. In a few days you will get to see both applications used by the Chiricahuas living in Mescalero,"* I told my kids.

After hiking and exploring the area, we sat under a tree for a well deserve break. There, I thanked the Creator for allowing us to witness and share such sacredness. The silence was broken, when my son asked, *"Dad is the owner of Red Paint Canyon an Apache Medicine Man?"* *"No son, the owners are white people. They are very kind and have welcomed us here and allowed us to stay at their home. We are very lucky to have them as our friends. Unfortunately they were not around to greet us, but hopefully you both can meet them one day,"* I replied.

Although I had captured their attention, I felt that I had given them a lot of history and information to digest. Realizing that too much information can be overwhelming, I concluded the history lecture by saying. *"Well this is it; I just wanted to bring you both here to see where some of our ancestors came from. Now let's go and have some fun hiking up to Ojo Caliente."* By the time we reached the head of the spring, we were ready to take a plunge. Once cooled off, I came out and sat on the old willow log, as they continued to soak. A few minutes later, I grabbed my drum from my backpack and began to sing while I watched them play. I finished my singing with a prayer as I gave thanks to the Creator for all his blessings.

While driving back to the cabin, I experienced the same feelings I had four years earlier. With each turn I took, I knew I was getting further and further from my sacred place. *"Will I ever come back? Will my children ever see this place again?"* I wondered with a sense of sadness. I soon realized that I was worrying too much, and missing all the beauty that surrounded us. *"Be thankful Siggy,"* I told myself, *"Enjoy the moment, who knows what tomorrow may bring."* Once we reached the cabin, we loaded our luggage in preparation for our departure the next day.

Early next morning, we left the Monticello Box Ranch and headed towards the town of Monticello. The smell of morning dew along with the laughter from my children put a grin on my face. As I continued to exit the canyon, feelings of joy and a sense of loss came over me. First I thought about the smile on my ancestor's faces when they first saw their descendants walking on their home grounds. On the other hand, I thought about how they must have felt when they were forced to march out of the canyon they called home. The three-week march across two states ended at the San Carlos Apache Reservation in Arizona, a place commonly referred to as hell on earth. The disgraceful event marked the beginning of the worst chapter in Chiricahua history.

The atrocities committed by the U.S government during that dark period remain among the most shameful events in American history.

I was almost out of the canyon when I realized that the mere thought of that horrible experience had sparked a sense of animosity and anger, I had never felt before during my previous visits. Not wanting my thoughts to affect my mood or behavior in a negative way, I began to pray. *"Grandfather please forgive me if I offended you with my evil thoughts. I am grateful for being here with my children in times of peace. I thank you for all your gifts. I ask that you give me strength and courage to overcome my worst enemy, myself."* Although my prayer was short and simple, it helped immensely, as shortly thereafter I regained my composure. Once back on track, I was able to see the beauty that surrounded us and focus on our next destination, the Mescalero Apache Reservation.

After driving north on Highway I-25, and west on Highway 380, we reached the towns of Bonito and Alto. While driving through those two small towns, I noticed a drastic change in the vegetation. The landscape went from a barren desert dotted with Yucca, Grease Wood, and Mesquite, to beautiful tall mountains covered with tall Pines and huge Oaks. Upon reaching Alto, we merged onto west Highway 70. Soon after, a huge billboard with a Crown Dancer welcomed us to the Mescalero Apache Reservation.

It was about 1:00pm when we entered the local community, where most of the tribal members lived. There my children met Carlos Enjady and his family. Unfortunately, Jack and Richard Wood were unable to attend. The four of us headed to the Feast Grounds where they met other tribal members, among them, Kathleen Kanseah. While sitting on the bleachers, I explained to my children what was going on. My daughter was delighted with the place and the people she had met. What a beautiful view we had from our seats. In front of us stood four tepees, each one representing a maiden. In the background were mountains covered with tall green pines, resembling a postcard. To our right was the Big Ceremonial Tepee where the young maidens would spend four nights in prayers and dancing. We enjoyed the schedule programs, which included a young Crown Dancing Group from East Fork, Arizona.

At about 3:00pm the announcement was made for War Dancers and Singers to get ready. A few minutes later, Freddie Kaydahzinne jumped started the show with his powerful voice. What a sight, the arena was filled with young men and women dancing in their traditional outfits. I quickly pointed out to my children the white stripe painted across the faces of the male dancers. *"Remember I told you guys that you would see it again? There, that's how the white clay was used in the old days,"* I said. A few hours later, when the show was over, I went downstairs and said hello to Freddie and the boys. Freddie asked if I was going to sing with them. *"Yes, I would like to. I am here with my family, but I would love to sing with you guys tomorrow,"* I replied.

As the evening progressed, the sacred fire was lit and shortly after the first Crown Dance Group emerged from the darkness. All four dancers' upper bodies were painted in black. Across their chest and abdomen were four mountains painted in white. Along their arms, lines resembling lighting were also painted in white. That particular group had two clowns, both completely painted in white. *"You see there is another use for the white clay,"* I said. I also explained to them, the meaning of each painted item and the meaning of the dance. They were fascinated with the spectacle and everything associated with it. Among the many things that impressed them most, was the enormous bonfire in the center of the dance arena. Its radiating heat was felt by all of us, even though we were sitting up on the bleachers.

141

Something else that caught my daughter's attention was the beautiful bright yellow dresses worn by the Maidens. After watching the Crown Dancers for a while, we headed to our hotel in Alamogordo where we spent the night.

The next day we returned to Mescalero. There we picked up Carlos and the four of us headed to the Feast Grounds. After shopping around through the vendors we proceeded to sit on the bleachers where we enjoyed the various groups of entertainers as part of the scheduled show.

At about 5:00pm, Freddie Kaydahzinne and the boys arrived to perform the much anticipated Apache War Dance. I grabbed my drum and joined the gang for a good time. While sitting at the end of the bench, I noticed that my friend Carson was missing. I soon learned that he was not going to be participating in any activities associated with the feast. I must admit, I felt lonely and unprotected without him by my side. Once the singing got going, I fell in rhythm with the rest of the group. Even though I didn't have Carson translating the songs and singing in my ear, I never felt better. There I was singing in Mescalero while my family watched from the bleachers. The vividness of that experience has not been erased by time. When our session ended, I thanked Freddie and the other singers and returned to the bleachers were my children eagerly awaited. With a big smile on his face, my boy said, *"Wow Dad, you did well! I can see why you love to come here so much!"* He said. *"I am very happy that you are here to enjoy it with me,"* I replied.

Not long after, chow was called. We stood in line and got some food, a courtesy prepared and served by the maidens' family. While feasting on the bleachers, the first Crown Dance group entered the arena. Once they blessed the fire from all four directions they began to dance. During the ceremony only the females were allowed to dance with the Crown Dancers. As the evening progressed, the number of female dancers increased. Among them, were four maidens, all of them where dressed in bright yellow buckskin dresses adorned with beautiful beadwork. Their loose shiny black hairs were complimented with either two eagle tail feathers or a single eagle plume. Their faces were covered with sacred pollen. All the females danced in line moving in a clockwise manner, around the huge arena. The Crown Dancers on the other hand, were free styling around the bonfire.

The beautiful and inspiring sight prompted a strong desire for my daughter to dance. With a sense of pride and a lump in my throat, I proudly watched as she put on her toe-guarded moccasins and pulled out her shawl from her backpack. She walked down the bleachers and stood on the eastern outer ring of the arena. There she waited for the dancers to come by. Because it was still early in the evening, the group was short of forming a full circle. Ironically, all the female dancers had stopped on the western side of the arena and were dancing in place. A few minutes later the group began to move again. Because their steps were slow and precise, it took a while before the last dancer reached the eastern entrance where my daughter patiently waited. I am sure those few minutes must have felt like an eternity to her. She was showing a lot of courage, and I was feeling very proud. When the last dancer went by her, she joined in. To my surprise, she immediately fell in rhythm with the rest of the group.

As the evening progressed, other Crown Dance groups joined in. In time, the dance arena was filled with dancers. The once gapped circle of female dancers had joined at both ends. That particular evening, things went a little different, as The Crown Dancers began to dance on the outer circle. The rare occasion forced the ladies to dance inside and therefore closer to the bonfire.

The fire was fueled by huge dry pine logs, measuring approximately five feet in height and about fifteen inches in diameter. On that particular night the fire had reached ten or fifteen feet in height. The enormous amount of heat radiating from them was felt by everyone, including those of us sitting on the bleachers. I could only imagine how it was affecting my little one. The change in arrangement was very different then what she had observed the night before. It was something I had never seen either. The Crown Dancers came from every direction and at times, very close to her. Not knowing if my little princess was scared or not, I began to pray to the Creator. *"Life Giver, please hear me, I ask that you give my little one enough courage and strength to hang on...."* After all she was only nine years old and all alone in a strange place. On top of that, there were more than a dozen Crown Dancers wearing two-foot tall horns on their black masked heads. In their hands they held two foot wands, which they used in a zigzag motion. Any one of those factors would have been enough to scare her away, but she didn't. Instead, she continued dancing as if she had been doing it her whole life. It was obvious that she had it in her blood. Oh how proud I felt sitting up high on those bleachers watching her like a nighthawk. I looked up to the skies and recited another short prayer, *"Thank you Grandfather for allowing us to be here and learn a little bit of what I thought to have been our lost culture."* I felt proud for being part Apache and for returning to ways that were long lost by my family through silence and shame.

About an hour later, my daughter came back. I told her how proud I was for her courage to continued dancing under the unusual circumstances. *"Dad, I was not scared at all,"* she said. She sat on the bleachers with us and we continued to enjoy the feast. Despite the radiating heat, the temperature began to drop to uncomfortable levels, forcing us to end the night early.

While driving west on Highway 70 towards Alamogordo, my daughter asked me for a favor. *"Sure, what is it?"* I asked. *"Is there any way we can go to church tomorrow morning?"* She asked. Although I had never attended church with them before, it was something they were used to doing with their mom. *"Of course we can,"* I replied.

The next morning after breakfast, we headed east on Highway 70. A few miles after crossing the Mescalero Reservation line, my daughter said, *"There Dad, that's the church I want to go to,"* as she pointed to a beautiful stone building on the right hand side off the main highway. The name of the church was St. Joseph, a catholic church. Although I was raised Catholic, I had not attended Church since age eleven or twelve when I completed my first, and last, Communion. I pulled over and parked in front of the old Church, built in 1887. Not totally thrilled, I began to follow my children up the wooden rail-road tie beam steps that led to the main entrance door.

Once inside, I realized that this was not an ordinary church. To my surprise, it was very different than any other one I had ever seen. The stone walls reached at least fifty feet in height. In the center, above the altar, hung a huge banner of a Chiricahua Apache dressed in traditional outfit. A bandana wrapped around his head, held his long black hair in place. The side walls were adorned with replicas of Crown Dancers' Horns. They were painted in the traditional black and white colors. Behind the entrance wall hung four framed paintings of Chiricahua leaders. From left to right were Chief Cochise, Victorio, Naiche and Geronimo. I must admit that I was in total shock and I felt somewhat angry and insulted. At first I thought, how far will the church go to lure you in? They had used sacred symbols and legends to accomplish their mission. As time passed I began to acclimate to the surroundings. The fact that we were the only ones in there, allowed us to move about and explore every corner of the building.

143

While looking at the paintings and different written articles on the back walls, I noticed one that was kept inside a glass case. It was titled *"Chiricahua Scouts who served the U.S. Army."* As my children walked towards the front of the church, I stayed back and read the names on the list. To my surprise, I saw the names Second and Jumper. Filled with excitement, I called my children over to show them my discovery.

Up until that day, I had never met anybody or seen anything bearing my family names, but there they were. The feeling was overwhelming, almost as if I had found proof, as to who I was. I finished reading the list that consisted of over one hundred names. At that moment, I humbled myself and realized that the Creator works in mysterious ways. I began to look at the church in a different way. With a big lump in my throat, I walked up to the last row of seats and dropped to my knees. There I asked for forgiveness for my initial hostile thoughts. I also asked the Creator to help me find anyone related to my family's name. When finished, I sat on the bench and watched my children as they knelt down for their own prayer. About fifteen minutes later, we headed down to the parking lot and quietly sat in the car while I digested what had taken place. I kept looking at the beautiful structure that had revealed so much to me. In a peculiar way it contained a piece of me. *"You see, aren't you glad we came to church?"* My daughter asked. *"Yes I am, thank you,"* I replied. From there, we stopped at Carlos house. I couldn't wait to tell him about our discovery at the church. That afternoon before heading to the feast grounds, we stopped at the church where I proudly showed Carlos the list that contained a piece of my identity. Once at the Feast Grounds, I sang some War Songs with Freddie and the boys. That evening, my daughter got to dance again and I felt just as proud.

Afterwards we returned to our hotel and began packing our luggage for our next day's departure. Early next morning, we began our descent towards Albuquerque. After driving through the town of Bonito, I looked through my rear view mirror and sadly saw the evergreen Sacramento Mountains as they got smaller and smaller with each passing mile. At that moment, the following words echoed in my mind. *Come back, you hear. There is a lot more here for you to discover.* A few hours later we arrived at the Albuquerque's airport, where we boarded our eastbound flight. Once home, my children told everyone about everything they had learned during the trip.

Siggy Second-Jumper on a Stallion named Sundance.
Sunshine Ranches, FL, ca. 2002

By late July of 2003, I was back in Big Cypress with my children riding and taking care of the horses. In order to further enjoy our equestrian activities, I purchased a two-horse trailer with sleeping quarters. Shortly thereafter, I joined a horse-riding club and looked forward to traveling to other Seminole reservations and state parks. I soon found out that I needed at least one more horse to accommodate our needs.

Taking turns riding my only transportable horse prevented us from going on excursions with other club members. My daughter Emily suggested calling Sam Frank to see if I could start boarding the horse that I had broken in for him. The young gelding roamed freely in an eighteen-hundred-acre pasture.

Lance, riding 'Star' at The Junior Cypress Rodeo Arena, ca.2004 ****

Her idea prompted me to make the phone call a few days later. I explained to Sam what my needs were, and my desire to bring the horse to the stalls for further evaluation. *"It sounds great, that way my grandchildren can also get a chance to ride him as well,"* Sam said. The horse's name was Star, a liver chestnut Arabian with a rare calm nature.

In less than a year, I went from one, to three horses under my care. A few days after Star's arrival, I learned that he was Geronimo's son, the Arabian Stallion. By pure luck, I was working with three Arabians. Even though, I had broken-in Star years earlier, he needed a lot of work.

Again, using Sam's techniques, I was able to get Star back in riding shape. Within weeks, my children were riding Star and Spirit and running barrels at the Junior Cypress rodeo arena. Once a month we rode at various state parks and private ranches. About four months after Star's arrival, I began to break-in horses for different tribal members.

By late spring of 2004, I found myself overwhelmed with work and responsibilities. I called Sam and told him that I was returning Star and if it was possible to keep Spirit in his parcel of tribal land. His pasture was about four or five miles from the stalls. *"Yes, of course,"* Sam replied. Soon after, both horses grazed among five hundred head of cattle. In exchange for the nice gesture, I helped Sam with cattle work.

It was during that time that I truly learned about Seminole culture. Sam was a great teacher who enjoyed reminiscing about the old days when his people lived in the swamps around Lake Okeechobee. He also taught me about the Tribal Cattle Program, which consisted of rounding, branding, yearly vaccinations, purchasing and sells.

Our arrangement turned out to be a good trade, not only was I getting a break by not having to pay for boarding, but I was learning about cattle work and having fun doing it.

One of my favorite activities was traveling with Sam to other ranches to purchase livestock. The most memorable trip was one that Sam and I took to a ranch in Lorida, Florida. The reason that trip was special was because Sam was purchasing a dozen head of cattle for his daughter Sunshine. Sam was proud of the fact that his daughter was willing to continue with the family tradition. The purchase and delivery of Sunshine's cattle marked a historical event, as she became one of the first Seminole female cattle owners.

By early summer, I began riding my horse Spirit back and forth between Sam's pasture and the rodeo grounds. During those trips, I rode along Josie Billie Highway, the main road that cuts through the Big Cypress Seminole reservation. On both sides of the roadwere beautiful open prairies that made up other tribal members' pastures.

Among those parcels of land was one in particular that caught my attention every time I rode by. It belonged to Moses Jumper Jr. Moses aka "Big Shot" is Betty Mae Jumper's son. He and I have a few things in common, but the most prominent one is our love for horses.

Moses "Big Shot" Jumper Jr. (Snake Clan)
Riding a Cracker Horse during the annual Shootout Seminole War Reenactment
Big Cypress Seminole Reservation, FL, ca.2006
Photographed by Gordon O. Wareham (Seminole, Panther Clan)

Big Shot's land was dotted with cattle and among them were his legendary Cracker horses. Moses is one of less than a handful of Cowboys in the country who takes pride in his unique herd. His Cracker horses are direct descendants from the original Spanish herd.

Spanish horses and cattle arrived in Cuba from Spain in the late 1400's. These animals were later shipped to North America through St. Augustine, Florida. The horse became an essential part of the cattle industry and those who worked on them became known as Cowboys. In order to drive the cattle more effectively, the Cowboys made leather whips. Because of the sound made by their whips cracking in the air, the Cowboys, along with their horses and cattle, became known as Crackers. Although other names such as Seminole Pony, Prairie Pony and Cow Pony have been used over the past five centuries to describe the Spanish horse, they have all faded away with time. Today the small but spirited Spanish horse is known as the Cracker horse.

Big Shot still uses them as they did back in the 1500's. Their easy, ground covering gait makes them ideal when working and driving his cattle. Many times while riding my horse, I would stop in front of Big Shot's property just to admire his herd, as they grazed peacefully throughout the open prairie. That was the easy part of the day, just riding along and enjoying the beauty of the Everglades.

Once I got to the stalls, the real work began. Preparing the horses and trailer for weekend getaways was not an easy task, but along with my children's help, it all got accomplished. These were special times for me indeed. Our favorite place to camp and ride was at a state park called DuPuis located in Martin County, about a three-hour drive from the Big Cypress Seminole Reservation. The park offered over thirty thousand wooded acres with lots of game, natural springs and various marked trails. It was there that we spent a lot of time camping and riding with friends. Our favorite thing besides riding all day was roasting marshmallows at night time by the campfire.

By midsummer, a new horse arrived at the Junior Cypress stalls. She was a beautiful young paint; mostly black with white patches. It was love at first sight for my daughter. She took one look at the sassy mare and wanted me to buy her. I quickly found out that she was not for sale. It belonged to a Seminole lady who had bought the horse for her ten-year-old daughter. I offered her a deal; I would break-in the young mare, in exchange for my daughter to ride her. The offer was accepted with a handshake, and a week later I began to work with the three-year-old paint. I soon found out this was no easy task. The sassy mare was a real handful that made me feel uneasy. As long as I could remember, I felt comfortable around horses; handling those that were wild or furious had always been easy for me.

For the first time in my life, I had come across one that would change that, and I was looking at it. That paint kicked with all legs and with a lot of precision, not to mention she could bite like an alligator. I worked with her with some hesitation and lots of pressure from my daughter. She was too young to understand what was on hand. On my first experience, I found it almost impossible to take the stubborn animal into the round pen without fear of getting hurt. The owner gave me full permission to do whatever I had to do. She explained to me that the mare had come from the neighboring Brighton Seminole Reservation, where they had unsuccessfully attempted to break her in. *"That's great! What have I gotten myself into?"* I wondered. Days went by and I continued working with her in the round pen, but I knew she was not ready for the saddle. I even tried giving her carrots and apples hoping to win her trust but it did not work.

On a hot summer day, I took the feisty mare to the round pen, determined that I was going to ride her that day. Although it was hot and humid, it didn't seem to make a difference; she remained just as mean and energetic. After working her for about thirty minutes, I decided to move on to the next step. With help from tribal workers, we were able to put a saddle on her. While being held by the men, I mounted her. Once they let go, she bucked like any other horse. In reality I found her bucking to be weak and not as explosive as others her age. After a while of having fun in the round pen, I walked the tired animal to the rodeo arena. By then a small crowd had gathered. A combination of tribal members, workers, and the owner of the mare, along with her children and mine, made the small audience. Held down again by a few tribal employees, I mounted the horse. Once they let go, the mare took off as fast as she could. A sudden stop and a quick buck sent me flying sideways landing on my right hip. Although I didn't hear anything crack, I felt a terrible pain upon landing on the ground. Practicing what I had preached to my children, that you always get back on the horse after you fall, I had no choice but to attempt to ride her again. With a slight limp and lots of pain I managed to get on her one more time. Luckily I was able to hold on without falling again. When it was all over, I noticed that my horse medicine bracelet was broken. *Medicine is a protective amulet, usually made for an individual's specific purpose.* Mine consisted of a silver bracelet in the shape of an Eagle feather with four pieces of turquoise running down the center. It was made for me long ago, and I was told to always wear it when breaking in a horse. Once the bracelet was broken, I knew that my horse breaking days were over. I walked away from the mare and approached the owner. I told her that I was done and sorry that I was not able to finish the job. My daughter had a hard time understanding why I couldn't finish the job. Despite my explanation, she remained unsatisfied.

The following weekend in spite of some hip pain, I loaded Spirit into my horse trailer and drove out to DuPuis Park by myself for a three day excursion. The first day went on without any incidents. On the morning of the second day, the pain in my hip had become intolerable, forcing me to cut my trip short. That evening, I checked into the emergency room, where I was admitted for the very first time. After having fluid removed from my right hip, the doctor had a serious talk with me.

I was informed that my type of injury required two years to fully heal. Any aggravation and I ran the risk of infection and possible hip replacement. It translated to no running, jogging, dancing and especially not riding horses. Without much to do, time moved slowly. Although the pain was gone, I managed not to dance or ride at all.

Instead, I decided to go into horse breeding. I purchased a beautiful mare, in hopes to breed her with Geronimo, the Arabian Stallion. The new challenge kept me busy and out of trouble. June had come and gone, and there was no sense in going to New Mexico, since most activities there required lots climbing and hiking.

By the end of July of 2004, my injured hip was doing better as most of the fluid had been reabsorbed. The doctor said that swimming and walking was ok. In time, I was allowed to hike, as long as there was no jumping or any type of heavy impact on my hip. Out of all the activities prohibited, the one that hurt the most was not being able to dance. A short time later, I was allowed to go back to full-duty at work.

On December 3rd of 2004, I drove home from work after doing a twenty-four-hour shift. Upon arrival, I found Carlos Enjady waiting on my front porch. I shook my head in amazement. After a few seconds, I began to accept that it was really him. Not only was his visit totally unexpected but his long hair was cut short and he had grown a mustache. *"What are you are doing here?"* I asked. *"I came to stay for a while,"* he replied. Although I found it odd, I asked no further questions. *"Stay as long as you like,"* I said.

The next day I drove him to Miami Beach. Carlos had never seen the ocean and he was excited to experience it. Our days were busy visiting friends and relatives. In the evenings we listened to music, watched television and shared family stories. One particular night, while talking about past relatives, the name Second came up. Carlos stated that to the best of his knowledge there were no Seconds' living in Mescalero. He mentioned that perhaps there would be some in Oklahoma.

His comments made me think of Ruey Darrow, she was an Apache from Oklahoma, whom I had met on my first visit to Mescalero. After hearing my story, she invited me to visit her and her relatives. Over the years, Ruey kept her invitation opened. She had since passed away and I didn't know what to do.

I told Carlos I was determined to find my relatives even if I had to go to Mexico. We spoke long into the nights, discussing the past, our heritage, and what future surprises lay in store. His visit came to an end a month later. He has always shared a special place in my heart and even today, when I think back on our friendship, I still see him as the Gate Keeper.

It was mid January of 2005, and the holidays were over. During quiet moments, I would think about Carlos and the special times we shared. His visit had a purpose. Our long conversations about our ancestors had inspired me to continue searching for my family. Mrs. Ruey Darrow's echoing words of going to Oklahoma to meet her family and friends kept haunting me. That little bird on my shoulder told me that the time was right. Determined, I searched the web for airline prices. To my surprise, a round trip to Oklahoma City, OK was only one hundred twenty dollars, about half the normal price. I really saw that as a sign to make it happen. Without hesitation I booked it. Knowing that Mrs. Darrow had passed on, I called Kathleen Kanseah in Mescalero to find out who I should see upon my arrival. I was told to make arrangements by calling an individual, who I will refer to as a Fort Sill Apache. A few days later, I called and spoke to the person that I was referred to. I informed that individual, that Mrs. Darrow had asked me many times to visit her family and other tribal members. We arranged to meet upon my arrival at The Complex, or headquarters of the Fort Sill Chiricahua Warm Springs Apache Tribe of Oklahoma, located near Apache, Oklahoma.

On the first week of March, I arrived in Oklahoma City in the early evening hours. It was 9:00pm when I checked into a hotel in Anadarko, the nearest town to my destination. To my surprise the small town had shut down, leaving me hungry with no place to eat. I was told by the front desk attendant that the nearest restaurant was a McDonalds', about twenty miles away. It was at that moment, that I realized how far a hungry man will go to satisfy his needs.

The next morning I went to the hotel's restaurant for breakfast. I sat at a table and placed my order. Not far from me sat a Dakota Indian from Minnesota.

Within minutes, his curiosity got the best of him. Finally he asked what I was doing there. I told him I was here to visit the Fort Sill Apaches. The blank look on his face let me know he had no idea what I was talking about. After joining him, I proceeded to explain who the Fort Sill Apaches were and how they got their name.

I told him, that in 1913, after more than twenty seven years of imprisonment, the Chiricahua Apache were set free by an Act of Congress. They were given the choice to remain in Oklahoma where they had been held for the past nineteen years or relocate to New Mexico with their kin, the Mescalero Apaches. The one third or eighty two of two hundred and sixty five Chiricahuas that chose to stay in Oklahoma became known as the Fort Sill Apaches. Once done with our meal, I asked the waiter for direction to the Fort Sill Apache headquarters.

After driving for a while through endless wheat fields and cattle pastures, I arrived at The Complex on time for my 10:00am appointment. It consisted of two almost identical buildings side by side with an adjacent parking lot and a separate building, perhaps a gymnasium.

Fort Sill Chiricahua Warm Springs Apache Tribal Office ****
Apache, OK

Nervous but determined, I entered the building. I introduced myself and informed the receptionist I was there to see the Fort Sill Apache. Apparently they were not aware of our pre-arranged meeting and had to call the individual at home. I was told that the person would be in within the hour. At about 11:00am the Fort Sill Apache showed up. After a quick introduction, I was taken into that individual's office.

There, I was told that the Apaches were nomadic people that followed the seasons, and migrated across the southwestern states and northern Mexico. I was also informed that they were divided into different bands.

After that, I was shown a paper that illustrated where those bands were found. According to the Fort Sill Apache, the same paperwork was used to lecture a group of boy scouts that had gone through on previous days. In amazement, I told the individual I was not here for that. *"I am Jose Second's great-grandson, and I am looking for any of his descendants or anyone related to the name,"* I said. *"There are no Seconds here and no relatives either,"* the individual replied. The individual referred to a book, which was in alphabetical order. *"See, Jose First came here, but Jose Second did not."* Sadly, only two sentences described Jose's lifetime of pain and suffering. It read, something like this: Jose Second, P.O.W. in Florida, Alabama, discharged and headed to Mescalero, New Mexico. *"As you can see, Jose Second never came here, so therefore you are not a Fort Sill. You are not one of us,"* the individual emphasized. So many thoughts went through my mind in just a few seconds. I couldn't believe what I was hearing. There, in front of me, sat an individual, not just an Apache but a Chiricahua, telling me I was not one of them just because Jose Second did not to go to Oklahoma. Stunned by those words, I remained speechless. I was saddened that such technicality was being used against me. Not by an attorney or a judge, but by the very own people that my great-grandfather fought and went to prison for. I didn't know what to make out of it. If that wasn't enough, the insults continued. The next thing I heard was, *"So you will not be able to seek enrollment with our Tribe."* Somewhat defensive, I replied, *"At what point did you hear me say that I came here looking for enrollment?"* It didn't take a genius to realize things were not going well. The last thing I mentioned were my plans to go to Fort Sill's Cemetery in search of any relatives possibly buried there. I was about to leave, when I was told *"Let me take you next door, we have a kitchen there that serves free breakfast to our Tribal Members. Since you're not one, it's going to cost you three dollars."* Although I came real close to denying the invitation, I said *"No problem, I think I can spare that."*

The inside of the adjacent building consisted of an open floor space, half living room, half dining room. The living room area had a TV and a sofa. The dining area consisted of a small kitchen with some dining tables, which reminded me of a sunroom at a retirement home. Apparently they had stopped serving breakfast at eleven, a few minutes before our arrival. Although the kitchen was closed, there were some tribal members still eating their meals and drinking coffee. Prior to meeting anyone, I excused myself to use the restroom. As I exited the coed bathroom, I noticed an older gentleman waiting to use it. I was told that his name was Benedict Johze, the last surviving Fort Sill Chiricahua P.O.W.

Upon my return, I stood in the center of the dining room, where I was introduced to the tribal members that were there, perhaps five or six of them. *"Everyone, this is Siggy, he is Jose Second's great-grandson. He came all the way from Florida looking for any Seconds' or relatives. Because there are none here, he would like to go to Fort Sill's cemetery to see if any are buried there,"* they were told.

Although I was formally introduced, I was unable to remember any of their names. I do recall an individual; he was a stocky gentleman with a spiky crew cut and grayish hair. I was told he was related to the Kaywayklas'.

The cold reception not only sent chills down my spine, but left me feeling awkward. Not a word was spoken, other than those of an older lady, who sarcastically said, *"Tell him, he is not going to find anything here."* I stood there not knowing what to do or say. The words 'numbed' and 'paralyzed' merely describe how I felt at that moment. Realizing I was not welcomed, I attempted to release them of their fears.

"Do not be threatened by my visit. I did not come here seeking any material things, nor a free breakfast. I just came to look for any relatives. " I said before heading out the door. Shortly after, the Fort Sill Apache caught up with me. *"I know a place down the road where we can go and get something to eat,"* I was told. Not letting my ego get in my way, I accepted the invitation.

As we drove towards the restaurant, I noticed a little church on the left hand-side of the road. It was the Apache Reformed Church, a place where the Fort Sill Apaches worshipped Jesus. I was later informed by local residents, that the wooden structure was built in 1920 and renovated in 1967.

Apache Reformed Church ****
Apache, OK, ca. 2005

A few minutes later, we arrived at a small restaurant where a buffet lunch was being served. I paid for both of us, and showed the same individual who would not treat me to a three dollar breakfast that I had enough to pay for the two of us. After finishing our meal, I handed a leather bag I had beaded years earlier for Mrs. Darrow. The bag which had her name on it was very personal and I felt it was the right thing to do. Just before we parted our ways, the individual expressed a desire to accompany me to the Fort Sill Cemetery. We drove down to the town of Lawton, where Fort Sill was located. After getting through a strict and thorough checkpoint, we entered the military base. A few minutes later, we arrived at Fort Sill's Graveyard. Two signs on a stone wall read:

Apache Prisoner Of War Cemeteries

"Here, beneath Oklahoma skies, far from their natives haunts in Arizona, New Mexico, and Northern Mexico is the resting place for more than 300 Apaches of the Chiricahua, Warm Springs, and Nedhi Tribes. During and after the Geronimo Campaign of 1886, these people, hostiles, friendlies, and scouts alike were sent as prisoners of war to Florida, then Alabama.

In 1894 they were brought to Fort Sill where they remained for the next 19 years. Living in 12 villages, with many of their leading men serving as soldiers and U.S. scouts, they built their own houses, fenced the entire military reserve, dug water tanks which still dot the landscape, raised 10,000 cattle and grew bountiful crops. Granted freedom by an Act of Congress in 1913, 183 returned to New Mexico while 82 settled on farms near here."

"This burial ground is a memorial both to their historic past and to their industry and perseverance on their long road to a new life." The sign on the other side of the stone wall read:

Apache Indian Cemeteries

"The roll call of Chiefs, warriors, army scouts and families buried here include the most famous names in Apache history: Geronimo, whose daring band performed deeds unmatched since the days of Captain Kidd. Chief Loco of the Warm Springs who stood for peace; Chief Nana, the original Desert Fox; Chief Chihuahua of the Chiricahuas; and sons and grandsons of Mangas Coloradas; Victorio; Cochise; Naiche; and Juh and of such noted scouts as Keahteney, Chatto, Kayitah and Martine. Here also lie 12 of the 50 Apaches who were U.S. soldiers and scouts at Fort Sill. Linked with these men in the Indian Wars was a Legion of Army Greats - Generals Crook, Miles, Howard, Crawford, Gatewood, Lawton, Grierson, and Leonard Wood. This cemetery on Beef Creek was established in 1894 by General Scott. Related cemeteries nearby are the Chief Chihuahua plot ¼ mile north and Bailtso plot just across the road. Scouts Mangus and Domeah, and white interpreter George Wratten are buried in the Post Cemetery."

Fort Sill, Oklahoma

After reading the signs, we proceeded through the cemetery's open gate. We walked quietly and respectfully, reading each headstone. There I was, in the final resting place of the men and women belonging to the once mighty and feared Chiricahua Tribe.

Fort Sill Apache Cemetery, Fort Sill, OK
Photographed by Barbara Holloway

In the middle of the cemetery was Goyathlay's grave, meaning *'One-who-yawns,'* better known as Geronimo. He was born in 1829, near the upper waters of the Gila River. Both his father, whose name was Taklishim *'The Gray One,'* and his mother Juana, were full-blooded Bedonkohe Apaches. His grandfather was Mahko, chief of the Bedonkohe Tribe. Geronimo died on Feb 17, 1909 from pneumonia. He was buried on February 18th in the Apache Cemetery on Beef Creek. The very same spot I was standing on.

Geronimo's grave
Fort Sill cemetery, OK
Photographed by Barbara Holloway

Among Geronimo's relatives buried in the Apache cemetery were his 6th wife Zi-yeh; Nah-dos-te (1819-1907), his full sister wife of Nana (1800-1896) of the Warm Springs Apaches; one son Fenton, one stepson Guy Amardo, one son-in-law, Dahkeya, two daughters Luly and Eva; two grandsons, Joe and Thomas Dahkeya; two granddaughters, Nina Dahkeya and Evaline Golene; two first cousins, Ish-keh (widow of Chief Juh, Chief of the Nednai) and Bonita (mother of Fun, Tsisnah, Jozha, and Jah-ken-ish-ishn); and six second cousins, Burdett Tsisnah, Jason Betzinez, sister Ellen Chachu, Jah-ken-ish-ishn, Nah-kay-gode-konne; and E-clah-heh (2nd wife of Chief Naiche of the Chiricahuas). Geronimo's only surviving lineal descendants as of 1962 were his son Robert Geronimo of Mescalero and Robert's offspring and the offspring of Robert's Sister Lenna Geronimo, also of Mescalero.[1]

From Beef Creek Cemetery, we drove a short distance to a much smaller graveyard. Among the Apaches buried there, was Chief Chihuahua (1822-1901) and his brother Ol-Sanny (or Jolsanny) (1821-1909). Once done visiting the smaller cemetery, we drove out to the other side of the base. Shortly after crossing Beef Creek, we entered the old village area, where the prisoners once lived.

The place was beautiful and tranquil, filled with rolling hills and covered with tall grass. The first former village we visited was that of Chief Apache Loco (1823-1905). He was the last leader of the Warm Spring Apaches. After his death, his son John Loco (1876-1945) who was enlisted as a scout at the fort became head of Loco's village[1].

The next campsite we visited was that of Roger Toclanny's (1863-1947), Tu-clanni meaning *"lots of water."* Roger was a Mimbreño Apache and is said to have had the longest record as a Scout in the regular Army that was held by an Apache. He never at any time bore arms against the US, serving instead as Scout against the hostile Indians. Yet, he was sent east as a prisoner of war along with the others to join the very people he had helped track down. He went with his third wife, Sy-e konne, a stepdaughter of Chief Loco. His land was still smoldering from a previous brush fire.

Adjacent to Roger's camp was the village of Chief Christian Naiche (1856-1921), last Chief of the Chiricahua Apaches. "The hereditary Chief was the youngest son of Chief Cochise and his principal wife Dos-the-she, *'Something–at-the-campfire-already-cooked,'* who was the daughter of Chief Mangas Coloradas of the Warm Springs Apache. At Mount Vernon, Alabama, Naiche enlisted as a Scout with Company "I" 12th, then transferred to the 7th Cavalry at Fort Sill, where he was made head of his village, and enlisted as Scout by General Scott in 1897 along with Geronimo, Chihuahua Mangus and others"[1]. I liked his property the most, as it contained the highest hills and huge rock boulders, resembling New Mexico's landscape. Our tour ended with Perico's Village, it was there that Geronimo and his 9th and last wife Azul lived[1].

After spending some time there, we headed back towards the town of Apache. It was close to 5:00pm when we arrived back at the Complex. I was asked when I was going home. *"I am here for five days,"* I answered. *"Five days! What are you going to do here for five days?"* I was asked again. *"Nothing, I just gave myself enough time in case I found something to do or someone related to me,"* I replied. Feeling awkward again, I said *"Goodbye,"* a word used by Indians only when a return is not expected.

An hour later, I was back in Anadarko. The unpleasant reception was nothing compared to the lonely and cold night in that hotel. I remembered lying in bed and saying to myself *"What am I doing here? I left my family behind for this!"* Unable to sleep that night, I went through the entire experience many times over in my mind. Although thankful by the individual's latter action, I was still unable to shake the negative feeling I had inside. The amount of hurtful words and the cold reception outweighed the efforts shown towards the end. Those sharp stabbing words *"You are not one of us,"* kept swirling in my mind. In order to ease my anxiety and disappointment, I began to pray. *"Grandfather, I was hurt today. I ask that you give me the wisdom to understand and the ability to forgive, along with the strength to go on with my search."* Within minutes after my prayer, I realized that the same words that had hurt me so deeply became words of blessings. Indeed, Jose Second had never gone there, and boy was I glad. Ironically, the same technicality used against me, served as my acquittal.

The next day with nothing to do, I drove back to Fort Sill in search of anything new. During my search, I found the Jail House where the defiant Geronimo spent time. I proceeded to enter the two-story museum, where I found myself all alone. The upstairs of the building consisted of officer's quarters and a court-like room, perhaps used for trials. Down in the basement, I found six prison cells and a display case showing various items belonging to Geronimo. Among them were an old wood frame saddle that he had left in Lawton for repairs, various beaded leather bags, a beaded walking cane, and an old hand gun.

Fort Sill's Jail House located in Fort Sill, OK, ca. early 1900's
Courtesy of Jail House Museum

Next to the display case was the actual cell, where the relentless and legendary leader spent some time. I proceeded to walk into the small square room, which measured approximately 10' x 10'. It contained a small window opening, blocked by iron bars. What really impressed me the most was the foot-thick wooden door.

Prison cell where Geronimo spent time ****
Fort Sill, OK

157

After the self-guided tour, I proceeded to drive around the military base and back to the Chiricahua camps to enjoy the serenity of the place.

By early afternoon I had run out of things to do and decided to drive to Oklahoma City, where I unsuccessfully tried to get an early flight back home. I stayed there and survived the next three days by attending a country fair. I was glad when the plane took off, and thrilled when it landed in Florida.

Eagerly waiting at the airport was my family. With both children in my arms, I prayed to the Creator for the things I had. It was there that I realized how rich I was. Later that day, I told everyone about the reception and my feelings about the whole experience. That evening while laying in bed, I thought about how different things would have been, had Fort Sill been my first experience instead of Mescalero. The love and warmth I received at Mescalero was so overwhelming that it allowed me to put the unpleasant experience behind me. I can only wonder how many other descendants like me have been rejected in a similar manner. Perhaps my story will encourage them to go to the right place, Mescalero. I hold no hard feelings for the Fort Sill people, I pray for their good health and prosperity.

Siggy Second-Jumper
Dressed in War Dance regalia. ca. 2005

In February of 2005, I received various emails from my friends in New Mexico. Among them, Jack Noel and other Monticello Canyon residents. They were asking for my help in reference to an awful event that was about to take place. I was informed that an out-of-state mining company was seeking permit from the State of New Mexico to explore and possibly mine Red Paint Canyon. It was there, that a rare earth mineral, Bertrandite was found. Although Bertrandite is considered nontoxic, it contains small fragments of Beryllium which is a highly toxic alkaline metal mainly used in circuitry and firing mechanisms of thermal nuclear devises.

The news came as a total surprise to me. *"How can any company seek permit without the owner's knowledge or consent?"* I asked. For the first time in more than six years, I learned that the people that had welcomed me to my ancestor's homeland did not own Red Paint Canyon, like I thought.

Instead, it belonged to a descendant of the family who conveniently took possession of most of the Chiricahuas' homeland after their forceful removal by the U.S. government. For more than a century, that family has made a fortune in the cattle industry. Over the years, the descendants of the original family abandoned the profitable livestock business and began to look at the lucrative real estate value of *'their land'*, in order to satisfy their endless hunger for greed.

While they sold parcels of land of one hundred acre minimum for hundreds of thousands of dollars, the Chiricahuas did not have a piece of land to call their own. A sad reality that continues to this day. Most Chiricahuas live below poverty levels and some still go to sleep hungry. I seriously doubt that any of the descendants of the original land grabbers even associate themselves with anyone of such status. I will go on to say that I am positive that none of them have ever gone a day without a meal. To add to their avaricious menu, some have allowed their greed to take them to the most pitiful of all sins. That is, selling their water and mineral rights to out-of-town companies. Their actions showed neither concern nor remorse to the fact that "their land" is sacred to the Chienne Apaches. It is a place where their ancestors were born and forever rest. Such actions by the greedy family also show no consideration to other canyon residents and/or future generations. The so common phrase *'me, myself, and I'* continues to apply over and over to this voracious bunch.

By early April of that year, most canyon residents were in total panic, their drinking water in possible danger of contamination and their property values in jeopardy. Despite countless efforts and previous violations for illegal drilling, canyon residents were unable to stop the process of permit application. The slow, but steady progression, which began in January, continued gaining strength.

The word was that the only way for the permit to be denied was with the help of the Apaches. How ironic, I thought, as I read the emails. How could they even think of asking the very own people that were expelled from there and treated like animals to come help them save the canyon. After all, it was that place that caused a lot of resentment between the two races.

The following factors influenced my decision to help. The first one was my gratitude to the O'Toole family who for six years had opened their doors to my family and me without ever asking for anything in return. The second one was the crisis itself. As I put things into perspective, I realized that for the first time in more than a century, the same canyon that so bitterly divided the two cultures, offered an occasion for embracement. Jumping at the opportunity, I made arrangements to meet with certain Chiricahua Warm Springs' leaders from Mescalero, New Mexico.

In May of 2005, I drove to Monticello Canyon in New Mexico, where I met with some concerned residents to discuss in detail some of the issues pertaining to mining at Red Paint Canyon. Later that day, while returning from a hike through the canyon, I noticed what appeared to be a group of people standing next to an SUV about a mile away. As I got closer, I was able to identify them as a man and three women. I approached the group and found them to be friendly. To my surprise, one of the women asked if my name was Siggy. *"Yes,"* I responded. *"We have a mutual friend, his name is Jack Noel,"* she said. The group had traveled all the way from England to show and express their opposition in reference to mining the Red Paint Canyon. After spending some time chatting, we parted ways.

The next morning, I drove to the Mescalero Apache reservation to meet with a small but concerned group of Chiricahua-Warm Springs descendants . After presenting the case and the significance of their involvement, I was told that they needed more specific information in reference to the matter, before getting involved. (I must mention that some elders were skeptical about any participation.) *"You are young and naïve, in time you will learn not to get involved in that mess. They will use you, and burn you in the end."* I was told. Against their advice, I continued with my involvement.

Once back in Florida, I notified all concern parties that the Apaches needed more detailed information in order to help. I suggested that Jack Noel be the one to present the case. I made arrangements for us to meet with the group of Apaches a month later.

On Thursday June 30th, I arrived in New Mexico. On the morning of July 1st, I drove to Kathleen Kanseah's home in Mescalero. There I met with a few Chiricahuas including the same individual whom I had met when I visited the Fort Sill Apaches in 2005 during my family search. I told the group that my friend Jack Noel was coming from Monticello to explain the issues pertaining to mining at Red Paint Canyon. At 5:00pm, I drove down to St. Joseph's Church in Mescalero and met with Jack as previously planned. He then followed me to the Feast Grounds' parking lot. From there I drove him to James' camp, and introduced him to some of the group members that were present. *"This is my friend Jack Noel from Monticello. He is the one that will explain what is taking place at the Red Paint Canyon,"* I said. At first they were apprehensive, as not many outsiders are normally seen that deep into the campgrounds.

A short time later, Jack began to speak of the devastating effects of mining Red Paint Canyon and the possible contamination of Ojo Caliente's water. As time passed, the tension began to ease. Present at the meeting were all Crown Dancers and the singers Carson Carrillo and Pete and Carl Kazhe. All three singers were direct descendants of Roger Toclanny, a notorious Warm Springs Apache and devoted advocate of Ojo Caliente and the Monticello Canyon.

Mr. Toclanny spent decades trying to convince the U.S. government to allow the Warm Springs Apache to return to their home. Everyone became very interested in what Jack had to say. His speech was short and straight-forward with a simple explanation of the desirable minerals found in Red Paint Canyon and their toxicology. Jack concluded by saying that without the Apaches coming forward, the permit for mining was unstoppable.

A while later, the rest of the singers and James Kunestsis showed up. James, our leader, was also a direct descendant of Roger Toclanny. I introduced Jack to them, and after hearing the facts of the matter, James asked *"How we can help?"* *"The only way to stop the permit is if the Apaches come forward and express to the Governor of New Mexico and to the Head of the Permit Department how important and sacred the canyon is to the Chiricahuas, especially to the Chienne band,"* Jack replied. James talked about the canyon's history and how much of the spiritual, as well as herbal, medicine came from there. Jack told the group that a meeting was coming up, and that he would notify me on the specific dates. It was obvious that Jack's short presentation was effective when the group responded *"Let us know, you have our full support."*

Shortly after, all singers and dancers began making their way into the tepee to prepare for that evening's fire dance. James told Jack that he was welcomed to stay and wait in the brush arbor while that took place. When preparations were done, we all came out of the tepee and I was able to meet with Jack again. He was invited to walk along with us as we made our way to the Feast Grounds.

Once there, I took Jack to meet with another group of Chiricahuas. Among them were Kathleen Kanseah and the Fort Sill Apache previously mentioned. *"This is my friend, Jack Noel, the gentleman from Monticello that I spoke about earlier today,"* I said, as I introduced Jack to the group of elders sitting at the V.I.P. section. The reception was kind and pleasant. Kathleen had brought an extra chair for the expected guest. They all wanted to hear what Jack had to say in reference to the proposed mining at Red Paint Canyon.

Once I left him in good hands, I returned to the eastern entrance and waited there with the group until James gave the OK to walk in. That night while singing, I felt an incredible sense of accomplishment, as I looked at Jack's silhouette reflecting from the glow of the fire. I felt great admiration not only for his efforts, but for his love of the Apache people. I knew the next step was up to the Creator and the only way to get there was through prayers. In between songs I prayed that things would fall in place and that our Sacred Red Paint Canyon would not be blasted and devastated. As the night progressed, I thought about life and how each and everyone I had met had a reason or purpose for coming into my circle of life. Who would have thought that one day I was going to be working together with Jack for such a cause?

Because our group was the first to perform that evening, our session ended at about 10:00pm. At that time, I went over and got Jack. Together we walked out of the Feast Grounds and onto the parking lot, where his car was parked. There, he thanked me for everything and expressed how special and significant the whole experience had been. *"I finally got to meet and share time with the people I love and hold in such high regards,"* Jack said.

After shaking hands, we both went our separate ways. I returned to the camp and spoke to different members of the group about Jack's presentation and request for help. Indeed, he had done a good job at explaining the issues and as a result had left the group in high alert and ready to respond.

A Special Day
Chapter Twenty Four

The next day was a beautiful Saturday morning and I was feeling great. I drove to the Mescalero Tribal gas station where my friend Carson Carrillo worked. Carson had asked me to stop by, before heading to the Feast Grounds. It was close to 11:00am when I arrived. The gas station was far from your typical modern facilities. It consisted of a single one-thousand-gallon fuel tank that sat above ground level with a manual metered pump.

With a grin on his face, he asked me to join him as we walked over to a shaded porch. I grabbed a plastic chair and sat in comfort next to my friend to talk. The first topic that came up was Red Paint Canyon and the damage cause by mining. Next, we talked about going to White Tail the next day. At lunch time, Carson's wife Carol stopped by to see how we were doing.

Carson and Carol Carrillo with their grandson Jalen (Jaybird) Burgess ****
Mescalero Apache Reservation, NM, ca. 2005

Every now and then, our conversation was interrupted by customers who stopped by to fuel up, which neither one of us seemed to mind. During those breaks, I followed Carson to the pump and watched him greet the people enthusiastically. Most of the customers were tribal members. Some of them I knew well, while others I met for the first time.

By noontime I had greeted quite a few. Among those I met for the first time, were descendants of Old Charles Martine and of his cousin Martin Kayihtah (1856-1934). Martine and Kayihtah were the two Apache scouts sent with Lt. Charles Gatewood to find Geronimo's camp in the Sierra Madre and convince him to surrender. The high risk mission was accomplished without incident. In 1886, Geronimo and Naiche surrendered for the last time. The eventful day, was full of surprises. Who would have thought that I was going to be meeting the direct descendants of two Chiricahua Apache scouts who lived that history.

Geronimo's Camp with Sentinel.
Sierra Madre, Mexico, circa 1886.
The site was Cañon De los Embudos, one mile from Crook's camp.
Courtesy of Lynda A. Sanchez from Eve Ball's photo collection

At around 1:30pm, a thin, tall gentleman with short black hair, wearing a cowboy hat, drove up in an old blue Ford Bronco. He was not there to get fuel, but to talk to Carson. *"Siggy, this is Windy Runningwater,"* Carson said. After shaking hands, he sat down to join in our conversation. Little did I know that the gentleman I had just met had the answer to my prayers. Windy was easy to talk to and by no means was he interruptive. On the contrary, he was full of Apache stories which I found fascinating. Windy had returned to Mescalero after spending years in Washington, D.C. and traveling abroad. His stories were recollections gathered from scattered Apache descendants that he had met during his travels. *"Man, there are Apaches everywhere. Some have no clue where they came from and I guess others don't really care to know. I have yet to find one that wants to come back,"* he said. *"Go ahead, Siggy, tell him your story,"* Carson said.

A SPECIAL DAY

Based on the topic and Carson's request, it appeared that Windy had come over to hear my story. Feeling cautiously comfortable, I began to tell Windy about my ancestor's journey and my long search for my relatives. After finishing my story, Windy said to me. *"Well, I am related to the Seconds, so we are related."* I could not believe what I was hearing. That was the second time I had heard an Apache say to me that we were related, the first was Katherine Kenoi. Although she had used the same words years earlier, for some reason they did not have the same effect. I sensed something was different when Windy said it. Mrs. Kenoi had passed away by then, and there in front of me was someone, perhaps the only one, I thought who could possibly be my relative. At that moment, I realized why I had traveled by myself. After all, who else could I had brought along that would spend their vacation time at a gas station in a hot July day. It was truly meant to be, I thought.

I told Windy about my negative and disappointing experience while I visited Fort Sill, Oklahoma in search of anyone related to me. I also informed him that there were no Seconds or any relatives there based on what I was told. *"I cannot believe they said that to you. The Mithlos' live there and they are related to Jose Second,"* he said. I simply left it at that, as I did not want to go into anything negative after what was turning out to be one of the most positive days of my life. *"It's OK, you are in the right place,"* Windy said with a smile. *"As a matter of fact, there is a lady who lives here in Mescalero and although she doesn't bear the name, she is a Second by blood. Her name is Lorraine. You should go and see her. She has been expecting you. Tell her that you spoke to me. She lives up in Second Canyon. Do you know where that is?"* Windy asked. *"No, I don't even know where the first canyon is,"* I replied. Windy laughed out loud and said, *"No, Second Canyon is named after your great-grandfather Jose."*

The whole thing was overwhelming to me. In all the years visiting Mescalero I had never deviated from my routine, which consisted of simply visiting my friends, Carlos, Carson and Kathleen, and a few other families. Ironically, they all lived less than a couple hundred yards from Highway 70. Needless to say, I was astonished to learn that there was a canyon somewhere in Mescalero in honor of Jose.

It was close to 4:00pm when Windy's visit came to an end. I stayed around until Carson finished his shift at 5:00pm. As Carson and I shook hands, he said, *"I will see you tomorrow morning. Can you be at my house at 6:00am? We are going to visit White Tail and I want to take you to meet Lorraine at Second Canyon."* *"Thank you very much, I will be there,"* I replied, as I headed to James' camp to prepare for the night.

That July marked three years since Carson had stopped singing with us. We were all pleasantly surprised when he showed up to join us that evening. He told everyone that it was I who had motivated him to return to the Feast Grounds. Due to personal reasons, Carson had stopped participating in any involvement associated with the Maiden's Feast. I had supported and respected his decision during his absence. Whether he was back for one evening or for good, it didn't matter. Regardless, we were delighted to have him back with us. An overwhelming sense of joy was felt by everyone. Needless to say, it felt good to have my old pal singing next to me again.

That evening, inside the sacred tepee, I found myself overwhelmed, as my mind was going a million miles per minute. In order to soothe my anxiety, I began praying to the Creator like never before. *"Hear me, Grandfather. You have guided me here. For years, I have found refuge in this camp. Now I ask for courage and strength. As you know, Grandfather, I didn't come here looking for riches. All I have ever asked of you is to guide me back to my family.*

A SPECIAL DAY

I just want my ancestors to rest in peace knowing that I had made it back to tie the broken loop." Somehow I don't remember the events of that evening. Before I knew it, our session was over.

That night I gave one of our singers, Lynn Hank, a ride home. Out of all the members in the group, it was Lynn who had taught me the most when it came to traditions and tribal history. Although his knowledge was impressive, his true gift was revealed that evening as we conversed in front of his home. It was there that Lynn told me that there were songs about my missing ancestors and that the group's prayers were answered the day I showed up. His revelation made me think of Catherine Kenoi when she told me the same thing upon my arrival in Mescalero. Based on hints during our conversation, I came to believe that Lynn knew what happened to my family in 1886 and what was about to take place after my meeting with Windy. Lynn was a true spiritual leader, his aura *(medicine)* and words of wisdom gave me the strength and courage I had prayed for. After a long talk, I drove down to my hotel in Alamogordo.

Once in my room, I took a warm shower and laid down. There, I began to think of the sequence of events that had taken place. One thing was for sure, it all happened because I had traveled alone. I kept thinking of Windy and his rather bizarre appearance. *"Would I ever see him again? Was it all planned? Who was Lorraine? What did she look like? Could she be the one I had searched for so long? How did it happen? Was it real?"* The anticipation was killing me. Between prayers and Lynn's words of encouragement, I was able to fall asleep.

White Tail

Chapter Twenty Five

The next morning by 5:00am, I was out of the hotel room and driving to Carson's house in Mescalero. Upon my arrival an hour later, I found him waiting on his front porch. Our first stop was twenty minutes later at the tribal casino, where we had breakfast. By 8:00am, we were on Highway 70 heading west. A short time later, Carson told me to make a left onto a gravel road. *"This is the way up to White Tail,"* he said. *"I can't believe I am here,"* I replied. I was about to see and experience real American history. My teacher, Carson, did not have a PhD, nor was he a Harvard professor; instead, he was a Chiricahua P.O.W. descendant and a White Tail Native.

The following information as to how White Tail evolved from a vacant canyon to one of the most significant pieces of land in Chiricahua history was provided by Carson Carrillo and the collected work of Eve Ball. Eve was one of the most prominent and respected writers in Chiricahua Apache history.

In 1911, a bill was introduced in Congress to expel the Chiricahua Apaches from Fort Sill, Oklahoma, the third and final place where they were kept as prisoners since their surrender in 1886. As a result, an active campaign was started to find a new place to relocate them. A committee was formed amongst the imprisoned tribesmen, who included Ace Daklugie and Eugene Chihuahua (Carson's grandfather) while Talbot Goody represented the Chiricahuas. James Kaywaykla and Roger Toclanny (Carson's great grandfather) represented the Chienne (Warm Springs). Accompanied by an army officer, the five member team was allowed to go to New Mexico to look for a permanent home. They visited Ojo Caliente and the Mescalero Apache Reservation. The Mescaleros graciously agreed to share their homelands with their kin. The offer was taken back to Fort Sill where it opened for discussion among the families headmen. After some confusion and disagreements, they voted. Two-thirds (183) of the prisoners decided that Mescalero was a good place to relocate. The other one-third (82), mostly young progressive men who had accumulated some property, were unwilling to start over again. Among those eighty-two were some that felt that by refusing to go to Mescalero they would be granted a home at Ojo Caliente.

On April 1, 1913, all Chiricahua prisoners of war were set free by an Act of Congress. Freedom came with a bitter taste as the 265 Chiricahuas found themselves homeless, a shameful and sad status that remains to this day. On April 2, 1913, the 183 Chiricahuas who accepted relocation to the Mescalero Apache Reservation boarded a special train with all their belongings and gave their final farewell to those who chose to remain in the Apache, Oklahoma area.

On April 4, the train arrived in Tularosa, New Mexico, the nearest depot to the Mescalero Apache Reservation. The newly-arrived refugees were greeted by their kin, the Mescalero Apaches. Within a day, they began to assemble a tent village near the Mescalero agency. A week after their arrival, Chief Naiche, son of Chief Cochise, Daklugie, son of Chief Juh and Eugene Chihuahua, son of Chief Chihuahua, requested their own village site. Three days later, the three leaders decided upon White Tail as their place of abode.

As Carson and I continued driving, I was captivated by the stories and the beautiful pines that covered the high mountaintops. After driving approximately ten miles, we began to reach heights in the eight thousand plus range. The thinner air was cool and filled with fresh pine aroma.

I couldn't help to think how those three men must have felt in the presence of so much beauty. At times, the views were spectacular, allowing us to see the peaks of many other mountains. One in particular was still partially covered with snow. Carson described it as one of the sacred mountains of the Mescaleros, known as *'Sierra Blanca.'*

Six miles later, we reached the outskirts of White Tail's once thriving community. There, in front of me, laid a pine tree-lined canyon, perhaps a square mile in size. Totally captivated by its beauty, I began to wonder again how the newly released prisoners must have felt upon arriving at such a heavenly place. Carson explained that the first few years were full of hardships, the limited resources and harsh winters would have broken anyone's spirits, but as a group they managed to endure.

A few years later, a community project was started. Neat four-room houses with galvanized-tin roofs were constructed. By 1937, most of the families had abandoned their tepees and brush arbors and were living in homes. What was probably perceived as a good accomplishment was actually the beginning of a new crisis. With the end of the construction boom came unemployment. Most of the arable land was occupied by homes. The situation got worse when Pearl Harbor was bombed, as many Apaches enlisted and went off to fight. Others went into industry and various types of war work. As a result, a big exodus occurred not only from White Tail's community, but also from the entire Mescalero Reservation. Shortly after, entire families began leaving White Tail to settle closer to the main town of Mescalero. Within a short period of time, White Tail became a ghost town.

One of the first properties we came across was a vacant lot on the right side of the road. It belonged to Geronimo's nephew, Japer Kanseah Sr. At the age of thirteen, Jasper was Geronimo's youngest warrior when they surrendered in 1886. He was the last survivor of Geronimo's band when he died at Mescalero in 1959.

Old man Jasper Kanseah Sr. is seen here standing next to Eve Ball's "wishing" well outside her home in Ruidoso, New Mexico. circa 1950's.
Donated by Lynda A. Sanchez from Eve Ball's photo collection

A few miles later, on the same side of the road, we came upon four cement-block structures that appeared to be in fairly good shape. One of them was used for storage, the other one was the community school and next to it were two houses. One of them belonged to the school teacher, Mr. Bob Ove, whom I had met in Albuquerque three days earlier. After spending two days with the former teacher, I learned a lot about White Tail and the people that lived there. In a peculiar way, Bob had prepared me for Carson's tour.

Across the main road, in front of the school, were the remnants of the home belonging to Old Lady Connie. The wooden structure laid crumbled on the ground, reduced to nothing more than pieces of lumber and scrap metal. Mrs. Connie, also known as Dah-des-ih (Tah-das-te), was born in 1860. She was the sister of Eugene Chihuahua's mother Ilth-goz-ey, and the wife of Chief Chihuahua. Tah-das-te was a member of Geronimo's band and the wife of Ahnandia, a warrior with Geronimo. Ahnandia and her, both surrender with Geronimo and Naiche in 1886. While prisoners in Mt Vernon Barracks, Ahnandia went back to his 1st wife Dahn. They both died there. Tah-das-te then married Connie, a scout and father of three children with his late wife Beteir. Tah-das-te was Scout Connie's last wife. She had no children with him but in addition to Connie's three children, they took in Connie's nephews, the orphaned Jolsanny's children Richard and Samuel, who went with them to Mescalero.[1]

According to Chiricahua oral history, Tah-das-te was known as a courageous and fearless horse rider with daring and skillful fighting abilities. Tah-das-te and Lozen, Chief Victorio's sister, were the warrior women in whom Geronimo had such faith that he sent them as messengers during surrendering terms with the U.S. Government.

Old Lady Connie's (Dah-des-ih) (Tah-das-te) home.
White Tail, Mescalero Apache Reservation, ca. 2005
****

As Carson and I walked on her property, a feeling of sadness came over me as I looked at the crumbled place where so much history lived. I could only imagined what her house looked like and wondered why nothing was done to prevent such casualty from occurring. Next to her fallen home was an old rusted metal body of a vehicle. It was all that remained of a pick truck belonging to Tah-das-te's step-daughter, Eliza Connie. Amazingly the headlight's chrome casing still shone like brand new.

Throughout the tour, I kept thinking of Bob Ove's stories concerning Mrs. Connie. Mr. Ove told me that when he arrived in White Tail in 1948, as a young teacher, Mrs. Connie was eighty eight years old. Although Mrs. Connie's and Bob's homes were across the road from each other, they might as well been miles apart. *"Even though she was well aware of my presence, she never in any way acknowledged my existence. The few times we came face to face, she looked right through me. Even though I was a member of the community and friendly with many Chiricahuas, I was an example to her of everything she and her people had suffered,"* Bob said. To her last day on earth, she refused to speak English.

He remembered Mrs. Connie as being very active and always riding her burro up and down White Tail's main dirt road. She also took care of many stray dogs. Her kindness towards those homeless animals was so well known that the tribal store's butcher saved all the excess bones for her dogs.

Old Lady Connie's (Dah-des-ih) (Tah-das-te) home.
White Tail, Mescalero Apache Reservation, ca. 1948
Photographed by Robert Ove

WHITE TAIL

Next to Mrs. Connie's property, was the home of Charles (Charlie) Istee. Amazingly, his house was still standing tall against nature's elements. Charlie was the only surviving son of the notorious Warm Springs Apache leader Victorio. He was about eight or ten years old when his father Victorio and most of his followers were killed at Tres Castillos, Mexico in 1880. Young Charlie was away in San Carlos, Arizona with Chief Loco when the tragedy occurred. He had also survived twenty seven years of imprisonment when he moved to White Tail in 1913 with his Chiricahua wife Dora Chaenedee. Shortly after their arrival their son Evans Istee was born.

Seventy Six year old, Charles Istee, son of Chief Victorio of the Warm Springs Apache
Sitting in front of Bob Ove's home in White Tail, New Mexico
Photographed by Robert Ove, ca. 1948

Like Charlie, his home was build strong and stood long after those around it had succumbed and crumbled. In 1993, Bob Ove visited White Tail and took a picture of Charles' home long after he had passed on. Sadly, it was starting to show early signs of deterioration. By 2005, during my visit, its condition was critical. Nonetheless, I was fortunate to see and experience such a place before it was completely gone. The following photographs show a moderate progression of deterioration in a period of twelve years.

Charles Istee's home in White Tail, Mescalero Apache Reservation. Photographed by Robert Ove, ca. 1993

Charles Istee's home in White Tail, Mescalero Apache Reservation. ****
Circa. 2005

As Carson and I walked in front of Charlie's property, I noticed that the ground was littered with artifacts, such as belt buckles, silverware, glass jars, etc. As we walked towards the rear of the house, we came upon a grassless sandy area. There, we found the remnants of what appeared to be Charlie's horse drawn wagon. Because it laid partially buried in the ground, it reminded me of a Navajo sand painting.

Charles Istee, son of Chief Victorio of the Warm Springs Apaches
Riding his horse drawn wagon on White Tail's school grounds
Photographed by Robert Ove, ca. 1948

Unlike Old Lady Connie, Mr. Istee was friendly to Bob, the teacher. Charlie spent many hours sitting on Bob's porch, reminiscing about the old days when the white settlers invaded Apache Country. Fifty seven years later, it was Bob who spent many hours telling me those stories. One in particular caught my attention, as I was able to personally relate to it. It had to do with an Apache ambush at a Box Canyon. As I heard Bob telling the tale, I couldn't help to think of my beloved place, the Monticello Box Canyon.

According to Charlie Istee, "*A few Apache decoys rode out on a ledge so that the U.S. Calvary soldiers could hardly miss seeing them. As soon as they had been spotted by the troops, they pretended to run away, staying just far enough ahead to be seen, but not close enough to be caught. According to plan, the decoys rode into a box canyon from which there was no exit.*

173

The other members of the band were waiting on the cliffs above with ropes, which they lowered to the decoys. The decoys grabbed the ropes and were pulled up to safety. When the soldiers came inside the box canyon searching for the vanished Apaches, the men above rained down rocks to block the entrance to the canyon, then picked off the helpless soldiers trapped below, often by shooting the horses from beneath them.[8]" According to Bob, Charlie would slapped his thigh, rocking back and forth with laughter as he recalled such exploits.[8]

Another structure that stood firm on his property was a storage barn. This was indeed a rare sight, as most of them had either collapsed or were relocated. As Carson explained, a lot of the families took their homes and barns with them when they moved from White Tail to Mescalero.

Typical storage barn built by the Chiricahua Apaches while living in White Tail
Photographed by Robert Ove, ca. 1993

Learning Chiricahua history from Carson and remembering Bob's stories made visiting those home-sites extra special. Once back in the car, we drove to other property-sites, while I listen to Carson describe who they belonged to, along with that particular family's history. One particular property that sparked my interest was that of Robert Geronimo Jr. His parcel of land was located on the right side of the road and about three quarters of a mile from the school. It was tucked away in a hill about an eighth of a mile from the main road. Although I saw no signs of his home, I couldn't help to wonder what it must have looked like.

Fortunately, Bob Ove gave me some insight as to what it was like meeting Geronimo Jr. and his third wife Maude Daklugie. Maude was the daughter of Asa Daklugie and granddaughter of Chief Juh, of the Nedhi Apaches and Chief Chihuahua, of the Chiricahuas.

A few weeks after Bob's arrival at the Mescalero Apache Reservation, he drove the school bus to the tribal store to shop for groceries and a few other supplies.

He was about ready to leave for White Tail when he was notified by the store clerk that Robert and Maude needed a ride to their White Tail home. *"How will I know them?"* Bob asked. *"They are the only ones out there. He's the son of the big Chief Geronimo. You better watch out,"* he was told.

A short distance later, Bob spotted the two; they were sitting beside the main reservation road, content to stay there for as long as it took to catch a ride home.[8] Bob admitted that he was a little uneasy when he spotted them. He described Robert as stocky and looking younger than he actually was and with a physical likeness to his father Geronimo. Maude was wearing a bandana that covered her head. According to Bob, they both looked very dignified. *"I pulled over and was about to get out and help them get in, but they had already opened the door on the passenger side and were climbing into the school bus as though they had been expecting me. I turned, introduced myself as the new teacher at White Tail, and got nods and silence in return,*[8]*"* Bob said. In time, that cold reception evolved into a warm friendship. The two met often in the front porch of Bob's house. It was there that Geronimo told Bob of his childhood stories while growing up in White Tail.

Robert Geronimo Jr.
Son of Geronimo, seen here in front of Bob Ove's home
White Tail, Mescalero Apache Reservation.
Photographed by Robert Ove, ca. 1948

"As a youth growing up on the Mescalero Apache Reservation, Geronimo would rise on cold winter mornings, dress in little more than a loincloth, grab a bucket, and run through the snow to the creek. He would break the thin ice with his bare feet by jumping right into it, fill the bucket, and run back to the family's wickiups. He said that he never got sick until he started to wear heavy sheepskin winter coats like the white men wear.[8]"

After many visits, Robert invited Bob to visit his home. Bob has never forgotten that memorable day when he first visited Robert and Maude Geronimo. *"As I got near their home, I noticed that their front porch was festooned with fragrant strips of beef jerky and red chile peppers hanging from strings. The colorful display reminded me of Christmas decorations. Once inside the house, a huge sepia-toned photograph dominated the back wall of the living room. It was an enlargement of the familiar picture of Geronimo crouching, wearing his scalp belt, and his riffle leaning on his shoulder.[8]"* Bob said. *"That's my daddy. I remember when that picture was taken,"* Robert added. *"A photographer came to the stockade one day and paid the soldiers some money. Then he paid my father to pose for him. Daddy was laughing because the scalp locks were 'coons' tails, but the photographer told him to look serious. So he scowled just as the flash powder went off. Then he started to laugh again.[8]"*

When not working in the fields around his house at White Tail, Robert made whittle bows and arrows to be sold to tourists at the tribal store. According to Bob, his work was fine craftsmanship.[8] It was during another visit that Bob learned more intimate details of Robert's life.

Recollecting what Bob was told by Robert Geronimo Jr. himself: *"Robert was born on August 2, 1889, in Alabama, and that the record of his birth was kept in the Indian Agency office at Mescalero, which burned in 1902 and again in 1908. He also said that in addition to Lenna and himself, Ih-tedda, his Mescalero mother had two other children by Geronimo, a boy and a girl, but they died in infancy before Robert was born.*

Ih-tedda was a prisoner in Alabama, but because she was Mescalero, she was allowed to return to her people, something her husband Geronimo was in favor of. She arrived in Mescalero with her son Robert. In 1905, Robert was sent to Chilocco Indian School located in north-central Oklahoma. His father Geronimo visited him there that year. It was their first acquaintance with each other. Robert remained at Chilocco a little more than two years and spent his summers at Fort Sill with Geronimo. They developed a close relationship, and Geronimo accepted Robert without question as his son. At the end of the 1907 school year Robert joined Geronimo in Oklahoma. Although he lived among the Apache prisoners of war, he was never considered to be a captive himself, and the government never restricted his activities. In 1910, a year after the death of Geronimo, Robert requested to be sent to Carlisle School for more education. In 1913, when the Chiricahuas were freed by an act of Congress, Robert was counted among those who chose to remain in Oklahoma. In 1914, he made White Tail his permanent home.[8]"

After looking at Geronimo's property, Carson and I continued with our tour. The next property, on the left hand-side of the road, belonged to Adrianne Hank. Her story will be covered in later chapters.

About an eighth of a mile later, I was told to pull over on the right hand-side of the road. Carson got out the car and proceeded to open a barbed wire gate. A few minutes later, I found myself walking behind him up a sloped hill. About a hundred yards later, we reached a cement foundation where Carson's home once stood. Amongst the pine trees growing there, Carson noticed an old bottomless metal tub.

Carson Carrillo Sr., standing on what is left of his childhood's home foundation. ****
To the left (center), a bottomless tub where he used to bathe.
White Tail, Mescalero Apache Reservation, ca. 2005

Overwhelmed with emotions, he walked up to it, and picked it up. After a moment of silence he said, *"Wow, this was the tub where I used to bathe as a kid."* About a hundred feet from the metal tub, was a stack of debris that still contained some of the home's furniture. Among the various items found in the pile, were Carson's rusted spring mattress and frame. With choking words, Carson began to tell me what each item was and what they meant. Unable to hold back my own emotions, I joined Carson in what became a very emotional experience.

In a fruitful attempt to change our mood, I asked Carson about a big old faded red home that stood about a hundred yards from us. With a grin on his face, he said, *"That was the home of Jasper Jr. and Berle Kanseah, let's go over and look at it."* Upon our arrival, I noticed that only the front of the house was standing. The rear part had caved inward except for one of the bedrooms. The only thing in it was a bare spring frame mattress laying on the dirt floor.

Filled with emotions, I stood there in complete silence trying really hard not to let Carson see the tears running down my face. Berle had passed away a year earlier and I really missed him. Carson spoke of the days when they played baseball in front of their homes. Berle was Bob Ove's brightest student and Vernon Simmons' friend and school mate. It was through Vernon, a singer among our group, that I also learned a lot about Berle. Vernon told me of one particular day, when the school bus was in for repairs and a pickup truck was used to take them home. Before leaving, Bob, the teacher, lectured the students to sit in the bed of the truck and away from the rails. Once the truck was clear from the teacher's view, Berle and Vernon sat on the rails despite the teacher's warnings. During a sharp turn, Berle fell off the truck, breaking his arm.

His only concern as they drove him to the clinic was facing his teacher the next day. No one knows for sure, whether Berle got in trouble at home with his Dad, Jasper Kanseah Jr. or not.

According to Bob, Jasper Jr. was a serene and good-natured man. He was born a prisoner of war at Fort Sill in 1908. He was Geronimo's nephew and the proud son of Jasper Kanseah Sr. While standing on the Kanseah's property, Carson pointed to the next property over.

Jasper Kanseah Jr, ca. 1948
Photographed by Robert Ove, 1948 White tail, New Mexico

It was the home-site of David Kazhe (1869-?). David and Jasper Kanseah Sr. were members of Geronimo's band. They were both inaugurated as warriors just before they surrendered. David had a half brother, Morgan Kazhe by the same father, and full brother of Os-kissay (Goth-Kyzhn), who was the wife of old Tissnolthtos. David and Os-kissay's mother was Ih-zey. David married Annie Juan (Annie Pedro), who was a daughter of Pedro Juan, Arizona Apache scout who died in Alabama.[1]

It was in front of those three homes that Carson used to play ball with Berle and other kids. He explained how happy every one used to be there, and how appreciative he was to the Mescalero Tribe for the opportunity given to his family as well as others from the Chiricahua, Warm Springs and Nedhi Bands.

While standing on Kanseah's property, Carson began reminiscing on that painful day when he was forced to leave such a happy place. Although he was only ten at the time of the exodus, he remembers it well. The painful memory still brought tears to his eyes.

One of the last properties we visited was that of Eugene Chihuahua, the son of Chief Chihuahua and Carson's grandfather. His parcel of land was the farthest from the school. It was tucked away in a pine forest where the breeze felt cool and refreshing. It was there that Vernon Simmons lived with his adopted father Eugene Chihuahua and his Comanche grandmother, Hermannie.

Eugene Chihuahua, son of Chief Chihuahua, his Comanche wife Hermannie, and her three-year-old grandson, Vernon Simmons, Mescalero Apache Reservation, 1943. From Robert Ove's collection.

A short time later, we got back in the car and continued visiting other sites. One of them was the Community Well named after Eugene Chihuahua. The well's water was pumped into a huge metal container.

"Chihuahua's Well"
A huge water tank that provided White Tail residents with their water needs.
White Tail, Mescalero Apache Reservation, ca. 2005
****

It was approximately ten to fifteen feet in height and about seventy feet in diameter. It provided most of the community's water needs.

As we continued driving around White Tail, its magic seemed to increase with every turn we took. The once opened canyon where everyone lived was slowly being claimed by Mother Nature, as a thick and lush pine forest was starting to emerge. I felt privileged knowing that I was probably looking at the remnants of an era. The fresh pine smell coming through the car's opened window reminded me of the Christmas tree tent sell back in Florida. It seemed as if most of the morning had gone by in a blink of an eye. I was saddened that the Chiricahuas were forced to endure twenty-seven years of captivity, but I was happy for those who chose to relocate to Mescalero.

I must mention that the one third who chose to stay in Oklahoma were removed from Fort Sill, where they lost everything they had worked so hard for. Some were given small parcels of land throughout various towns/counties in or near Apache, Oklahoma. Those who remained in Oklahoma in hopes to live at Ojo Caliente were never relocated.

At around 11:00am, Carson decided it was time to leave. It was at that moment that I understood what he meant when he said how hard it was for him and his family to leave White Tail during the mass exodus. Amazingly, in just a few hours, I had fallen in love with White Tail myself. Driving away was also hard for me to do.

In July of 2010, the Creator blessed me with a special gift and responsibility, as I became the keeper of Bob Ove's White Tail photo collection along with the stories just mentioned. The following list of family names and home-site maps was composed by the late Berle Kanseah and provided by Vernon Simmons and Bob Ove. It will give a clearer understanding of the order in which Carson's tour was conducted on that memorable day.

WHITE TAIL

1) Jasper Kanseah Sr.
2) W.K. Maurice and Melvin Kanseah
3) Geo. M = 0
4) Neva Lester, Guitz = 0
5) Clara Mea and Art Johnson = 0
6) Paul Guydelkon = 0 (a son away at school)
7) Mrs. Connie = Natheniel and Delphine Connie, Kazhe.
8) Wheeler Tiss. = 0
9) David Kazhe Sr. = 0
10) Minnie Wilson = 0 Arthur Johson
11) Charley and Dora Istee = 0
12) Henry and Henrietta Kane = 0
13) Hugh Connie = 0
14) Hugh Chee = 0
15) Glydes Chee = Myron Buster,Frederic Fritz, Jonathan
16) Julian and Rachel Venego = Harold, Virgil, Blanche Chee
17) Emelia Naiche = 0
18) Christian Naiche = 0
19) Levi and Leeh Hosetosavit = 0 (Eugene step son)
20) John Allard = 0
21) Clarence and Isabel Enjady = 0
22) Richard Jolsanny = Ulyses and Verna, Leta Mae.
23) Berney and Rosalind Naiche = Adriann Marden
24) Maude Geronimo = 0 (Robert)
25) Asa Daklugie and Ramona = 0 (grandson Ralph O. Shanta. Jr.)
26) Wallace Enjady = 0
27) Wyne Enjady = Wynelle,Zeno, Collins (Delores)
28) Charlie Smith = Zeb Smith
29) Agnes Chihuahua and Pesiwonit = Carol Anita, Viola
30) Mrs. Goody = 0
31) David Kazhe Jr. = 0 (Belle)
32) Myrtis, Berle, Velmahee-Jasper Kanseah Jr.
33) Isaac and Dorcie Kazhe = 0
34) Evans Istee

Note from author: I do not know what the "= 0" stands for but it is transcribed here just as Berle had created it.

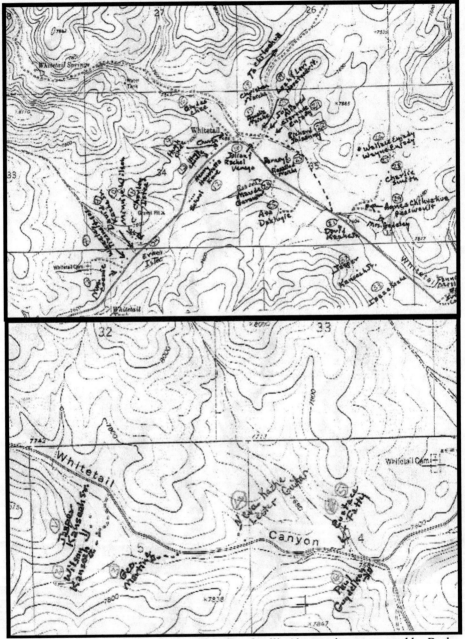

White Tail Maps showing various Chiricahua families' home-sites composed by Berle
Kanseah and provided by Vernon Simmons.

Arrival at Second Canyon

Chapter Twenty Six

In less than half an hour we had reached Highway 70. Once on the main highway, I thanked Carson for the sharing of knowledge and for the time he had spent with me. I asked him to join me for lunch. I was confused by his answer, when he said, *"Are you ready?"* *"You bet, I am hungry as a bear!"* I replied. It had been hours since we last ate. *"No, I meant, are you ready to meet Lorraine?"* He asked. *"Yes, of course!"* I replied.

We drove northeast on highway 70 and we made a left at the entrance to the 'Inn of the Mountain Gods', the reservation's state-of-the-art Hotel and Resort on a golf course that overlooked a beautiful lake and the sacred Sierra Blanca Mountain. As the road forked, we made a left and instead of heading towards the hotel, we entered a community where tribal members lived. A sign read *'Residents Only Beyond This Point.'* Once passed the sign, Carson pointed to a canyon on the right. *"That is Second Canyon, also known as Medicine Canyon,"* he said.

Shortly after, we made a right and entered a dirt road. About an eighth of a mile later, we arrived at a modest-looking home. Carson and I got out of the car and proceeded to walk towards a roof-covered porch. I felt my legs getting weak as I walked behind him in complete silence. After opening a small wooden porch door, Carson proceeded to knock on the front door. A few minutes later, the door was opened by a beautiful young girl. *"Hello, is your grandma home?"* Carson asked. I couldn't help but to stare at what I perceived to be my own blood. *"Yes,"* she replied with apprehension, as she ran away, while calling out for her grandmother. Within minutes, the little girl and a woman with silver streaks running down her long black hair appeared at the door. Carson spoke to the woman in Apache. A short time later she said to me *"I am Lorraine and this is my five-year-old grand-daughter Hailey."* The beautiful little girl who was showing signs of shyness would glance at me while clinging to her grandmother's dress. Lorraine asked us to come in. She addressed me again and said, *"I have heard a lot about you. Windy said that you were coming by today."* I was completely surprised when she said that one of her late brothers had already spoken to her about me. As a result, she had been expecting my arrival for many years.

Once inside the house, Lorraine and I began exchanging stories about our families. I told her about the hardships that my loved ones endured and my determination to find my relatives. Once I was done, Lorraine began telling me about her family and how our grandfather, Jose Second had remarried after his arrival in Mescalero in 1895. *In the Apache culture, as it is in most Indian cultures, there is no difference between a grand or great-great grand.* Lorraine who came from Jose's new family in Mescalero told me that she was the only one left from her generation. *"I am so happy that you are here. Everyone is gone, including my siblings. It is nice to have an addition to the family for a change,"* she said while glancing at the floor. After pausing for a few seconds, she looked at me with teary eyes and said *"What took you so long to get here?"* I wanted to say so much, but instead I found myself overwhelmed with emotions. I looked at Carson in hopes to regain my strength, but my protector appeared to be equally affected by the circumstances. Soon, the three of us found ourselves hugging and crying together. Little Hailey, perhaps scared after seeing three grown adults crying, began to cry herself and ran towards the back of the house. She returned with her grandfather, who came to see what was going on.

ARRIVAL AT SECOND CANYON

After a quick glance, he turned around and left; probably knowing that it was not the proper moment to stay or say anything. I did not feel embarrassed about breaking down and showing my emotions, just a few hours earlier Carson had experienced the same feelings without shame. After we all calmed down, Lorraine's husband and Haily came back and joined us. *"This is my husband, Hugh Evans. He is a Navajo from Ganado, Arizona,"* Lorraine said. Afterwards, the five of us sat in the living room and had coffee, sodas, and doughnuts. Upon the conclusion of my visit, Lorraine said *"I want you to go to the Feast Grounds later, so I can introduce you to the rest of your relatives."* She concluded by giving Carson directions on how to get to her camp.

On our way to Carson's home, we drove to the Feast Grounds, where I was shown Lorraine's campsite. To my surprise, it was located inside the fenced-in area. At that moment, I realized why I had never seen it before. The typical Apache arbor with a white tepee behind it sat in a section away from the general public's view. I asked Carson, why her camp was so far away from the others. *"This is the V.I.P section, your aunt Lorraine is a Medicine Woman. Her main responsibility is guiding the young maidens' through the four-day feast,"* he said. (*In the Apache culture, as it is in most Indian cultures, an aunt or an uncle is not necessarily the brother or sister of an individual's parents. It is simply a title given to the oldest person in that family. That individual, at times, may play the role of a parent/mentor providing guidance and support to younger members of their family. Lorraine, who is by blood my cousin in the white culture, is my aunt in the Apache way.*)

After learning more about her role, Carson and I stopped at a restaurant to eat and digest all that had taken place. After dropping him off, I returned to the Feast Grounds and headed to Lorraine's camp. Upon my arrival, I found Lorraine, Hugh and Hailey inside the arbor, sitting by a table. A few minutes after joining them, Lorraine's nephew showed up. *"This is your cousin, Warren Mendez,"* she said.

L to R: Siggy Second-Jumper, Lorraine Evans, Hailey Ahidley, Warren Mendez
Second Canyon, Mescalero Apache Reservation, ca. 2005
Photographed by Hugh Evans

ARRIVAL AT SECOND CANYON

Warren and I bonded immediately, as if we had known each other since long ago. As the afternoon progressed, I told everyone that I needed to head on over to James' camp to prepare for the evening's Fire Dance. I arrived at the camp only to find it empty. I took advantage of that solitude and entered the Crown Dancer's tepee to pray and analyze all that had taken place in the last twenty-four hours. After taking a pinch of tobacco and addressing all cardinal directions, I fell into a deep thought. Suddenly, a sad feeling came over me, as I began to wonder if the finding of my relatives meant that I had to walk away from James's group. My newly-found family had come across as being Mescaleros. That made me wonder if I had the right to continue singing among the Chiricahuas and sharing their most sacred moments.

Not knowing what to do or expect, I prepared to break the news to James and the rest of the group. *"What will the outcome be?"* I asked myself over and over. I remembered the old saying, *"Be careful what you wish for, because you may get it."* Suddenly, I began to pray like never before. *"Life Giver, hear me please; I humble myself in your presence, as you know I have asked for your guidance on this journey. Only you know how much I have bargained with you on this issue. I have told you that I was not seeking enrollment nor dividends or anything like that. All I asked was to find my relatives and nothing more. Thank you for answering my prayers and please don't get me wrong but what started as a happy day has suddenly turned into sad one. I didn't know that my family was Mescalero. I always thought I was a Chiricahua descendant. I was wondering if you can grant me one more wish. I asked that somehow you can keep me with James' group. They have given me so much and it is among them that I can talk to you with ease. Please have pity on me. Give me the strength to approach James and to accept the outcome."* The silent conversation with the Creator went on for a while. Once done, I stepped out of the tepee and sat in the arbor awaiting James arrival.

He showed up at about 6:00pm. Ironically James picked up on my mood immediately. *"What is going on? Is everything OK?"* he asked. *"I don't know how to tell you, but today I found my family right here in Mescalero,"* I said. After telling him who my relatives were, I expressed my concerns and the fear of having to walk away from his group. *"Why do you have to walk away?"* he asked. *"Because I believe my family is Mescalero,"* I replied. *"Let us have a seat,"* James said. *"I want you to relax. Even if you were a Mescalero, you could still stay with us, but you're not. You are a Chiricahua and you have always been in the right place. We all knew who you were, but could not show you the way. It had to come to you as a gift from the Creator, as it did. Lorraine feels Mescalero because of her mother's side, but she is a Chiricahua from her father's side,"* James said.

He proceeded to tell me more about my grandfather, Jose Second. *"While serving time as a prisoner of war in Mount Vernon, Alabama, Jose became friendly with the soldiers at the barracks. He promised the soldiers beautiful wild horses that roamed free in the mountains of Mescalero. Old Man Second had horse medicine, which meant he had a way with horses. The officers trusted him and allowed him to travel to Mescalero to round up the ancestors of the wild horses that still roam this reservation. Jose kept his promise, he captured a handful of horses and sent them back, but he never returned. He settled in Mescalero where he married a Mescalero Apache woman and began a new life for himself. Lorraine comes from that lineage. Jose became a powerful medicine man among the Mescaleros. His grandson, Bernard Second, Lorraine's late brother was also a powerful medicine man. It has been said that rest of the prisoners resented Jose for his escape and success. That resentment may still go on today.*

It is perhaps why you were treated as you were in Fort Sill. Jose was a full-blooded Chiricahua and that makes you a Chiricahua, just like you always have been. You are in the right place and can sing with us as long as you wish." James concluded his speech with a hand shake. I wanted to say so much in response, but a lump in my throat barely allowed me to say thanks.

By then, Lynn Hank and the rest of the group had arrived and gave me the same support. With a smile on my face, I grabbed my drum and walked into the tepee where preparations went as usual. While inside the tepee, I prayed to the Creator and humbly thanked Him for all His gifts. Indeed, he had granted me both wishes, not only did I find my family but I got to stay with my group. I couldn't help but wonder what I had done in this life to deserve so many blessings. That night I felt invincible, unconquered and most of all, Apache. I thought about my ancestors and how they must have felt seeing me there.

After the preparations were done, we all walked out of the tepee and headed towards the Feast Grounds. We arrived at the eastern entrance and waited for the fire to be lit. We then proceeded to sit on the benches as usual. That evening, things felt different; I had never felt so proud. The brief silence was interrupted by James' first song, and the arrival of the Crown Dancers. Soon after, groups of women joined in. I was so concentrated on my singing that I didn't pay attention to any of the female dancing groups that went by. Half way through our fourth song, a group of ladies remained dancing in place in front of us. It was at that moment that a strange thing happened, when I noticed a small hand make contact with mine. Surprised by the unusual action, I looked up, only to find little Hailey dancing in front of me. Besides her radiant smile, she wore a pink dress, fully beaded moccasins and a predominately pink and purple dancing shawl. Although she was only five years old, she was able to stay in perfect rhythm with the rest of the group. The strange coincidence and her warm action brought tears to my eyes. *"How ironic,"* I thought. How could a five-year-old girl make a grown man cry? A few minutes later, her group began to move. Every time it came back around, she smiled as if letting me know that everything was going to be alright. That evening, I sang as if I had tears in my throat. Somehow I felt as if I could reach and touch the million of stars that gave light to a clear New Mexican sky. Caught between thoughts, prayers and tears, our session came to an end.

Afterwards, I went to Lorraine's camp and told her I was heading home the next day. She offered me to stay with them for the night, but all my belongings were back at the hotel in Alamogordo. Once back at the hotel, my patience couldn't wait. I called home and let my family in on my day's events. That night, unlike the previous, I slept peacefully and relaxed. At last my family search had come to an end.

The next morning, I woke up eagerly and ready to reunite with my newly found relatives. The hour long ride to Mescalero seemed longer than ever. Not only did I want to get there fast but I wanted to make that final day last forever. I remembered asking myself why that magical experience had to be so short. Why couldn't I have met them a week earlier, when I first arrived? I caught myself and retreated to my old rule, be humble, and be thankful.

I arrived at Lorraine's home close to 9:00am. While sitting in the living room, I noticed a blanket hanging on the wall. Ironically, it had the same cross and crescent design that I had seen in an old family picture sent from Cuba. When I asked Lorraine about it, she said *"that blanket belonged to my late brother, Bernard Second, and the cross and crescent on it was a family design."*

I was about to tell her that I had seen the same design in my family's picture, when Warren Mendez showed up. A few minutes later Lorraine brought out multiple family albums and had them laid out on the living room table. Warren and I looked through many pictures. Among them were Lorraine's late brothers and sister. Lorraine expressed how most of her family had passed away, along with the family name Second. *"I was born Lorraine Second, but became Evans after my marriage decades ago,"* she explained.

Just when I thought I was done looking through albums, Lorraine pulled out a copy of an old photograph taken at a studio in Arizona in 1884. It consisted of two Indians next to each other. One was sitting with a rifle on hand and the other one stood empty handed. *"The one standing up is Jose First (1859-1913) and the one sitting down is Jose Second, our Grandpa,"* Lorraine proudly said. I held the photograph in my shaking hand and took a look at something that no one on my side of the family had ever seen.

L to R: Jose Second, Jose First
San Carlos Apache Reservation, ca. 1884

187

In the back of the photograph an article read: *"Jose Second, Itsah-Dee-Tsa, Saditsa, Indian name meaning "talking two ways". Itsa-Dee-Tsa was enumerated as Jose among Chief Naiche's band in the 1884, San Carlos Census, age 35, 5'5", married and talks Spanish. Jose Segundo (Jose Second) was his Mexican name and was used to distinguish him from another Apache, Jose Primero (Jose First) not related to each other, both were full-blooded Chiricahuas. Both had been captured by Mexicans as young boys and both had escaped as grown men and found their way back to their people.*

In 1876, the Chiricahuas had been removed from their own reservation and permanently resettled in at San Carlos Agency. Itsah-Dee-Tsa participated in the break out of 1885 along with Chief Chihuahua's band. He surrendered at Cañon De Los Embudos, Mexico in March of 1886 and was sent to Fort Marion, Florida, with Chief Chihuahua's group, totaling 77. Both Joses' served in company 1, 12th infantry regiment at Mount Vernon Barracks in Alabama.

In 1894, Jose Second (Itsah-Dee-Tsa) along with Chiricahua Jim (Ish-Kay-Znn) went to Mescalero in search of wild horses, both of them stayed and never returned. Jose First stayed in Alabama and was relocated to Fort Sill with the rest of the P.O.W. "Jose First's first wife was Maria Jose. He married her at Fort Apache"... "She died at Ft Sill, 1900. No children. Jose First was re-married again at Ft Sill to Zeh-golth-che-de (Reddish Lips), who died at Fort Sill 1912."... "José First went to Mescalero with the group in 1913 but died in May or June, within a month or two after arriving.[1]"

While holding the old photograph in my hand, I learned in detail all that had taken place after my grandpa's arrival in Mescalero. Soon after his arrival, he married Carabuda, a Mescalero. They had three children, Manuel, Frank and Philip. His son, Manuel, was born in 1898; he married May Peso, the daughter of a Mescalero Apache Chief. Manuel and May had no children. Frank was born in 1899; he married a Mescalero by the name of Aletha Choneska, Lorraine's parents. His youngest son was Philip, born in 1905. Jose Second was listed as a widower in the 1915 census. He is regarded as one of the best medicine men ever.

I was delighted to learn all that family history, and saddened by the fact, that Lorraine was the only living descendant from her generation. I asked Lorraine if I could borrow the photograph to make a copy. She said, *"Of course."* At 2:00pm I left Lorraine's house and headed to Albuquerque for a flight back home to Florida. At last, my dream had materialized, as Jose's children were finally reunited.

A few weeks after arriving in Florida, I was notified by Jack Noel that an official meeting over the mining permit at Red Paint Canyon was going to be held at the fire station in the town of Monticello, New Mexico. Desperately seeking additional support, I contacted a member of the Chiricahua Apache Alliance, a group composed mostly of unrecognized Chiricahua Apache descendants out of Silver City, New Mexico. In an e-mail, I explained what was happening in Monticello. I notified Jack Noel and told him to drive to Silver City, New Mexico and explain to the group what was taking place.

On August 4, 2005, the infamous public hearing took place. Over one hundred people showed up to express their opinions.[6]

Present at the meeting were:

Apaches from Fort Sill, Mescalero and members of the Chiricahua Apache Alliance.
Bill Brancard, New Mexico Division of Minerals and Mining (responsible for issuing the permits)
Karen Garcia, New Mexico Mine Regulatory Bureau
Holland Sheppard, Program Manager, Great Western Mining and representative hired to obtain the permit
Representatives from New Mexico Department of Game and Fish
Jeff Houser, Fort Sill Chiricahua Warm Springs Apache Tribe of Oklahoma
Holly Hougton, Mescalero Tribe Historical and Preservation Officer
Naomi Saenz, Secretary for the Mescalero Tribal Council
Alta Mae Branham, Mescalero Tribal Member
Oliver Enjady, Mescalero Tribal Council
John Wheeler, Mescalero Tribe attorney
Steve Darland, Representing Monticello Canyon Residents
Bob Haozous, Warm Springs/Fort Sill Apache
Jack Noel, Monticello Canyon Resident

During the public hearing, those who wanted to express themselves had the opportunity to do so. Not one person spoke in favor; the following people were just a few of the ones that stood up and spoke against the permit:

Steve Darland clearly explained the possible hazards to canyon residents, including heavy metal toxicity, lung cancer, and various other lung diseases. Among other issues of concern were the economic impact caused by contaminated water. Mr. Darland reminded the board that canyon residents depended on the Alamosa water to irrigate their crops and obtain drinking water.[6]

Holly Hougton expressed the sacredness of the Canyon and how Apaches have continued to go there to gather different things. She hoped that the fight to prevent the mining in the canyon would not have a negative impact and affect the existing relationship between Apaches and the land owners.[6]

Naomi Saenz expressed great concern and mentioned that the Apaches were still an integral part of the canyon. She hoped that everyone could work together to save the canyon.[6]

Jeff Houser spoke of the sacredness of the place and about his great-grandfather, was born there.[6]

Jack Noel offered a plan which he called "The Monticello Proposal." In his plan, the landowner would be paid market value for his land, and all companies and agencies involved would be compensated for time and labor. Mr. Noel ultimately wanted all involved agencies to work on a bill that would leave the land alone and protected forever. He also wanted to see the various Apache groups involved as caretakers of the land.[6] Based on the applause he received; the majority of the people present supported him. Jack later explained to me that the proposed bill would have benefited all parties involved.

Bob Haozous, a Warm Springs Apache from Fort Sill, stated that he had been given twenty acres within the canyon by a gentleman who felt guilty for owning Apache stolen land. Mr. Haozous expressed how he had returned his land back to nature and would like to see the canyon returned as well.[6]

Oliver Enjady, a Chiricahua from Mescalero, stated that the only reason Apaches were not living there was because the government removed them and forced them to live elsewhere. He spoke of the strong spiritual connection that existed there, and how the prayers, blood, and spirit of his forefathers were still present as part of the dirt and rocks that made up the canyons and the mountains.[6]

The Apache message was loud and clear, *"This is Sacred Land! Leave it alone, and deny any permit that disturbs it in any way shape or form."* Their statements were the deal breakers. It was obvious that Minerals and Mining along with Great Western Mining had heard enough. The meeting ended three hours later. Ironically, it came down to the people that had been herded out of the canyon to come back and protect it.

L to R: Siggy Second-Jumper, Jose Second, Jose First
Painting by Jack Wood and titled "The Protectors"

CHIRICAHUAS TO THE RESCUE

That evening, canyon residents celebrated as the threat of mining appeared to be over. A sigh of relief was felt by everyone, knowing that their drinking water and the air they breathe would remain free of any contaminants. As the smell of victory lingered in the air, suggestions were made to have a plaque erected to honor those Apaches that lived and died in the canyon, along with those that came forward to save it. The proposed plaque was to be erected near where the sacred water from the springs enters the Monticello Box Canyon. I was honored when asked to write it. I, along with other Chiricahua descendants from Mescalero, came up with the following inscription:

"This sanctuary, as you see it today, remains as it was when the Chiricahua Apaches called it Home. They lived here in peace and harmony. That balance was disrupted by a new mass of white settlers moving into the southwest, causing the Chiricahuas to subdivide into four groups. The group that remained here called themselves Chienne (Red Paint People). Their name derived from the traditional band of red clay drawn across the warrior's face and in honor of the Red Paint Canyon. To outsiders they were known as the Warm Springs - Ojo Caliente Apaches. Some of their latest leaders were Mano Mocha, Cuchillo Negro, Mangas Coloradas, Victorio, Nana, and Loco.

In the mid 1800's this sanctuary and the Chiennes were threatened again, this time by the U.S. Government. Pressure from the new settlers prompted a declaration of war on all Apaches. The conflict lasted many decades. A reservation was established here in 1874 by order of President Ulyses. S. Grant. The notorious Geronimo was arrested and jailed here in 1877.

Eventually the Chiennes were removed and sent to another reservation. As a result, some joined the warpath led by Geronimo, Naiche, Chihuahua, and Mangas. In 1886, under false promises, the mighty Chiricahuas surrendered to the U.S. Government at Cañon De Los Embudos, Mexico. The new prisoners of war were joined by the rest of the Chiricahuas including those that remained peaceful and others who served the U.S. Government as Scouts. In April of that year, they were herded into eastbound trains and sent to Florida, later to Alabama and ultimately to Oklahoma.

In 1913, the prisoners were set free by an Act of Congress. Almost twenty-eight years of captivity had taken their toll; only 265 had survived to enjoy their freedom. The survivors were given a choice, remain in Oklahoma or join their kin, the Mescaleros, in New Mexico. Eighty-two of them chose to stay in Oklahoma, and became known as the Fort Sill Apaches. Today the Chiricahua-Warm Springs descendants visit this place to pray for their ancestors and pay homage to their old sacred land.

In 2005 this sanctuary was threatened again by destruction and devastation caused by mining. Ironically, the descendants of the Chiricahuas that were once expelled from the canyon were appealed to help save it. For the first time, Apaches, canyon residents and supporters united for the same cause. We are thankful for the miracle of unity perhaps never seen before between the two races.

The success of their efforts allowed the beauty of the canyon to remain as it has from the beginning of its creation. May your steps tread lightly so that this land remains as is for future generations to see and enjoy. May the Creator bless us all."

Sadly, to this day Mr. Noel's proposal along with the idea to erect a plaque was never fulfilled. Those Apaches that came from Mescalero, Silver City, Oklahoma and Florida were disappointed but not surprised. Their love for the land and good intentions have been historically documented and preserved in these pages. Indeed, the skeptical elders were right, when they said, *"I was young and naïve."*

191

Feast at Second Canyon
Chapter Twenty Eight

On August 10th of 2005, I received a phone call from my aunt Lorraine Evans inviting me to be part of a feast honoring her son and his wife. They were both active in the U.S. Army and being deployed to Iraq to serve our Country. *"The feast will be here at Second Canyon in Mescalero. I have hired James Kunestsis' group and Freddie Kaydahzinne, this way you cannot say no. You are welcome to stay here with us. Hugh can pick you up at the airport if you like. So what do you say?"* Lorraine asked. Humbly honored, I accepted the invitation without hesitation. After hanging up the phone, I called my friend Jack Noel and extended the invitation.

A few days later, I visited an old Seminole friend, Mrs. Mary Jane Storm, the mother of Thomas Storm. Thomas was the lead singer of the Cypress Prairie drum, the last Seminole drum I sang for. The reason for my visit was to purchase a Seminole patchwork jacket and a few grass baskets to take to the feast as gifts.

Mary Jane Storm (Otter Clan)
Hollywood Seminole Reservation, ca. 2005
****

FEAST AT SECOND CANYON

Nine days later, on August 19, 2005, I arrived in Mescalero, New Mexico. I drove to Second Canyon where the feast was to take place. I arrived close to noon as preparations were just getting started. Lots of work needed to be done, and I was eager to get my hands dirty. After meeting the headman (the person that oversees all operations), I was given a choice to either help with the making of the dance arena or the building of the cooking arbor. Building of the dance arena consisted of making a huge circle marked with stones and setting benches for the singers to sit during the ceremony. The construction of the cooking arbor consisted of assembling a rectangular arbor/structure for the purpose of cooking. I chose to participate in the building of the arbor. It was something I always wanted to learn to do. I became part of a group of men assigned to that task. Using freshly cut oak, we began building the arbor from scratch. About half an hour into it, Lorraine came up to me and said that Windy Runningwater and his two sons, Eagle and Bird had arrived. I was happy to see him again, and pleased to meet his family. Windy and I worked together and talked about all that had taken place. About four hours later, we had finished what turned out to be the biggest arbor I had ever seen. It probably measured 30 x 50 feet and easily twenty feet in height. Once the arbor was built, we dug two fire pits at each end of the arbor. They both consisted of a hole in the ground, about a foot deep and approximately 5 x 4 feet large. Four-legged steel grills were placed on top of the two pits, for the purpose of cooking.

L to R: Windy Runningwater and his son Eagle. ****
Photographed in front of Lorraine Evan's house in
Second Canyon, Mescalero Apache Reservation, ca. 2005

FEAST AT SECOND CANYON

Feast at Second Canyon, Mescalero Apache Reservation, ca. 2005 ****

Building the arbor and digging those holes was relatively easy when compared to next job. It was a task that separated the boys from the men. It consisted of splitting pine logs in half. These were the logs to be used later in the evening as fuel for the Crown Dance, *sometimes referred as the Fire Dance.* Most of the wood pieces measured approximately five feet in height and about 15" to 20" in diameter, some weighed as much as two hundred pounds. The wood was brought to the Feast Grounds by the truckload and dumped into a large pile. They were later carried by hand to an adjacent area, where the splitting took place. The task was simple but extremely physical. It consisted of striking the logs in the center using a flat headed axe, which created a split, commonly known as a bite. After that, a steel wood splitter was inserted into the bite. The next step was the one that required a lot of energy. It consisted of striking the splitter by swinging the axe until the log split in half. Granted, in more than two decades as a firefighter, I had swung an axe quite a few times, but that was something. Some logs required dozens of strikes before surrendering. Just when I thought we were putting a dent on the pile, a truck would come to dump another load. The brutal workout went on for hours. I can't speak for the other guys, but it definitely put a hurting on me. By 5:30pm all the work was done and chow was called. Nothing tasted better than that open fire-cooked meal. It was great to sit around and enjoy the laughter of family and friends.

An hour later, Freddie Kaydahzinne showed up. I asked him if I could sing with him. *"Of course, you can,"* he replied. I assembled my drum and sat next to him on a wooden bench, as we waited for the War Dancers to show up. To my surprise, some of the dancers were the same guys that were splitting logs with me. With a dozen dancers or so, Freddie and I began to sing. Like a bolt of lightning, Freddie's thunderous voice echoed throughout Second Canyon. Oh, how proud I felt, to be singing with my mentor, accompanied by my family, in a canyon named after my Grandpa. The singing and dancing went on for a good hour. Where those dancers found energy to dance was beyond me.

L to R: Bo, Freddie, and Siggy singing Apache War Songs
Second Canyon
Mescalero Apache Reservation, ca. 2005

Upon the conclusion of the singing and dancing, Freddie stood up and gave a speech in the Apache language in honor of the two soldiers. I remained sitted on the bench listening to his words. I looked around and couldn't help but feel what it must have been like in the old days.

There I was, deep in Second Canyon, listening to my friend, teacher and mentor. To my left stood a traditional Apache camp with two columns of smoke rising in the air. More than a dozen dancers dressed in old traditional clothes gathered around me. In the far distance stood four tepees, each representing the groups of Crown Dancers hired for the feast. To top it off, Freddie was speaking in Apache. No words can describe or express what I saw and felt that day. As Freddie continued on, I began to pray, *"Oh Grandfather, I thank you for your many gifts, but most of all, I ask that you look over this couple and that you guide and protect them in their times of need. Most of all Grandfather, I ask that you bring them home safe."* Shortly after my prayers, Freddie's speech came to an end.

The dark orange, cloudless sky let me know it was time to head on over to James' camp to begin preparations for the Fire Dance. Upon arrival, I found everyone inside the tepee in the early stages of preparations. Because the temperature was dropping quickly, I took it upon myself to start a small fire in the center of the lodge.

As a result, I got teased with humorous remarks by the native New Mexicans who could not relate to the fact that I was uncomfortably cold. Regardless, my action was tolerated and later appreciated as the temperature dropped with the arrival of the night. The warmth from that fire felt good, especially to the dancers, whose upper bodies were only covered by wet paint. Once the paint dried, and the donning of the Crowns was done, our conversations and laughter came to an end. James' rapid beating of the drum let us all know it was time to bow our heads and pray. After the opening prayers, the dancing and singing began.

When finished, we all came out of the tepee and waited for James' signal to move on. That particular night, things went a little different. About fifty feet away from our tepee, both soldiers dressed in their military uniforms sat patiently waiting for us. Standing behind them were their families. We all followed James as he walked up and stood in front of the small crowd, where he gave a small speech followed by a prayer. After that, he began to bless Lorraine's son using the sacred yellow pollen. With the fine powder he marked a cross on the right foot, followed by the right shoulder, forehead and down the left shoulder finishing with the left foot. He then moved on to the female soldier and proceeded to bless her in the same fashion.

Once he was done, everyone present stood in line and performed the same ritual on the young soldiers. I have never forgotten that special moment when my turn came to bless my new family members. These were my prayers along with my blessings. *"Oh Life Giver, guide this warrior and his wife in their times of need. Give them strength and protect them from harm, and most of all bring them back home safe...."* Once done, the next person in line came to give their blessings. It was none other than little Hailey. It was incredible to see her do the blessings so naturally. While other kids her age ran and played around, she stayed focused watching everything. When everyone was done, the modern warriors, along with their families, moved on to the other three Crown Dancers' camps to receive their blessings. As the family walked away, our group headed to the dance arena and waited on the eastern entrance for the fire to be lit.

After the logs were ignited, we entered the arbor and sat on the wooden benches, where we waited for our Crown Dancers to bless the fire. Once that was done, James' began to sing. His voice echoed through Second Canyon, sending chills down my spine and goose bumps all over my arms. Next to me sat Vernon Simmons and Lynn Hank. With both of them singing in my ears, I was able to pick up the lyrics with ease. Because it was a warrior's feast, the songs we sang were different than the ones I was used to singing during the maiden's feast in Mescalero. Even thought, every feast I ever sang at was special, this one felt different. After all it was my family I was singing for. A constant reminder of that was watching little Hailey dance among the women. It was at that moment that I began to think of the day when her feast would take place. *"Will I be around for that one?"* I thought to myself. After realizing that only God can predict the future, I consoled myself with the fact that I was around for one just as important. About half an hour later, our dancers were joined by the other three Crown Dancer groups. It was an incredible sight to watch sixteen dancers and eight clowns all dancing in one place. On both sides of the arena, family members and special guests sat on lawn chairs, while others watched from the comfort of their cars. It was a great feeling knowing that all that hard labor had paid off. I felt privileged for being part of something so special.

After our singing session was over, I walked into the cooking arbor, grabbed a plate of food and proceeded to join Carson and Carol Carrillo.

They were both sitting on lawn chairs among a small group of Apache tribal members. It felt great to share such a meaningful moment among two individuals who shared a very special place in my heart. Running around with other kids were the Carillo's grandchildren. It was truly a time of celebration and everyone was having a good time of their own.

L to R: Carson and Carol Carrillo's grandchildren.
Jalen L. (Jaybird) Burgess, Nathan J. (Nana) Borgess, Raymond D. (Jubby) Carrillo
Mescalero Apache Reservation, ca. 2005
****

By midnight, I had totally run out of energy. After excusing myself, I headed back to my hotel to get some much needed rest.

The next morning I headed up to Mescalero again. I arrived at Second Canyon early enough to have a hot breakfast. This was the second and last day of the feast. All the work was done, except for the ladies who were busy cooking. I sat around and enjoyed conversing with friends and family members.

At about 1:00pm, I headed to St. Josephs' Church to meet up with Jack Noel. I arrived close to 1:30pm, when I realized that we had agreed to meet at 2:00pm. A few minutes after sitting at the church's administrative building, I decided to walk into the church that had touched me so deeply years earlier. The occasion marked the first time in my life that I had walked into a church on my own will, for the purpose of praying.

Once inside, I found myself alone, I thought about my kids, and the first time we visited. I knelt down and began to pray. I thanked the Creator for the many gifts and opportunities. After my humble prayer, I quietly exited the church and proceeded to wait for Jack.

Upon our arrival at Second Canyon, I introduced Jack to everyone. A lot of them he had met previously during his plea for help to stop the mining at Red Paint Canyon. Soon after, he began to help by carrying loads of the much needed cooking wood. Later that afternoon, Jack was served food by Lorraine and we sat around and caught up with what was going on at Monticello Canyon.

It was close to 5:00pm when James Kunestsis showed up. Jack wanted to talk to him. Together we walked over to his camp, where we found the rest of the group eating. Once there, Jack thanked James and the group for their support and involvement in the Monticello mining issue. Jack's action touched me deeply. Not only did he show courage when he asked for help, but he showed gratitude and respect when he returned to give thanks. It was something no other Monticello Canyon resident had ever done in any way, shape or form.

L to R: Lorraine Evans, James Kunestsis, Warren Mendez, Siggy Second-Jumper
Second Canyon, Mescalero Apache Reservation, ca. 2005

Half an hour later, Freddie Kaydahzinne showed up and shortly thereafter he and I began to sing war songs. Among the many dancers present were Freddie's kids, Bo and Kristen. While the war singing and dancing went on, Jack sat on a lawn chair and enjoyed the special moment. When we were done, I walked over to James' camp and began to prepare for the evening's fire dance.

FEAST AT SECOND CANYON

Once done, we came out and headed over to the eastern side of the arbor. The sky was beautiful with streaks of dark orange and bolts of lightning on its western horizon. We took our positions on the wooden benches and waited for James to jump-start the group into motion. The energy in the air was indescribable. Our dancers performed harder than ever and we sang like each song was our last. When the session was over, Jack walked up to me and said that words could not express what he saw and felt. I knew exactly what he meant. He gave his farewell to everyone, and I watched as he drove away.

The next day I arrived at Second Canyon at 1:00pm. After a nice lunch we began the breakdown of the camp. When finished, I was chosen to dispose of the medicine used during the feast. That part was taught to me by the headman. He and I penetrated deep into Second Canyon, and accomplished what was a vital part and conclusion of the ceremony.

Sadly, the time had come for me to head on back home to Florida, but not before I would bring up an issue that was heavy on my mind. It had to do with the changing of my name. It was there at that feast in Second Canyon that I decided to join so many other tribal members who had changed their names to honor and pay homage to their ancestors. With family approval and blessings, I added Second to my last name.

Apache Crown Dancers in Big Cypress
Chapter Twenty Nine

In November of 2005, Yellow Bird, the Arizona Apache dance group led by Ken Duncan was hired again by the Seminole Tribe of Florida. Like the previous year, I headed out to Big Cypress, accompanied by my children to watch them perform. After a quick greeting, we headed to the bleachers to get good front seats. Ken opened the show with a prayer, followed by the Come Home song, just like the previous year. Before Ken had finished singing the song, I told my children that the next performance was a hoop dance done by Ken's youngest son. Instead, and to my surprise, a group of four Crown Dancers emerged from the back of the stage. As Ken's voice echoed through the P.A., the dancers began to dance in sync with each other. Every now and then they would break away and walk on their wands.

Chiricahua-Coyotero Crown Dancer ****
Ken Duncan lead singer
Big Cypress Seminole Reservation, Big Cypress, FL, ca. 2005

APACHE CROWN DANCERS IN BIG CYPRESS

My daughter quickly asked how come they danced like that, and why their head crowns were different than those worn by the various groups in Mescalero. Proud of her observations, I explained that their style of dance, just like the shape of their head crowns was typical of the Arizona Apache groups.

Upon the conclusion of the show, Ken and I sat down to talk. During our conversation Ken asked if I knew Berle Kanseah. *"Yes, I knew him and had the pleasure of singing with him when I joined his son's Crown Dancing group in Mescalero. He was always concerned about his people losing the Apache language,"* I said.

"It's funny that you mention that, I have some Apache language tapes made in Mescalero. They were given to me, but I don't have any use for them, since I speak the language fluently. I will give them to you if you like," Ken said. *"That would be great!"* I replied. Ken and I exchanged information, and he promised to send the tapes as soon as possible. As I drove home that day, I thought about what had taken place. How ironic, the mentioning of Berle's name brought me what he had preached and emphasized so much, that being the importance of learning the Apache language. The following month, I received the tapes, as Ken had promised.

In 2008, I had the pleasure of running into Ken Duncan and his family as they were hired by the Mescalero Tribe to perform during the Fourth of July Feast. While conversing with Ken, I learned about something he wanted since he was a little boy. *"When I was young, growing up in San Carlos, I would follow my Grandpa over to our Crown Dancers' tepee and listen to the songs from a near-distance. Since then, I have always wanted to go inside that tepee and see what goes on."* Ken said.

It was at that moment that I realized I had the ability to give back to someone who had given me so much. A few hours later, I took Ken over to meet the members of my group. With James' permission, Ken entered our Crown Dancers' Tepee joining us in our prayers and songs. Later that evening, Ken looked at me with teary eyes and said. *"Thank you, Siggy! I will never forget you; I have fulfilled my lifelong dream."* Today I think of Berle and Ken every time I listen to those tapes.

Family Reunion in Florida
Chapter Thirty

In December of 2005, Lorraine and Hugh Evans along with their granddaughter Hailey Ahidley came to visit me and their daughter Nena and her family who were also living in Florida. Eagerly waiting for their arrival, my family and I set out to prepare a huge feast. By the time they arrived at my house, everything was cooked and waiting on the table. There, for the first time, I met Hugh and Lorraine's daughter Nena and her husband, along with their two children Camren Myron Reed and two-month-old Aiden Second Reed.

L to R; Lance, Camren, Emily, Hailey, Nena, Lorraine, Aiden
Hollywood, FL, ca. 2005
Photographed by Hugh Evans

It felt great to sit and enjoy such a special moment. The next day we visited the Seminole Hard Rock and Casino in Hollywood, Florida. After a nice tour of the facility, we headed down to Hollywood Beach. There, under the shade of swaying coconut palms, we watched the children play on the sandy shores of the beach.

The next day, we drove to the Big Cypress Seminole Reservation, which was located about an hour northwest from my home. We arrived at B.C. close to noon; where various pre-arranged VIP tours awaited.

L to R: Rear Row: Nena, Lorraine, Camren, Jesse
Front Row: Siggy, Emily, Hailey, Lance
Big Cypress Seminole Reservation, Big Cypress, FL, ca. 2005

The thrilling adventures began with an airboat ride. On that particular day we boarded a 16' aluminum craft, with three benches capable of accommodating three to four people each. The conductor was my friend Rey Becerra. He sat in a single seat pedestal perhaps three or four feet above the rest of us. Behind him, a huge V-8 motor roared through open headers. The lack of mufflers created a very loud noise that sounded very intimidating indeed. A spinning wood propeller generated enough air force to push the boat in motion. Protecting everyone from any flying debris was a steel cage that covered the motor and propeller.

For all of them, this was their first-time experience. As anyone who has ever ridden in one knows they can appear to be very intimidating at first. If that wasn't enough, the vessel sat on the murky waters of the Everglades, with dozens of alligators floating nearby. Once all of us gave the OK, Rey untied the boat and away we went. I really had a good time watching everyone's facial expressions as we left the dock. Within minutes from take off, the airboat began to hydroplane, thus allowing the driver to make 360 degree turns. Those daredevil maneuvers added to the thrill.

As we penetrated deeper into the land of the Seminole, the sawgrass got thicker and taller, at times reaching ten to fifteen feet. Everyone was amazed to see how the powerful boat cut through it like a knife. Rey informed us that we were navigating through old Seminole canoe trails and entering areas where tourists were not allowed, thus making the excursion extra special. After arriving at a cypress head, Rey shot down the motor so everyone could enjoy some of the hidden natural beauties of the swamps. There, the wildlife thrived, as otters played in the water and Anhingas stood still while sun-drying their open wings. Soon after our arrival, dozens of alligator approached the vessel looking for treats; many came just inches from the boat.

That was the first time that the New Mexicans came face to face with the prehistoric beast. It was at that moment that I was able to see the kid in everyone, as their faces revealed a combination between panic and joy. After capturing those special moments with my camera, we headed back to the other side of the park for a swamp buggy ride.

The buggies were custom made, some were able to accommodate up to thirty people. They consisted of a flat bed on wheels with many rows of seats. A steel cage-frame served as side-rails and support for the canvas roof. A big block V-8 powered all four wheels along with its huge tractor tires. Those buggies were made for one thing only, and that was to travel through the swamps. That particular tour consisted of traveling through Billie Swamp Safari, an enormous fenced-in area that was home to thousands of exotic animals from all over the world. As mentioned earlier, it was originally built as a hunting expedition for the rich and famous.

L to R: Rear: Hugh, Emily, Lorraine ****
Front Row: Lance, Hailey, Camren
Big Cypress, Seminole Reservation, ca. 2005

The exotic park was later turned into a preservation safari and ultimately became a tourist attraction. The first part of the tour consisted of crossing a deep water canal. Again their facial expressions were priceless. Once we got across, a sigh of relief was heard from everyone. As we traveled deeper into the swamps, we began to see all kinds of wild life. Most animals remained ambivalent to our presence, while others appeared somewhat interested.

There, we had the opportunity to see them in a natural habitat. Among the animals we saw were deer from all over of the world along with water buffalo and the once almost extinct American Bison. Shortly after, we crossed an open prairie filled with snowy egrets, tricolored herons and roseate spoonbills. After crossing the wet land, we entered a cypress hammock. At times, our path was completely covered by a canopy of a variety of trees. Rey Becerra, our tour guide described the many medicinal plants found throughout and how they were used by the Seminoles.

Hidden deep in the hammock was an old Seminole Camp. The site still maintained some of its original characteristics, such as a Sabal Palm Chickee, surrounded by a slew of citrus trees. A dugout Seminole canoe lay nearby as part of the display. The tour took about an hour from start to finish.

When done, we headed over to Billie Swamp Restaurant where we ordered some traditional Seminole foods. The menu offered a variety of exotic treats, such as buffalo burgers, alligator bites, which consisted of pieces of alligator meat breaded and fried. Also available were frog legs, Seminole fry bread and Indian tacos. After a long and fun day, we hugged each other and went our separate ways.

My children and I had a lot of fun that day. Even though we had done both tours many times before, they never ceased to amaze us. The Everglades is an incredible place, and only those who had the pleasure of experiencing its power and beauty can relate to it.

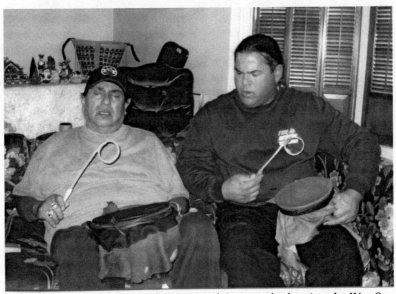

L to R: Freddie Kaydahzinne, Siggy Second-Jumper singing Apache War Songs
Artesia, New Mexico, ca. 2005
Photographed by Vincent Kaydahzinne

Back in July of 2005, Freddie Kaydahzinne invited me to be part of a project that involved singing and traveling. I eagerly agreed and accepted the offer. In late December of that year, shortly after Lorraine's visit, Freddie called me up and said, *"Well, the time has come. Can you make it to Mescalero? "Yes of course,"* I replied. A week later, I flew to New Mexico and drove to a hotel in Alamogordo, where I found Freddie waiting for me in the parking lot. We spent most of that day singing and synchronizing our voices.

The next morning, I drove up to Mescalero where I picked up Freddie and his son Bo. Freddie wanted to visit his brother Vincent who lived in Artesia, New Mexico, a small town located approximately two and a half hours away. After driving out of the Mescalero Reservation, we entered the neighboring town of Mayhill, where we stopped to get fuel and a bite to eat. Unfortunately, the only thing they had to eat that looked fresh were mini honey buns. Not a very healthy choice, but it was the only thing eatable at the only store in town.

About an hour into our trip, we entered some beautiful country with gorgeous valleys and rolling hills. Along the way, Freddie would point out areas of interest, including one where Apaches frequently visited to gather Mescal. As we continued our drive through open country, my hunger began to increase. That feeling quickly disappeared when Freddie picked up his water drum and began to sing. After a few songs, I joined him in his singing. Freddie's arsenal of melodies was impressive; he was the proud keeper of hundreds of Apache songs. A lot of them I knew from years of singing along with him back in Mescalero. In-between songs, he explained how some of them came to him.

"The majority of these songs have been passed down from generation to generation, but a lot of them came to me in dreams," he said.

While on the subject, I confessed to Freddie about the dream I had back in 1999, where an Apache by the name of Freddie was going to teach me to sing old Apache songs. We were both proof that indeed dreams can become a reality. Freddie and I continued singing while Bo listened to his iPod in the back seat. Never had driving such a long distance on an empty stomach been such a pleasure.

We arrived in Artesia, a small town known for its oil wells and refineries. There we picked up Freddie's brother, Vincent Kaydahzinne and the four of us headed out to get something to eat. We returned to Vincent's house where I met his wife Carol and I got to see some of Vincent's artwork. His home was mostly decorated with an impressive collection of paintings and statues. Vincent was a multi-talented individual, who specialized in the art of painting, carving, singing and flute playing. A tour of his workshop revealed many stone pieces in various stages of carving. That afternoon, we sat in Vincent's living room while Freddie and I sang.

After a full day of singing and laughter, we drove back to Mescalero. It was during that time that Freddie began to express how he felt about his grandfathers, Chief Cochise and Scout Chatto. Freddie is a descendant from an incredible bloodline of Chiricahua Chiefs. From his father's side, he was directly related to Cochise. The legendary Apache Chief was known as one of the greatest Chiricahua leaders of all times.

That side of the family was easy for Freddie to speak of. He started by telling me that Cochise had a daughter, named Dash-den-zhoos. She was born in 1862 and was half sister to Naiche and Taza.

FREDDIE'S FAMILY TREE (COCHISE SIDE)

Cochise's daughter, Dash-den-zhoos

207

SCOUT CHATTO'S STORY

Chief Cochise & Wife (Unknown name)
I
Dash-den-zhoos (1862-?) married Tim Kaydahzinne (1862-?)

Dash-den-zhoos was "half sister to Chief Naiche, same Father, and full sister of Naithlotonz. Naithlotonz married Fred Gokliz and after his death married Chiricahua Tom.

I
Dash-den had the following children:

- Sadie Kaydahzinne (1882-1896)

- Her sister Naithlotonz married Fred Gokliz and after his death married Chiricahua Tom

- Hanna Kaydahzinne (1897-?)

- Lena Kaydahzinne (1898-?)
Lena married Maurice Chatto (1891-1913) son of Scout Alfred Chatto (1854-1934) and his 3rd wife Be-gis-cley-aihn (Mrs. Helen Chatto)
Maurice Chatto died soon after arriving in Mescalero.

- Eunice Kaydahzinne (1901-?)

- Nelson Kaydahzinne (1903-?)
Nelson had a son named William, Freddie's father.
Freddie married Edith, a Mescalero, and had Bo (son) and Kristen (daughter)

After listening to Freddie speak of Cochise, I noticed that there was something bothering him about his mother's side of the family. Freddie is the maternal grandson of Scout Albert Chatto; perhaps the most hated and misunderstood Chiricahua Apache of all times. One who paid the ultimate price for the love of his people. Freddie felt that his grandpa was unfairly condemned by his peers and for many years has wanted to express his feelings on this matter. I am honored to have been chosen to do so, on his behalf.

Parts of this story were told to me by Freddie himself and the rest came from an interview conducted by Mr. Herbert Welsh, *Corresponding Secretary Indian Rights Association* while he visited the Apache prisoners in 1887 at Fort Marion, Florida.

Chatto (Spanish for Flat Nose) was a Chiricahua Apache Indian born in Arizona in the 1840's. He measured 5'8", had long black hair, black eyes, copper complexion, and loved to dress well. He had a reputation for being a ferocious warrior who participated in many raids against the U.S. and Mexican governments. That was the good Chatto by Apache standards, but the good Chatto, whose political ambition was to become Chief of the Warm Springs-Chiricahua band, quickly realized he was fighting a losing battle. Knowing that the warpath would certainly end in the annihilation of the entire Chiricahua tribe made the feared warrior come to terms. Determined to see his people live, he chose to give up rather than perish.

Chatto, Chiricahua Apache.
Chatto headed a delegation to Washington
for a conference on July 26th, to appeal to
the Secretary of War regarding the
removal of the Apache from Fort Apache
to the panhandle of Oklahoma.
Courtesy of St. Augustine's Historical Society Library

In 1883 he surrendered to U.S. Army General Cook, in the Sierra Madre Mountains of Mexico, just south of the Arizona border. There he made promise of good behavior which he kept for the rest of his life. He joined the U.S. Army and served as a Sergeant Scout under General Crook, the founder of the Battalion of Indian Scouts. After years of fighting Apaches, U.S. General Crook figured, that *"The only way to catch an Apache was with an Apache,"* especially catching one named Geronimo.

Chatto's decision to become a Scout, and join the enemy was influenced by his dislike for Geronimo. Because of that, he was assigned to the campaign against hostile Apaches, also known as the Geronimo Campaign. *"Very few people, including Apaches, were willing to go against the mighty and feared Geronimo, a powerful Medicine Man."* Freddie said.

Chatto's knowledge of Apache warfare tactics and familiarization with every possible refuge and watering hole made his services extremely valuable to his officers in command. He joined Lieutenant Britton Davis of Company B of Indian Scouts. He enlisted as First Sergeant on July 1, 1884, where he served for six months and received "Honorable Discharge" after term served. Chatto signed up again on Jan. 1, 1885, as 1st Sergeant under Lt Faison's Comp B of the Battalion of Indian Scouts. In May of that year, Jose First joined Comp B and served under Chatto. After serving another six months, Chatto was discharged with honors. His honorable service to the U.S. army was seen as a disgrace by other Apaches, including those that remained peaceful. As a result, Chatto became perhaps the most hated Apache ever. The mentioned of his name, which is smeared to this day, was repulsive to his peers.

This hideous reputation bothers Freddie greatly. *"I wish that everyone would understand that my grand-father Chatto changed his ways in the name of the people. He was able to place the best interest of all Chiricahuas before his own personal needs, the complete opposite of what Geronimo was doing. Chatto was a brave man indeed. He had the guts to go against Geronimo, a medicine man and the most feared Apache ever,"* Freddie proudly said.

The following story will bring light to Chatto's life as a Scout and prisoner:

By 1886, Chatto was used to living at Fort Apache, Arizona but he was unable to forget the place he loved most, Ojo Caliente, in New Mexico. He worked hard as a farmer in his fourteen-acre parcel of land; there, he owned a home several horses and mules. In July of that year, Mr. L.Q.C. Lamar, Jr. visited Fort Apache and held conference with Chatto, and asked him to visit Washington.

"No hint was given to Chatto that he was under suspicion of wrong-doing, or that his proposed journey to the Capital was to terminate within prison walls. On the contrary, Chatto thought he was going to talk with the authorities concerning the possible removal of himself and his people to a better reservation.[3]"

Apache Scouts who participated in the Geronimo Campaign
Courtesy of St. Augustine's Historical Society Library

General Crook's Apache Scouts
Expedition into Sonora, Mexico in 1883
Courtesy of St. Augustine's Historical Society Library

Scouts in picture—back row, left to right: Hola, Charley Yazza, Sanguine, Guerito, Tom, Casa Miri, Jake Segunda, Papel, Hosteen Nez, Navajo Phil, Pete, Marianito, Natchi, Viurito, Jose Chalaco, Jose Chiquito, Enrika, Calavasa. Middle row: Bega, Pasado, Chiquito, Mosto, Kisane, Charley No. 1, Mava, Chatsosee, Moqui, Choski, Navajo John, Francisco, Mamuzza, Pinto. Front row: Sam Nelson, Dine Chili, Apachito, Nas te ga, (C. R. Franks, Spl. Pension Examiner), Vicenti Baca, (S. F. Stacher, Supt. Eastern Navajo Agency, Crown Point, New Mexico), George, Casa Miri No. 2, Kohnine, Panteleon, Santiago, Dick White, Beneto Cloi. Above Indians served as Navajo Indian scouts, 1885-6, Companies A, B, C, with Captains B. H. Rogers, Albert B. Scott, and C. B. Hall; 2nd Lieutenants Pasada, Vicenti Baca and Benetocloi served as scouts in 1876 or later. All enlisted at Fort Wingate, New Mexico. Thirty-seven of the above are receiving pension with other claims pending. Picture taken September, 1926.

Apache and Navajo Scouts -- Picture taken in 1926
Courtesy of St. Augustine's Historical Society Library

"On July 15, Chatto and thirteen other Indians-men, women, boarded the east bound train to Washington. Upon their arrival, Chatto had interviews with the President, Secretary Lamar, and Secretary Endicott. Secretary Lamar told him if he needed anything in the way of farming implements to ask for it. Chatto told him of his needs in this respect, and Mr. Lamar told him that if he would return he should receive them. Chatto informed the Secretary that he did not wish to leave his old home at Fort Apache.

He was told to go home, to work, and to behave himself. Mr. Lamar further told him that he could return by way of Carlisle, because many of the men in his party had children there. Capt. Dorst, the army officer who had charge of them, then took the Indians to Carlisle. After remaining there some time, orders came for them to return to the west. They started westward and journeyed three days and three nights, when the car they were in was detached from the train. Chatto was feeling happy and bright at the prospect of reaching his home, when the first thing he knew, he was back at Fort Leavenworth. There, Capt. Dorst received orders from General Miles to meet him at Albuquerque. Upon his return, Capt Dorst said that General Miles would give them a reservation of so many square miles (60) and that they would lose none of the property they had left behind. The new reservation, he said, would contain better land than the old. Chatto assumed that they had taken pity on them because of their poverty.

The photo is circa 1880 - 1883. They are White Mountain Apache Scouts. Only 1 person is identified, so far. The first on the left as you look at the photo is Ha-teth-la, a Pinal Apache Chief.

Courtesy of St. Augustine's Historical Society Library

On this new reserve, the new Chief was to receive $50 per month, and others, according to their station, $30 and $20 per month. The Indians were again started on their journey and finally arrived. Not upon the new and better land promised them, but within the narrow limits of their prison.... Chatto naively said, *"I do not think this place looks as though it contains sixty square miles."* Chatto and the others had no clue they had just arrived in Fort Marion, St. Augustine, Florida, to join the rest of the tribe as prisoners of war. He was still wearing his heavy and beautiful silver medal attached to his vest by a brass chain given to him by Secretary Lamar when he was in Washington. The action by the government made no sense; there among the hostiles were the Scouts, some still on government payrolls.[3]"

Among the imprisoned scouts were Charles Martine(z) (1858-?) and his cousin, Martin Kayitah (1856-1934),"the two Scouts commissioned by General Miles, shortly before the close of the last autumn's Campaign in the Sierra Madre Mountains, to visit the camp of Geronimo and his band in order to induce them to surrender.[3]" The high-risk mission ultimately resulted in the surrender of Geronimo, Naiche and his followers.

The following story was told to Mr. Herbert Welsh, *Corresponding Secretary Indian Rights Association* by scouts Martine(z) and Ki-e-ta (Kayitah) while imprisoned in Fort Marion, Florida in 1887. I am hereby recording it, as it pertained to none other than the surrender of Geronimo.

"In payment for their mission, General Nelson Miles offered the two scouts ten ponies a piece if they would find Geronimo, enter his camp and persuade him to surrender. Accordingly, they went out with Lt. Gatewood, who had with him 10 or 12 men, and after marching several days up hill and down, searching for the trail of hostiles, they finally founded. Leaving the Lieutenant and soldiers eight miles behind, the two Indian scouts went unattended into the camp of Geronimo. They spent three days with Geronimo trying to persuade him to leave the war-path and to surrender to General Miles. Geronimo finally consented to give himself up, and, in company with the scouts, he joined Lt. Gatewood and his detail of soldiers; but on the journey to General Miles, Geronimo went off on another raid into Mexico, rejoining Gatewood on his march.

Once the mission was accomplished, the two scouts received $100 each, but that they did not deemed equivalent to what had been pledged. It was further stated that they were at first given $60, but a military officer increased the amount to $100 out of his pocket.[3]"

"Scout Roger To-Klanni was also in confinement. He was a Chiricahua who married a White Mountain Apache woman, and consequently left his people to live with hers. He had not been on the warpath for many years, certainly not since 1872. He was one of General Crook's most trusted scouts in the Sierra Madre campaign.

Another scout was Sergeant Major George Noche (1856-1914), his knowledge of the terrain was a contributing factor for the success of the Geronimo Campaign. Noche was Captain Crawford's chief of scouts in the attack upon Geronimo's camp.

'Dutchey,' a Chiricahua also in captivity, was at Captain Crawford's side when the officer was murdered by the Mexicans. A year and a half later, he shot the Mexican by whom Crawford was killed.[3]"

Part of a letter by Herbert Welsh, dispatched by the New York Times in March 22, 1886, may shed some light into why such despicable actions were taken.

"There was an imperative demand from the people of Arizona that the Apaches should be removed, as they were bad Indians, likely to go on the warpath at any time, and their presence was a constant menace to the lives and security of the people.[3]"

In the end, "Chatto was seen as a blood-thirsty murderer and no injustice would have been done to him if he had been hanged or shot, either of which events the people of Arizona would have properly rejoiced.[3]"

Despite Mr. Welsh's efforts to release those scouts that had served with honor and distinction, not one of them received any consideration by the U.S. government, instead they remained prisoners for twenty seven years.

"This was one of the many injustices endured by the Chiricahua Apache people. Chatto went on to marry Helen in Fort Marion. They endured the long and painful journey of imprisonment for almost 28 years." Freddie said.

Helen and Alfred Chatto
Photograph donated by Freddie Kaydahzinne

After being released in 1913, Chatto along with his family chose to move to Mescalero. He was killed in an auto accident in Mescalero in 1934. Freddie still sings songs that belonged to his grandmother Helen. As our drive continued, I began to tell Freddie about my family, and how I ended up arriving in Mescalero. I also told him what James Kunestis said to me upon my arrival there. *"You are like the Morning Star. You come from the east and bring knowledge to us."*

After hearing my story, Freddie told me of a song he had composed years earlier, titled "Suss Bine" meaning Morning Star. *"The song became very popular and is sung by other groups in Mescalero."* A few minutes later, he began singing the song to me. I made him sing it a couple of times, until I learned it.

From that day on the song became very special to me. With the end of that song, came the conclusion of our trip. After dropping Freddie and Bo off, I got on Highway 70 and began to drive back to the hotel. During that long drive, the following thoughts came to me: *"I believe that all Chiricahua leaders wanted the best for their people; some went about it in their own way. It is easy to criticize their actions after the fact. We should praise them all; perhaps their actions, good or bad, created a balance that made it possible for us to be here today. I hope that this story will help ease some of the pain, and bring harmony and understanding among families and individuals that still resent Chatto's ways."*

Regardless, they lit and carried the torch that still gives light to our path. We must accept the passing of the torch; it is up to us to give light to the next generation. I pray that we can put past differences behind us, and accept each other regardless of our painful history. Let us devote our energy and efforts embracing each other and preserving the beautiful Apache culture and language.

Siggy Second-Jumper dressed as an Apache Scout
Hollywood Seminole Pow Wow, ca. 2006

In January of 2006, I was medically cleared from my hip injury. As a result of good compliance, I had healed completely and faster than expected. Almost two years had passed since the dreadful fall from the wild painted horse. I was eager to make up for the time lost without dancing.

I began training immediately for the biggest Pow Wow in Florida, the Seminole Tribal Fair, which was held each year on the second weekend of February. My training went well, and without any incidents or pain. All my moves were still there and I just needed to work on my cardio. Time moved on fast, soon I found myself at the registration booth, signing up in the category of Men's Northern Traditional. To add to the excitement, the Pow Wow was going to be held at the Hard Rock Live, a brand new state of the art indoor arena. It was located inside the Seminole Hard Rock Casino, in Hollywood, Florida, less than three miles from my home.

DANCING FOR SCOUTS

Inspired by Freddie's feelings and Chatto's story, I dressed up like never before for Friday's grand opening. I showed up in a typical Apache Scout outfit. My attire consisted of toe guarded moccasins, cotton pants, a leather breach cloth, and a blue army coat with Sergeant Stripes. It was tied at the waist by a fully loaded cartridge belt. I let my hair loose and wrapped it with a red bandana, a scout's trademark. In hand I carried a Yellow Boy Winchester Rifle.

My intentions were not to come across as being pro-Scout or anti-Geronimo. I simply wanted to pay homage to those who in their own way, right or wrong, wore the blue coat and the red bandana for the love of their people. While wearing the Scout's uniform, I wondered which side I would have chosen under those circumstances. I seriously doubted that many of the people in the audience knew or understood the meaning of my outfit. The judges obviously did, when they awarded me second place in my category.

Apache Scouts, 1925 posing in White Tail, Mescalero, New Mexico
Back Row: L to R, # 3 Alfred Chatto wearing hat, tie and metal. # 6 Martine, #7 Kayitah.
Middle Row: # 4 Roger Toclanny, wearing suit, tie and mustache. Extreme right is Perico with black hat.
Front Row: Kneeling down in the middle of the women, wearing white shirt and black blanket with gray hair, Dash-den-zhoos, Chief Cochise's Daughter
Photo donated by Freddie Kaydahzinne

Visit to St. Augustine, Florida
Chapter Thirty Three

In April of 2006, I decided to look further into my families past history. More specifically, I was interested in learning about my grandmother, Jose Second's wife. She was only known as a number, and I wanted to know what she looked like, or at least try to find her name. I figured the first place to start was by calling Castillo de San Marcos (Formerly Fort Marion) in St. Augustine, Florida.

On May 1st, I called the Fort's Library and spoke to a Park Ranger by the name of Amy Harper. After introducing myself, I asked her if they had a way to identify the former female Apache prisoners, other than by numbers. Ms. Harper informed me that they did not have a lot of records regarding any of the former Apache prisoners. She suggested for me to contact the St Augustine's Historical Society Library to find out if they had such information.

Minutes later, I found myself hearing the same thing from the librarian, a gentleman by the name of Charles. He told me that very poor records were taken, and assured me that a list that compared names with numbers never existed. Somewhat disappointed, I was about to hang up when I was informed of something that cheered me up and made the call worthwhile.

I was told by Charles, that a gentleman had just donated a photo collection never before seen. It contained some rare shots of the first group of Apache prisoners arriving in Fort Marion in 1886. To top it off, among those pictures were some of Geronimo. Excited about the news, I made an appointment for three days later.

On May 4th after a five-hour drive, I arrived in St Augustine, Florida, the oldest City in the United States. It was 1:00pm when I entered the Historical Society Library and met Charles, the librarian. A few minutes later I was given a pair of white gloves and escorted to a private room. To my surprise, all files pertaining to the Chiricahua Apaches were waiting for me at a table.

In those documents I found all kinds of information, ranging from personal letters written by the prisoners, local residents and military officers. There were also lots of photographs. The only list of names I found was in a file titled "Apache Prisoners in Fort Marion, 1886-1887" by Historical Aide Omega G. East

BACHLON=BECOTHLA=BENDER=BESTHUAY=BASHOZEN=BEZENAS=BIZHU
= COYONHE=CATIA=CONAENATO=CHARLIE=COQUINA=CHATTO=CISNER=
CATHENAY=CHEOO=CHIHUAHUA=CHECHET=COHA=DUTCHEY=DONSHED
AN= EESKENEY=FATTY=FRITZ=GOZO=GOODYGOODY=GERONIMO=
MARION, (Daughter of Geronimo)
HAOZOUS, SAM, (Son of Geronimo)
HUERI, called Francisca at Fort Marion.
HARRY, DICK=HAHALEY=HOSANNAH=JOSHYA=JOHHIE=JIM=JOSE=
JOSANNA=KASHONAR=KASOCHON=KAEETINAE=KATAR=KARETNAE=
NANA=KALESON=KEROZONA=KIETA=KROSHECA=LANZEA=LOCO=
MARTINEZ=NICHARZEH=NAUSEN=NOSLIN=PARLO=PHIL=SPUDY=STON=SO
CORRO=SHUNARCLAY=STALOCH=SOZOHE=ZILI=SOZ=SIELE=SIZZEN=
SHILTINOO=TO-DAY=TOKLANNI= WENOSHE.

In another file, I found the following letter. It was sent to the library back in 1988 by a P.O.W. descendant by the name of Harry Mithlo Mitchell living in Anadarko, Oklahoma. The fact that it related to the Mithlos' caught my attention. Once I read it, I found the information to be worth noting for its historical value.

November 22, 1988

Indians

Page Edwards, Director
St. Augustine Historical Society
271 Charlotte Street
St. Augustine, Florida 32084

I have been seaching for information on the Apache Indians, who were send to Fort Marion, St. Augustine, Florida. My dad was a prisoner there and he is alive and well.

I need information on the following;
   Lawrence Mithlo (arrival - age - departure)
   Bill Watson Mithlo (DOB - infant - mother)
   Eugene Chihuahua (brother to Bill Mithlo)
   Photos of prisoners (working - sick - hangings)
 ✓ Geronimo (arrival - departure - age)
 ? List of adults (names) (photos)
 ? List of children (names) (photos)
 ✓ How the Quakers helped the Apaches.

I am putting a family history together to honor our father, Bill Watson. I will be awaiting your reply.

Harry L. Mithlo Mitchell
Educator

P.S.
Info. on Ceremonies
while at Fort Marion

Courtesy of St. Augustine Historical Society

Saint Augustine Historical Society

271 Charlotte Street • Saint Augustine, Florida 32084 • (904) 824-2872

Dec.2 . 1988

To Harry L.Mithlo Mitchell

ANADARKO , OKLAHOMA 73005

Dear Sir ,

We assume , that in your letter from Nov. 22 nd you are refering to the Apache tribes , who were at Fort Marion in1886 and 1887.
A group of 72 Indians were confined here in 1875 , but they were of different tribes.
To answer your questions one by one :

1. We have no information about Lawrence Mithlo or Bill Watson Mithlo , as there are no list of names in our possession .

2. A chief Chihuahua arrived at Ft.Marion in April]886 . We do not know , if " Eugene " is said chief or a member of his family.

3. We are including with this letter some copies of photographies of Apache prisoners and children. 108 children were sent to the Carlisle School for Indians in Philadelphia .The picture of the children is a copy from the book " Battlefield and classroom " by Richard Henry Pratt. We can provide you with a group photograph from the Apaches for $ 30.-

4. Geronimo (1829 - 1909) was not at Fort Marion in St.Augustine .He arrived at Fort.Pickens , Pensacola on Oct.26 , 1886 . However , his 3 wives were at the Fort in St.Augustine and his daughter Marion was one of the 12 Apache children born here . A son , named Sam , was also a fort prisoner .

5. As there weren't any Quakers in St.Augustine , the probability of them helping the Apaches in any way was nonexistent.

6. Concerning ceremonies - prisoners drew pictures of an Apache Fire Dancer on the wall , so we are aware of one of the oldest ceremonial dances performed here . Of course , there were occasions for a medicine dance , performed by the medicine man .

For detailed information about the Apaches we recommend the St.Augustine Historical Society's EL ESCRIBANO 1969 : " APACHE PRISONERS IN FORT MARION " by Omega G.East . We can mail it to you for $ 8. - plus $ 2.50 for shipping .

Please let us know , if we can be of further assistance to you .

Sincerely yours, *H.E.Martinsons*

(W.E.Martinsons,Genealogy)

Courtesy of St. Augustine Historical Society

The above letter was written in response. Just like I was told on the phone three days earlier, it reflected on the fort's poor record keeping during the Apache imprisonment. Indeed I was not able to find a list to compare names and numbers for the female prisoners, but instead I found Mr. Mitchell's letter. It was through his correspondence that I learned that Bill Watson Mithlo and Eugene Chihuahua were brothers. Since the Mithlos' and the Seconds' were related, it made me wonder if the Second's were related to the Chihuahuas'.

I have since learned a lot about the Mithlos' of Oklahoma through Lorraine, as she still stays in contact with them. In July of 2010, Lorraine introduced me to some of them while they visited Mescalero. During that meeting, I had the pleasure of meeting Watson Mithlo's daughter.

Another file contained newspaper articles, showing what Watson Mithlo looked like. Standing next to him was Benedict Jozhe, the last survivor of the Fort Sill Apache P.O.W. He passed away on September 25, 2005.

Daily Oklahoman

Sooners Find
Indian's Grave
APR 1 2 1960
(Oklahoman-Times Washington Bureau)

WASHINGTON — Two Oklahoma Indians have found the grave of the eldest son of television's most famous Indian warrior, Cochise.

They found the unmarked resting place of Tazhay in an old Washington cemetery about a mile from the Capitol building.

Benedict Jozhe and Watson Mithlo, of Apache, said they hope to obtain a suitable marker for Tazhay's grave.

Jozhe, chairman of the Fort Sill Apache Indian tribe, is a descendant of Cochise, who led the Chiricahua band of Apaches in the southeastern part of Arizona.

Recently Jozhe, who has spent much time gathering and publishing historical accounts of the Apaches, heard that Cochise's eldest son had died in Washington while on official business for his tribe.

When Jozhe and Mithlo came to Washington for an annual board meeting of the National Congress of American Indians, they began a search. It took them through military burial records, the Library of Congress, and the bureau of American ethnology.

Tazhay supposedly had been buried in Arlington National Cemetery, but the Oklahoma researchers found his unmarked grave in a little-known cemetery.

Standing before the unmarked grave of Tazhay, oldest son of the famous Indian warrior, Cochise, are (left to right) Oswald C. George, Coeur d'Alene, Plumm Idaho; Ida Moore, Oneida Indian originally from Wisconsin and son Randy; Helen Peterson, Oglala Sioux and director of National Congress of American Indians; Benedict Jozhe and Watson Mithlo, both of Apache, and Irene Dixon Mack, Menominee, a regional vice president of the NCAI.

Watson Mithlo with suit and wearing glasses, to his right Benedict Jozhe.
The group was photographed as they visited Cochise's son, Taza in Washington, D.C.
Courtesy of St. Augustine Historical Library, St. Augustine, FL

Once I finished reading and making copies of documents, letters and newspaper articles, I was escorted to a separate building to see the photo collection previously mentioned. After entering a room that appeared to be someone's office, I was asked to sit by a computer while I waited for the librarian to turn it on. With the touch of my fingers, images began to emerge. I could not believe what I was seeing. There in front of me, for the first time, I got to see Chief Chihuahua's group posing in the Fort Marion's courtyard. Standing in the middle of the group was the Chief himself, to his right, stood the powerful Medicine Man, Nana. Standing on Nana's right, was none other than Jose Second. Filled with excitement, my hand began to shake. I was almost afraid to click on to the next image. Since the pictures had just been turned in, I knew that I was the first descendant to lay eyes on them. I felt so privileged. The next photograph was that of the City of St. Augustine in 1886. It showed less than a dozen family homes surrounded by vacant land with Fort Marion in the background.

Chiricahua-Warm Springs Apaches in captivity at in Fort Marion, FL, ca. 1886
Pictures from F.W. Bruce Collection - Donated by his great-grandson, Cleve Powell.

In the middle was Chief Chihuahua wearing a black suit, and holding a piece of paper, to his right was Nana, wearing a hat. To Nana's right was Jose Second holding another piece of paper. The warriors were surrounded by the women and children. I spent a long time trying to see if any of the children resembled my great-grand parents, KuKah and Florentino.

St Augustine, FL, ca. 1886
Pictures from F.W. Bruce Collection - Donated by his great-grandson, Cleve Powell.

The next photograph showed various types of Sibley tents set up on Fort Marion's north rampart. I had heard about them, but to see them was worth a thousand words. My next finger click revealed something even more special. It consisted of an Apache Crown Dancer carved on the fort's coquina wall. A part of me wanted to look at each image slowly and re-live the moment. On the other hand, I wanted to click through and get to the controversial picture of Geronimo.

The dilemma had to do with the fact that Geronimo was taken to Fort Pickens, in Pensacola, Florida, where he supposedly remained throughout his confinement. Again, that was according to military records. As mentioned, records were poorly kept, to say the least. To my surprise, the next image that emerged on the screen was the famous picture in question. It showed Geronimo next to a gentleman. Indeed both men stood on the north rampart of Fort Marion. Behind them were four Sibley tents and the fort's wall, which was partially covered with Indian blankets. The gentleman next to Geronimo was wearing a suit and hat. Geronimo was also wearing a hat and what appeared to be a traditional white with black stripes prisoner's shirt.

A rare picture of Geronimo in Fort Marion, Florida with F.W. Bruce, ca. 1887
Pictures from F.W. Bruce/Cleve Powell collection

The next photograph was a close-up of the same photograph of Geronimo and F.W. Bruce. As a result, I was able to observe in detail various personal details such as a ring in each middle finger and the way in which the individual tucked his pants in his socks. The manner in which he stood was also very distinctive, along with his hat and shoes.

Geronimo and F.W. Bruce at Fort Marion, FL, ca. 1887
Pictures from F.W. Bruce Cleve Powell collection.

The next shot showed Geronimo standing on the same spot with a small group of people. To Geronimo's left stood a white lady under the shade of an umbrella. Standing in front of her was an unknown Indian lad and to her left, an unknown Indian woman. Needless to say, the photograph forced me to stop and dig deep into my memory bank. One thing was for sure, Geronimo had two wives and children that were sent to Fort Marion, Florida. They were In-tedda and Zi-yeh and her children.

While staring at the photograph, I wondered if the feared leader was visiting his family at Fort Marion under special circumstances. After all, what could have been more significant than the birth of his daughter, Marion, named after the fort. *"Could the Indian woman in the picture with lad been Zi-yeh and her children?"* I wondered.

L to R: Geronimo, Unknown Lad, Mrs. Bruce, Unknown Apache woman,
Mr. F. W. Bruce, Fort Marion, FL, ca. 1887
Pictures from F.W. Bruce/Cleve Powell collection.

The following records give a broad glance into Geronimo's family history. "After his father's death, Geronimo and his mother left the Bedonkohes and joined the Nednai Apaches in northern Sonora led by Chief Juh (Long neck, born in the 1820's-1883). There, Geronimo married for the first time to a Nednai girl named Gee-esh-kizn. In the summer of 1858, his wife, their three children, and his mother were slain by Mexican troops in the "Massacre of Kas-ki-yeh" in the town of Janos, northern Chihuahua, Mexico.

Geronimo then moved north and rejoined his Bedonkohe Kinsmen. There he acquired another young wife, a Bedonkohe named Chee-hash-kish. In 1864, she gave birth to his son Chappo (1864-1894) and in 1865 to his daughter Lulu (1865-1898). Chee-hash-kish remained with him until 1882, when she was captured by Mexicans at Casas Grandes. She was never again seen by her people. Shortly after his marriage to Chee-hash-kish, Geronimo took a 3rd wife, Nana-tha-thtith, who was also a Bedonkohe. They had one child. In the fall of 1861, their home camp in Arizona was attacked by Mexican Troops. Many were killed including Nana-tha-thtith and their child. Geronimo and Chee-hash-kish managed to escape. During that time, Geronimo and other Bedonkohe took up residence among the Chiricahua Apaches and married into that tribe. Geronimo then acquired his 4th wife; she was a Chiricahua/Nednai and a sister of Edwin Yahnozha (1865-?). Both siblings were closely related to Cochise and Naiche. After a stay at the Warm Springs reservation, Geronimo and his group eventually settled in the area of Apache Pass, Arizona. During that period, he took on his 5th wife, Shtsha-she, a Bedonkohe Apache. Subsequently he married his 6th wife, Zi-yeh a Nednai Apache. Geronimo and Zi-yeh had two children, a son Fenton Geronimo (1882-1897), and a daughter Eva Geronimo, born in 1889, both of whom died at Fort Sill.

In August 7, 1885, while camped in the mountains of old Mexico, west of Casas Grandes, they were attacked by Indian scouts under Major Wirt Davis's command. One boy was killed and nearly all the remaining women and children were captured. Among those captured were Geronimo's 6th wife Zi-yeh, and their son Fenton and his daughter Lulu by his 2nd wife Chee-hash-kish.

In Nov of 1885, Geronimo took several women from Fort Apache, among these were Ih-tedda, "Young Girl," a Mescalero, whom Geronimo took as his 7th wife and who later became the mother of Lenna and Robert Geronimo; and Biyaneta Tse-dah-dilth-thlilth, whom Perico took as his wife and who later became the mother of Dolly and Isabel Perico.

In Sep of 1886, when Geronimo and Naiche surrendered to General Miles, Geronimo's wife Ih-tedda and his son Chappo and Chappo's family surrendered as well.[1"] Chappo's wife Hohchlon (Nahd-clohnh) and their infant daughter died mysteriously in Florida. By then, Zi-yeh and her children had already been shipped to Florida as prisoners of war. Zi-yeh died in Fort Sill in 1904.

In 1889, while in the Mt. Vernon Barracks, Geronimo consented to let Ih-tedda return to her people at the Mescalero Agency in New Mexico, which the authorities permitted her to do so. This separation was equivalent to a divorce and she remarried soon after she got there. She also kept their two small children Robert and Lenna. Robert was the youngest and was born the year that Ih-tedda went back. Geronimo then married his 8th wife name not recalled *(perhaps Francesca)* but they could not live in harmony and separated about December 1905.

In 1907, he married his 9th wife Azul, a Chiricahua Apache. Azul lived with Geronimo in Perico's Village at Fort Sill, Oklahoma until Geronimo's death from pneumonia on Feb. 17, 1909.[1"]

Filled with excitement, I asked the librarian if I could make copies of the photographs. I was told that the collection's donor did not authorize the library to do so. Unfortunately they did not have a contact number for him. Honored but disappointed, I continued looking through the rest of the photographs. A lot of them pertained to the fort and other unrelated issues. I left the library with a sense of ambivalence not knowing if the Apache in question was the feared leader or someone else.

The next day I headed to the library at Castillo de San Marcos, formerly Fort Marion. There, I met with Officer Amy Harper, the Park Ranger I had spoken on the phone days earlier. She appeared to have a great deal of knowledge about the former Indian prisoners kept there, which included the Apaches, Kiowas and Seminoles. I told Ms. Harper that I had seen Mr. Bruce's collection at the Historical Library and expressed to her my disappointment when I found out I was not allowed to copy any of the photographs. To my surprise Ms. Harper said *"I know the gentleman that dropped them off. I have his information and will gladly give it to you. He may allow for you to make copies."* After getting his name and number, Officer Harper proceeded to give me a tour of the fort. It included a visit to a cell-room where an Apache Crown Dancer had been carved on the coquina stonewall. The carving was so faded that unless shown, I would have missed it. Indeed, it appeared to be the same figure I had seen in a photograph a day earlier at the Library. Once done, I thanked Officer Harper for her time and the sharing of such historical information.

Carving of Crown Dancer on Fort Marion's prisoner's cell wall
Pictures from F.W. Bruce/Cleve Powell collection.

Fort Marion's Prison Cell, where Crown Dancer was carved ****
Circa. 2006

227

VISIT TO ST. AUGUSTINE, FLORIDA

That evening while in my hotel room, I called the gentleman who had donated the photo collection. His name was Cleve Powell, a retired Corps Engineer and the great-grandson of F.W. Bruce. Mr. F.W. Bruce was also an Engineer with the U.S. Army in St. Augustine, Florida in 1886 and was titled "Fort Keeper." Mr. Powell remembers his mother telling him about her grandfather, F.W. Bruce, having met Geronimo at Fort Marion.

Mr. Powell explained how he received a box belonging to his great-grandfather. In it he found a bound book with letters and pictures dating back to 1885-88. A few days later, I received an e-mail from Mr. Powell repeating how the photo collection came to him. *"I am glad I took the time to dig through a box belonging to my great-grandfather's nearly rotten clothes. In it I found an old valise lined with a 1932 newspaper (dated a few days after he died) with at least 200 miscellaneous photos stuffed in it, no order and very few marked."* Among those pictures were the ones he turned over to the St. Augustine Historical Society Library. His contribution is greatly appreciated. I am honored for the trust he bestowed upon me, when he allowed me to share with the reader those rare and special captured moments.

In May of 2006, Hugh and Lorraine Evans along with their grand-daughter Hailey Ahidley returned to Florida. They came to visit their daughter Nena, who lived with her husband and two children in St. Petersburg, Florida. On the first weekend of May, I along with my children drove up to meet with them. Our much anticipated reunion was filled with joy, laughter, the sharing of stories and food. That evening, prior to going to sleep, we made plans to go to the beach the following day.

The next morning after breakfast, Nena suggested going to a park in Pinellas County called Sandy Key. It was known for its beautiful native landscape and pristine shores. With enough food to feed an army we left Nena's home and drove to the beach. Upon arrival, we were greeted by dozens of coconut palms that gently swayed with the early morning breeze. The sand was mixed with multicolor shells that glittered in the sunlight. After unloading our coolers and beach chairs, we proceeded to set our umbrellas. Under their cool shade, the adults sat and enjoyed watching the children play in the shallow waters of the Tampa Bay.

Jose Second's descendants relaxing at a Florida Beach, ca. 2006
L to R: Emily, Siggy, Lance, Hailey, Lorraine, Aiden, Camren, Nena.
Photographed by Hugh Evans

While sitting on that white and glittering sandy beach, I thought about the gifts that life had given me. It was amazing to see how the family had reunited. I thought about my grandfather Jose Second, and how his sacrifices were not in vain. It was his will to live that made it possible for all of us to be there that day. The sharing of food and laughter brought us closer together. I felt a sense of happiness and accomplishment knowing that I had mended my family's broken circle.

Finally, I could rest assured that at least for a few more generations it would stay that way. Our get-together went well, the family bonded and a sad feeling was felt by all of us when the time came to part ways. The children began to smile when they found out that a month later they would see each other again in Mescalero.

Monticello – Mescalero

Chapter Thirty Five

In the summer of 2006, my children Emily and Lance were off from school and counting the days to go to New Mexico. They could not wait to see Hailey, Camren and Aiden and the week-old addition to the family, Hailey's newborn sister Rema. We flew into El Paso, Texas on the 27th of June. We then drove to Monticello, New Mexico. We arrived at the Monticello Box Ranch in the late afternoon. Upon our arrival, we were treated to a homemade cooked dinner by Denny and Trudy O'Toole, the owners of the ranch. While sitting in the dining room, we experienced a rain shower that lasted approximately fifteen minutes. That was the first time in all the years of visiting the canyon that I had seen any rainfall at all. The O'Tooles informed me that they had seen a lot of rain, and that there was plenty more to come.

After dinner, we sat and watched a brand new DVD movie about Lozen "Warrior Woman". The well-made documentary was mostly filmed at the Monticello Canyon. The true story covered accurately some of the events that took place in the late 1870's when Victorio, Lozen's brother, was in charge of the Warm Springs Apache band. In the film, a young Lozen was portrayed by none other than Lozen Enjady, a descendant from Victorio's bloodline. An all Apache cast, along with interviews with other Victorio's descendants , made the movie into a memorable and historical masterpiece. A touching moment was during an interview with Victorio's great-granddaughter. As tears ran down her face, she spoke of the struggles and sacrifices encountered and endured by Victorio and his band. The movie depicted lots of memorable and sacred places along with sad scenes, but it was Victorio's great-granddaughter's stories and tears that touched me the most.

Another piece of footage of great value was played by Harlyn Geronimo, as he showed how the sacred red clay of the Chiennes was mixed with water prior to its application. He also demonstrated how the paint was drawn across the warrior's face before going into battle. *"It must be applied, from left to right, like the rotation of the earth,"* Harlyn said. By doing so, it provided the warriors with a psychological shield that assured them success in battle and a safe return home.

In another scene, the narrator stood on the grounds where the old Warm Springs Apache Agency once stood. In the background one could still see what was left of the old adobe walls that once made up the Agency building. That scene made my mind wonder, as I had unsuccessfully searched for that site for many years. At that moment I knew I had something out there to look for. After watching the stunning documentary, my children and I headed back to our guesthouse, where we called it a night.

The next morning we woke up at sunrise and after a light breakfast we headed out in search of adventure. The unusual heavy rains from the previous days had turned the canyon road into a muddy and challenging drive, even for our Jeep. Also affected by odd amounts of rain was the beauty of the landscape that surrounded us. I was amazed at the variety and number of blooming flowers along the river's bank and the lush and colorful vegetation growing on the mountains. The overwhelming presence of life made the canyon look more beautiful than ever. The Alamosa River water was deeper than normal but still low enough for a safe drive.

Half way through the canyon, we decided to stop and do some rock climbing. My son Lance wanted to hike up a familiar trail that led to a series of caves. His determination and skills not only impressed me but made me feel proud.

231

Siggy teaching Lance the art of climbing
Monticello Canyon, NM, ca. 2006

After our climb, we got back in your vehicle and continued our drive. The rough and challenging excursion ended a few miles later, when we reached the open valley, which had turned into a field of flowers.

First on my mind was to find an undiscovered spring. Ironically, I had learned about it through my English friends, the ones I had met in the canyon back in April of 2005. According to instructions, the hidden spring, similar to Ojo, laid behind some rolling hills.

Siggy and Lance standing in front of a spring, Monticello, NM, ca. 2006

I parked my vehicle and the three of us followed the directions I had been given. Sure enough, after a strenuous hike, we reached a mound that covered the old spring, which measured approximately fifteen square feet. The foot-deep water was mostly covered by a thick layer of algae. Before touching the water, I had a prayer, which is always done in the presence of such a life giver. I found the water to be slightly cooler than its neighboring Ojo Caliente Spring. It was obvious that the new-found spring had not seen much human activity. After drinking the water, and taking some memorable picture, we proceeded to return to our Jeep.

Although a couple of hours had gone by, we still had a whole day ahead of us. After a short drive, we began hiking in search of the old Warm Springs Apache Agency ruins. After a couple of miles of mountaineering in different directions, we came upon a mesa. Once on it, I was able to see the ruins that once made up the entire government agency. Some of the crumbled walls had turned into small mounds of dirt. Others still retained their definition, clearly showing multiple rows of adobe bricks. The tallest wall stood about five feet tall, its "L" shape revealed what was once the corner of a room or building.

Out of all the places in the canyon that I had visited over the years, this one felt different, as an uneasy feeling came over me. Somehow I felt I was looking at a battlefield. Afraid to walk on such fragile archeological site, we satisfied ourselves by taking pictures from a distance.

Knowing that time waits for no one or nothing and that all we are is dust in the wind encouraged me to captured the moment as a testament of time and a witness to something that inevitably will be gone.

Warm Springs Apache Agency Ruins
Monticello, NM, ca. 2006
****

While standing on those sacred grounds, I took the opportunity to teach my children about the origin of our bloodline. For some unknown reason, I felt a connection with the place and its ruins. I told them that it was there that our ancestors were born, lived, fought and died on. While telling those stories, I realized that despite all the misfortunes that happened there, it was also a place of joy and birth. Among those possibly born there was the one that gave us our genes, our great-grandmother Kukah, Jose's daughter. With a sense of joy we made the long hike back feeling like a walk in the park.

We then drove to Ojo Caliente Spring for a much needed soak. While soaking and relaxing in the warm pool, I noticed lots of black clouds moving in. Knowing that the ground was already heavily saturated from previous monsoons, I decided it was best to return to our cabin.

Shortly after our arrival, the heavy rains began. In less than an hour the slow moving water of the Cañada Alamosa River became raging white water. With just enough food to last a few days, I began to think of stories I had heard from canyon residents where people were trapped in their homes for weeks due to flash floods - not a foreign concept for me, as I was used to similar circumstances that we Floridians have experienced during hurricanes. Although both catastrophes are different, they share a similar concept. They both required preparation and patience. That night our small meal left us all hungry. I wanted to stretch our food, just in case we got stranded for a prolonged period of time. My children and I were aware that some rough days laid ahead.

While in bed that evening, I could hear the river's roaring sounds intensifying. The next morning we got to see and experience a raging river out of control. I placed a stone on the river's edge to monitor the water level. Two days later, I noticed that the water was slowly receding. To my surprise on the third day, we woke up to a cloudless blue sky. The river's water was back to normal. Without hesitating, we packed and drove out. The twenty-mile drive tested our Jeep to its limits. More than three decades of four-wheeling through the Florida swamps paid off. Although I came very close to getting stuck, I managed to get out of the canyon without getting my feet dirty.

Once on a paved road, we counted our blessings, and began our drive towards Mescalero. A few hours later, we entered the dreaded Valley of Fire. Upon our arrival at the visitor center, we were greeted by some folks who began taking pictures of the Jeep; it appeared that they were more impressed with the looks of our vehicle than that of the Valley. Once we stepped out of the Jeep, I realized what the big deal was about. Ironically, our vehicle looked like a camouflage war tank; the only spot not covered with dry mud was made by the windshield wipers. After the much needed break, we continued our drive towards Mescalero, passing the small towns of Bonito, Alto, and Ruidoso. In Ruidoso, I drove the muddy Jeep through a car wash and brought back to life its original silver color.

We then drove to Second Canyon, arriving at Lorraine's house close to 2:00pm. As soon as Hailey saw my kids, she ran towards them and gave them a hug. Within minutes she had produced two other bikes for all of them to go riding. It was great to watch them ride up and down the dirt road being chased by the three house dogs. That evening we sat at Lorraine's house and caught up with the latest.

The next day, feeling good and rested, we drove out to visit the Carrillo family. I wanted my children to meet them and vice versa. While Carson and I talked about the first time we met, my boy Lance and Carson's grandson Raymond played in their front yard.

MONTICELLO - MESCALERO

It felt great introducing my children to a family that meant so much to me.

After lunch, we headed to the Feast Grounds. That year, James' camp was built inside the sacred grounds. Also different was the fact that the brush arbor and the Crown Dancer's Tepee were adjacent to each other. Both structures were located about two hundred feet from Lorraine's camp and the eastern entrance of the dance arena. After showing my children where the camp was, I told them to sit at the bleachers while I prepared for the evening dance.

Upon entering the arbor, I found all singers and dancers gathered around a wooden table. Although I was greeted with enthusiasm, I sensed that something was wrong or different. Soon I found out what it was. Leroy Coonie, our oldest singer, had fallen ill and was not doing well.

James said that he had gone to the hospital to see Leroy and that he wanted for us to carry on and sing with or without him. I also learned that Leroy was sent home to be cared by his family. After talking for a while, we entered the tepee and began our preparations for the evening's Crown Dance. It was hard for me to look at the spot where Leroy normally sat. His absence left me with an empty feeling. I prayed that my old friend would pull through. I thought about his soft demeanor and the pictures we had taken together years earlier. The pleasant memories brought a grin to my face. Once our preparations were done, we headed out. That year our group was the first out again, and by 10:00pm we were done for the night.

The next morning, an overwhelming feeling came over me. I wanted to see Leroy but did not know where he lived, other than deep in the mountains of White Tail. I also thought it would be a great opportunity for my children to see and learn about such a significant place.

By 10am, we found ourselves driving on the dirt road that led to White Tail. As we drove up, the beauty intensified with each mile driven, thus making the trip an enjoyable experience. In a blink of an eye, we had reached the outskirts of the former Chiricahua Village, a place lost in time and rich in history. It was hard for my children to find much amusement there, as most of the structures that once made a vibrant community lay crumbled on the ground. Just like Carson had done with me, I told them of the importance of the place. I am not sure if they were able to grasp so much history in such a short amount of time, but I told them anyway.

I drove around White Tail for a while, but I was not able to find Leroy's home. Even after stopping and asking one of the few residents for directions I was still not able to locate it. Embarrassed to ask again, I continued driving in vain. One thing was for sure, I was getting to know my way around White Tail pretty good. Its immense beauty was overwhelming and I really didn't mind the adventure.

While coming down a mountaintop, I spotted a pickup truck driving on a nearby canyon. After a long pursuit, I caught up to the vehicle driven by a local resident. I asked the gentleman for directions to Leroy's place. *"Follow me, I will take you to it,"* he kindly responded. Amazingly, he drove to the only place I had missed. About an eighth of a mile later, he pointed to a gate and waved at me as he drove away. Once at the gate I was able to see Leroy's blue Ford pickup truck. I drove to the house and I told my children to stay in the vehicle. I walked up to the front door, where I was greeted by Leroy's family. Shortly after, I was taken to one of the bedrooms to see him. There I found my old friend laying in bed watching a small black and white TV. I grabbed his hand and I said, *"Well, here I am again, I heard you were sick so I came up to say hello."* He nodded his head and whispered *"Thank you."*

L to R: Siggy Second-Jumper, Leroy Coonie, Carl Kazhe, Joey Kazhe
Mescalero Apache Reservation, ca. 2004

Not knowing what else to say, I sat quietly and watched TV with him for a while.
Coincidently they were showing a hunting program that was filmed in Indiantown,
Florida. It consisted of a few camouflaged hunters getting ready to shoot a water buffalo.
Nothing was wrong with that, except that the animal grazed peacefully in a fenced-in
farm. A few moments later, one of the hunters knelt down and whispered into the camera
how he was going to shoot the animal. He looked through the scope of his rifle, held in
his breath as if he was shooting a hummingbird. Instead he was shooting at a motionless,
two-thousand-pound beast, less than three hundred yards away. I took advantage of the
comical opportunity to break the silence. *"Leroy, let me tell you something, that's not
how we all hunt in Florida,"* I said. Although too weak to talk, I was able to bring a grin
to his face. After ten minutes or so, I got up and stood next to my mentor and friend.
*"Leroy, I have started to write a book about the Chiricahuas and I would like to write
about you and perhaps use the picture that we took together. Would that be OK with
you?"* I said. He nodded his head, squeezed my hand and whispered *"Yes."* I said
"Thank you." Not knowing what else to say, I excused myself by telling him that my
children were waiting for me outside. *"Thanks,"* he whispered again. I walked out of his
room, half choked up. I acknowledged his family and made my way back to mine. Once
back in the Jeep, my children wanted to know how he was doing. *"He is very sick, but he
is in good hands. His family is taking good care of him,"* I said.

We drove down the mountain, reaching Lorraine's home in less than an hour.
Once there, my children were able to run and play and burn some of that endless energy.
After a few hours of fun, we all headed out to the Feast Grounds as we did on the
previous day. Once I got my children situated, I headed out to James' camp. There, I
told everyone I had visited Leroy.

After talking for a while with the other singers, I headed back to the bleachers to spend time with my children. While sitting on the bleachers, I noticed Kathleen Kanseah walking in. We all sat with her in the V.I.P. section to talk. She was as kind to my children as she has always been to me. During our conversation, Kathleen invited us to come to her eightieth birthday in September. I told her, I made no promises, but that I was going to try really hard to make it.

Later that afternoon, I reported to James' camp with my children. Both of them were welcomed and fed by the group. After a nice warm meal, they returned to the bleachers, as I stayed behind to prepare for the evening dance. Right as the sun set, our group was ready to go. Soon after the sacred fire was lit, we entered the dance arena.

We sat on the wooden benches facing east. To my right sat Vernon, on my left sat a new singer, a young teenage boy with long hair and wearing glasses. James introduced him to me and said that the young man was related to me. I looked at him and couldn't help to think of our oldest singer Leroy Coonie. In a bizarre way the young man was there to carry on for Leroy and we all knew it and welcomed him. A few minutes later, James' voice echoed through the night and the dancers fell in rhythm to the beat of our drums. Being thankful for the moment, I began to sing my heart out. One thing was for sure, I could not predict nor control the future, but at that moment the Chiricahuas were alive and well and I felt proud and rejoiced. Our session ended by 10:00pm. Once done we all headed back to our hotel. There, my children wanted to know who the young man that sat next to me was. I told them that the new singer was related to us.

The next day, we drove up to Cloudcroft, a small town that borders the reservation. Once there we enjoyed the beauty and serenity of a waterfall at a public park. After spending time there, we drove down to Second Canyon where we met up with our family. Again, my children enjoyed playing and riding bikes under the watchful eyes of the three family dogs. Once they got tired, we headed down to the Feast Grounds where we fell into our routine.

While we were eating, the new singer showed up. I introduced him to my children and we enjoyed each other's company. I explained to the young man how significant his timing was, somehow he knew. When the time came for me to go into the tepee, my children walked over to the bleachers and waited for our group to finish with preparations. The night moved on and a short time later, it had all come to an end.

The next day as we prepared to return home, Vernon Simmons said he had something for my children. After a short walk to his car, he opened the trunk and gifted them some custom-made T- shirts. They read "Chiricahua Warrior" and it showed a War Dancer dressed in an old traditional outfit. *"Here, wear this to school and show them who you are,"* he proudly said. His noble action touched me deeply. With a sense of sadness, my children and I walked away. It was obvious they didn't want to leave.

As we drove away on Highway 70, my children began to express to me what I had been feeling since the first day I arrived in Mescalero. They both couldn't wait to return the following year. What impressed them the most was the love and warmth they had received. Knowing exactly what they meant I said, *"Well, we will just have to come back for more."* While driving through the Tularosa Valley, I saw bolts of lightning shooting across the Sacramento Mountains. It was obvious that heavy rains were coming. Within days of our departure Leroy passed away. He will be greatly missed.

That summer, New Mexico experienced record-breaking rainfall. One monsoon after another brought rains for weeks without a break. Down in Monticello Canyon, some of the residents were trapped for weeks in their homes.

The tamed Alamosa River which normally runs inches deep and no more than six or eight feet in width, became a raging white river. Water levels reached fifteen hundred feet wide, and fifteen feet deep. Elderly Canyon natives did not recall ever seeing anything like it during their life time. Fortunately, by early September the rain stopped. Within days, the water levels and life in the canyon returned to normal.

On the evening of September 14, 2006, I arrived in Mescalero, New Mexico with my friend, Cristina Bilardello. The purpose of our trip was to attend Kathleen Kanseah's birthday. The following day, we drove around the Reservation visiting family and friends.

Among the many people we visited were Carson and Carol Carrillo. It was during our visit that Carol brought out an old photo album filled with memorable pictures. One was of Carson's grandfather, Eugene Chihuahua. The resemblance between Carson and his grandfather was stunning.

Eugene Chihuahua, son of Chief Chihuahua
White Tail, Mescalero.
Photograph donated by his grandson, Carson Carrillo Sr.

L to R: Sam Kenoi, Robert Geronimo, Jr., Eustice Fatty,
William Magoosh, Davis Spitty, Emmit Botella, Art Botella,
Donald Blake, Jess Campbell - Dance Troop from Mescalero
Photographed in Chicago in 1936, and donated by Carol Carrillo

Another photograph that caught my eye was one from 1936. It consisted of a group of Apache dancers from Mescalero. Among them was Sam Kenoi. How ironic! There for the first time, I held in my hands two photographs of the two men who meant so much to me.

Mr. Samuel Kenoi and Mr. Eugene Chihuahua were among a few Chiricahuas who came forward to reveal their recollections to Morris Opler and Eve Ball, two respected writers who wished to tell their tales using their words and account of events. Their valuable stories included seeing ships leaving Florida with Apache children. They also revealed Chiricahua traditions and the location of sacred places.

Their willingness to come forward helped me immensely during the search for my family and my arrival in Mescalero. At the time of their revelations, they were criticized by their peers for publicly sharing such information. Today, their contributions are greatly appreciated not only by me, but by all tribal members. By destiny or fate, it was Samuel Kenoi's daughter, Catherine Kenoi, and her grandson Carlos Enjady, that brought me to Mescalero in the first place.

After leaving the Carrillos', we drove to an open field off Highway 70. It was there that Kathleen's birthday feast was to take place. By the time Cristina and I arrived, the camp was already set. It consisted of a huge arbor surrounded by four tepees. There, we met Kathleen who was sitting inside the arbor surrounded by her family and friends.

KATHLEEN KANSEAH'S BIRTHDAY

Kathleen Kanseah's 80th Birthday Feast
Mescalero Apache Reservation, NM, ca. 2006
****

She was dressed in a blue calico dress and looking more beautiful than ever. Her usual reception was as warm as the fire she sat next to. *"I am so glad that you are here,"* she said, as she welcomed us with a hug and a smile. *"Are you guys hungry?" She asked. "Please allow me to serve you something to eat,"* she said. After spending time with her, I walked over to James' camp to prepare for Kathleen's birthday ceremony. Once done, we came out of the tepee and found a group of Kathleen's family members walking her towards us. They sat her on a chair in front of our lodge as the family stood around her. The look on her face revealed her joy and happiness. James addressed the family and spoke of how honored he was to be part of such a special celebration. After a beautiful speech James proceeded to bless Kathleen, while the Crown Dancers danced for her and her family. In return, Kathleen and her family blessed all the Crown Dancers.

Once that was accomplished, we proceeded towards the dance arena. A few minutes later, our dancers emerged from the darkness of the night. As the dancers did their blessings, the fire grew to a fifteen-foot bonfire. The enormous amount of generated heat felt good on what turned out to be a very cold night. To my left sat the new edition to our group, the young singer, who was related to me. Sitting on my right, was Vernon Simmons as usual. Next to Vernon was Lynn Hank, followed by James Kunestsis. Once the fire was blessed, James' voice thundered through the silence of the night. The dancers danced like never before and our voices grew stronger as the night progressed. Our group's performance ended just before midnight. Vernon and I headed towards his car where we found Cristina and his wife, Della, wrapped in blankets and uncomfortably cold. As we prepared to leave, Vernon asked if we had any plans for the next morning. He wanted to take us to the nearby town of Lincoln to learn more about Billy the Kid.

Chiricahua Crown Dancers at Kathleen Kanseah's Birthday Feast
Mescalero Apache Reservation, ca. 2006
****

As planned, Cristina and I arrived in the early morning hours at the Simmons' home. After crossing the reservation line, we entered the town of Ruidoso, which is adjacent to Lincoln. After leaving Ruidoso's congested area, we entered Lincoln's open country. With each mile driven, an unbelievable beauty began to emerge. The unusual heavy rains from the previous months had created fields of flowers as far as the eyes could see. Vernon told me that all that beauty that surrounded us was once part of the Mescalero Apache Reservation.

In the far horizon, the Capitan Mountains stood as a landmark. A while later we arrived in downtown Lincoln. The place was very small but beautiful. It consisted of approximately ten to fifteen buildings, most of them historical in nature. Among them was the old courthouse. It was there that Billy the Kid, an American Legend, was taken as a prisoner to be hung. Days later, he shot his way out as he escaped leaving behind two dead lawmen.

The four of us entered the old courthouse and proceeded with the self-guided tour. It was great to experience so much American folklore and western history with such dear company. After an enjoyable morning, we headed to the neighboring town of Capitan, another small town made famous by Smokey the Bear, a mascot the United States Forest Service created after a 1950 wild fire in the area of Capitan Gap in the Lincoln National Forest of New Mexico. When the smoke cleared, firefighters found an orphaned tiny black bear cub, burnt and afraid, clinging to a tree. They named the cub "Hotfoot Teddy". The little bear gained nationwide attention and was renamed "Smokey". It has since become a symbol for fire prevention.

In the town of Capitan, we found every form of bear impersonation imaginable. It was obviously the town's theme. After having lunch there, we headed back to Mescalero.

During that drive, Vernon Simmons began to tell stories about the old days. He started with his childhood, as he grew up in White Tail living among his grandmother Hernannie and his adopted grandfather Eugene Chihuahua. Hernannie was a Comanche from Oklahoma who married Eugene Chihuahua, the son of Chief Chihuahua, and a direct descendant of Chief Victorio and "grandson of Katie Kaydahzinne.[1]" Eugene Chihuahua was ten years old when his father, Chief Chihuahua surrendered at Cañon De Los Embudos in 1886. Listening to Vernon speak of his grandfather Chihuahua was important to me. After all, my entire family was among his group.

L to R: young Eugene Chihuahua, son of Chief Chihuahua, next to his uncle Jolsanny, unknown Apache, Apache Curley. Fort Marion, FL, ca. 1886-87
Courtesy of St Augustine Historical Library

Eugene Chihuahua on right working cattle, Fort Sill, Oklahoma
Photograph donated by Lynda A. Sanchez, from Eve Ball's photo collection

Eugene Chihuahua, along with the rest of the Warm Springs/Chiricahua prisoners, summoned enough will power to endure twenty seven long years of imprisonment. The last nineteen years of confinement were spent at Fort Sill, Oklahoma where he worked hard raising cattle.

When freedom finally came in 1913, he was a grown man. Eugene and his family were among the two thirds of the group who chose to move to Mescalero, New Mexico. It was Eugene, Naiche and Ace Duklagie who picked White Tail as the site to build their homes and form a community. Vernon began by describing the location of Eugene's four-room house. It was there where he grew up surrounded by love and beauty. As a small boy, Vernon's grandmother forced him to attend Sunday Church in White Tail. His grandfather Eugene on the other hand, did not attend, as he did not believe in praying to the Creator through walls, instead he preferred nature's open space. According to Vernon, Eugene got up every morning at sunrise and walked to his favorite spot for his morning prayers. Vernon remembered a particular Sunday morning when he refused to go to church with his grandmother. Instead, he wanted to follow his grandfather. Although he was only eleven years old, he was able to convince his grandmother of his choice.

That morning, young Vernon followed his grandfather Eugene to his favorite place. There, he learned by watching his grandfather pray the old way. When the prayer was over, he was asked, *"Do you know what I was doing?"* *"Yes, you were praying,"* Vernon replied. *"Yes, I have prayed for water and for the good of the people."* Eugene told young Vernon.

244

On that particular year, a serious drought had left the hayfields with no grass to cut. *"Most of White Tail's community made a living by selling hay and oats."* Vernon said. *"A few days after my grandpa's prayer, a gentle rain fell, which brought some hope and relief to the people and their crops."* Vernon said. From that moment on, Eugene began to patiently teach young Vernon new ways to communicate with Ussen, the Apache God. Under the guidance of his grandfather, Vernon's faith grew stronger. Eugene was a well-respected Medicine Man who took on a huge responsibility as the leader of the White Tail Chiricahua Crown Dance Group. Proudly and with a sense of joy, Vernon began to recollect: *"One morning, my grandfather asked me if I was willing to enter a higher level of spirituality by joining his Crown Dance group. I eagerly accepted the responsibility and became a Clown, a position of power and prestige."* Vernon added.

Eugene Chihuahua's Crown Dance group performing in White Tail, New Mexico.
Robert Ove's photo collection
Photographed by Robert Ove in 1948

Vernon went on to tell me the name of his grandfather's singers. They were Claude Enjady, John Eller, Richard Jolsany, Acie Shanta, and Arnie Mendez. After dancing for four years as a clown, Vernon began to Horn Dance. When his grandfather passed away in 1965, the group was carried on by the late Melford Yuzos. Vernon continued dancing, eventually making his way to lead dancer. A position he held for many years. He retired from dancing and began singing in the late 1960's.

Eugene Chihuahua, visiting his camp-site at Fort Sill, Oklahoma, 1960
Photograph donated by Lynda A. Sanchez from the Eve Ball's photo collection

He also remembered his grandfather going on a trip to Oklahoma to visit his old camp site. Vernon left White Tail when he was approximately sixteen years old. Today, he loves to go there and reminisce about the old days.

After crossing the reservation line on Highway 70, we came upon the tribal gas station. Vernon pointed (south) across the street and showed me where his land was located. *"That area used to be called Snow Spring, named after a spring behind my property,"* he said. As we continued driving on Highway 70, Vernon pointed to Leroy Coonie's White Tail home, which was also located on the southern side of the road, a short distance further. Vernon explained that a lot of the White Tail homes were moved into town. Shortly after, we came across the entrance to the 'Inn of the Mountain Gods' resort and casino. He said the area used to be called 'Pigeon Tank'. While heading west on Highway 70, Vernon told me to pull over as if heading into the Feast Grounds. *"I want to show you something special,"* he said, as he pointed to a green house sitting on a hill. Vernon explained that the structure we were looking at was Eugene Chihuahua's home. Just like Leroy's home, it was brought down from White Tail. It was in that house, that Vernon grew up and received lots of love and warmth. After taking some pictures of Eugene's house, we decided to head on down to Vernon's present home in Mescalero.

KATHLEEN KANSEAH'S BIRTHDAY

Vernon Simmons standing in front of Eugene Chihuahua's home.
It was there that he lived with Chief Eugene Chihuahua and his grandmother Hermannie.
Mescalero Apache Reservation
Circa. 2006
****

Unfortunately, our trip had come to an end. It was a great day, filled with good old memories. I was thankful for the privilege of spending such quality time with a wonderful couple and for the sharing of such historical knowledge. The following notes were given to me by Vernon: Chihuahua's wife Ilth-goz-ey had five children Eugene, Ramona, Emily, Osceola, Tom and probably one more by the name of Mable. Chief Chihuahua was closely related to Kanesewah, Tissnolthtos, and Kaydahzinne. Probably through marriage, to Kaahteney all of whom were regarded as "Uncles" by his children. From Chief Chihuahua's family, only his wife Ilth-goz-ey, his son Eugene and three grandchildren survived to go to Mescalero.

From the Simmons' residence, Cristina and I drove to Lorraine's house where we spent most of the remaining afternoon. Prior to the sun setting, we drove over to the Kathleen's Birthday feast grounds. That evening, everything went as planned and in the same order as on the previous night. The only difference was that we sang and danced harder than ever before. We wanted Kathleen and her family to know how much they were loved. That evening as things came to an end, I sat on the bench with my drum on hand and gave thanks to the Creator for all His gifts. I prayed for my family, Kathleen and everyone dear to me. Upon the conclusion of the feast, Cristina and I began to give our farewell to everyone.

It was during that time that Lynn Hank asked me if I could stop by his house on my way out to Alamogordo. *"I have a gift for your children,"* he said. I arrived at Lynn's house close to 11:00pm.

There I had the pleasure of meeting his mother, Adrianne Hank. It didn't take long for me to see where Lynn got his gifts or Medicine as I called it. *"I finally get to meet you. I have heard so much about you. Berle Kanseah told me of the Cuban-Apache long ago when you first arrived in Mescalero. Have a seat make yourself at home,"* Adrianne said. Besides her warm reception, I sensed that I was meeting someone special, and definitely very traditional. Within minutes she had captured my full attention. Adrianne was full of stories from White Tail. I sat on the couch and listened to her for hours. It was close to 2:00am when I left the Hank's home. Indeed Lynn had a souvenir for my kids, but the true gift was meeting his Mom.

The next morning, Cristina and I drove to the town of Truth of Consequences. After checking into our hotel, we decided to visit Monticello Canyon. I wanted to see what it looked like, after the unusual heavy rains and flooding. Upon our arrival, we found complete devastation; the landscape was totally rearranged by Mother Nature. For the first time, I found myself unable to drive through it. Variable size holes stood in place of the old rocky road. It was obvious that some major force had gone through. Indeed, the canyon had changed. The natural transformation had made the canyon look more beautiful than ever. Its mountains were covered in green, and multicolor flowers never before seen, bloomed under a cerulean sky. Because we were unable to travel through Monticello Canyon, we decided to return to T or C to enjoy some of the activities that the small town offered. We visited the famous Geronimo Springs along the Rio Grande and enjoyed soaking at one of the local hot mineral springs.

Next on our agenda, was visiting Silver City. To get there, we drove across the small towns of Kingston, San Lorenzo, and Mimbres. The beautiful forested area was surrounded with tall mountains covered in green. *"We are now entering the heart of Apache country. To be more specific, it once belonged to the Mimbreños-Warm Springs Chiricahua Apaches. To break it down even further, it was home to Mangas Coloradas and Victorio. Two of the greatest leaders the Warm Springs Band ever had,"* I proudly said to Cristina.

We were about to enter Silver City when our beautiful and scenic ride suddenly ended when we came upon a very ugly and sad scene. It consisted of a huge hole in the ground, with similar characteristics as the Grand Canyon. The only difference was that the canyon we were looking at was made by Man out of greed, instead of God's creation out of love, like the Grand Canyon of Arizona. It was hard to believe that I was looking at an area once covered by the same sacred mountains and forest that Mangas Coloradas fought so hard to preserve.

Cristina who was not aware that such devastation was caused by mining thought that the multi color layers on the scratched rocky walls looked beautiful. I on the other hand saw it as the type of sacrilege that would make any Indian cry. Not a single tree lived in such devastation. Sadly in the background, a line of tall pines awaited their fateful day.

A brochure at a local store gave specific information in reference to the ugly truth behind such destruction. The free pamphlets made for tourists revealed how hundreds of thousands of copper pounds were produced by those mountains yearly. It proudly stated being the second biggest producer of copper in the world. I felt ashamed in the presence of so much greed. Immediately, I thought about Red Paint Canyon. What my eyes were seeing was the perfect example of what Red Paint Canyon could have looked like had mining been permitted. As feelings of sadness and bitterness came over me, I started thinking about today's American issues, such as terrorism and immigration.

09/19/2006

Copper Mine, Silver City, NM
Circa. 2006
****

There in front of us was a perfect example of the countless acts of terrorism that started in 1492 and continued to this day. Plans of erecting a fence across the Mexican-U.S. border to control immigration are supported by most Americans. An act designed to prevent the rightful owners of the southwestern states to enter their native homelands. Indeed a fence should have been erected, long ago. Just ask an Indian or a Mexican what happens when you don't control immigration.

Luckily, a short distance later, I began to see the beauty of the Gila Wilderness in the distant horizon. I allowed that beauty to embrace my spirit, leaving behind all that ugliness and negative energy. We continued our trip until our arrival at a beautiful cabin tucked deep in the pine forest of Piños Altos, a small town north of Silver City. Once settled in, we sat on the porch and enjoyed the serenity I yearned for.

The next day we drove into the Gila Wilderness, the heart of Apache country. Hidden deep in that forest was the Gila Dwellings. Although I had visited it before, it never ceased to amaze me. After visiting the dwellings, I decided to show Cristina the other side of the park.

It was there in that area along the Gila River that Geronimo was born. Like all Apache boys, he began to learn the art of warfare and survival. A necessary required to face the many challenges that life would present him with. Little did he know that such training would forge him into the most feared Indian in American history.

Small monument honoring Geronimo's birthplace, Gila, NM ****

After giving Cristina a brief introduction, we began our hike towards the Middle Fork Springs, a trip that required crossing the Gila River multiple times. During the first crossing, we found sudden drops in the bottom of the river, perhaps caused by the previous flooding. By holding our hands and using walking sticks we managed to make it on to the other side. Once back on solid grounds, we continued our hike in search of the hidden spring. A while later our trail came to an end, forcing another cross-over. That time the water came above our waist. We held hands again and made it safely to the other side. After a few more crossings we reached the hot springs.

Gila Hot Springs after the big floods in summer of 2006 ****

That time, they looked very different, as the manmade soaking pools made out of stones were gone. The previous floods had swept them away, thus returning everything to nature's way. A small but steady stream of steaming water protruded from the mountain's edge. It ran about a foot wide and about thirty feet long and into the cold water of the Gila River. The spring water was so hot that just a light touch could have easily scalded. That same hot water used to be cooled off by various manmade dug out trenches from the Gila River. The mixture created different water temperatures which allowed people to sit where they felt most comfortable. Since the soaking pools were gone, we consoled ourselves by sitting on the banks of the river, where the two streams met. There, we enjoyed the surrounding beauty under a partly cloudy sky. After an hour of total relaxation we began our hike back to the car and ultimately back to our cabin.

The next morning we headed out towards the Gila again. Before getting there, we decided to stop at a local restaurant in downtown Piños Altos. Once done, we walked across the street to visit an old fort named Santa Rita del Cobre-Fort Webster. It was built in 1834 by Francisco Elquea as a private Mexican fort to protect the Santa Rita Copper Mines from Apache attacks. In 1851, it was renamed Fort Webster to control the Apaches and to protect the US-Mexican Boundary Commission.

Santa Rita del Cobre Fort 1834-185 later renamed Fort Webster in 1851 ****
Piños Altos, NM, ca. 2006

After a short visit of the old fort and shopping through the various gift shops in the area, we headed out. Shortly after, we found ourselves on Mountain Spirit Highway, a road that cuts through the middle of the Gila Wilderness and one that took us to Lake Roberts. The manmade reservoir sat in the middle of a forested oasis. It provided all sorts of water-related activities, which we took advantage of.

From there we headed to Mimbres, and ultimately to San Lorenzo. In-between the two small towns a beautiful waterfall caught our attention. The natural beauty was known to locals as Bear Creek Waterfall. The forty-foot water drop and an azure and cloudless sky in the background made the sight look like a postcard.

Bear Creek Waterfall, Gila, NM
Photographed by Cristina Billardello

Once out of San Lorenzo we got on the main highway and back to our lodge. We sat on our cabin's porch, and reminisced on all that we had seen and experienced. The next morning, a sad reality set in as we drove back east towards El Paso, Texas and ultimately to Florida.

Seminole Cattle Drive
Chapter Thirty Seven

In November of 2006, I was called upon to help my Seminole friend Sam Frank with a cattle drive. I along with my children arrived at the Seminole Big Cypress Reservation, where I met with a group of about fifteen other people, mostly Seminole tribal members. That cattle drive was primarily done for the purpose of counting the newborns. The hard but fun work involved flushing about four hundred head of cattle from thousands of swampy and wooded acres into large holding pens.

On that particular drive, a combination of the old and new ways was applied. The old ways consisted of cowboys on horseback and flushing dogs, aided by the modern ways of Sam and me flushing cattle with our trucks.

Sam Frank's Cattle Drive
Big Cypress Seminole Reservation, ca. 2006
****

The combined way was a different experience for me, but I must admit it was a lot of fun. I am not sure which part I liked most, the driving of the cattle or four-wheeling through the thick splashy mud. At any rate, the work got done and within a couple of hours, we had the entire livestock rounded and heading towards the holding pens.

Once there, the cowboys separated the newborns away from their mothers. My daughter kept a head count of the young steers and heifers. While pinned on the ground, all of them got their ears cut while the young bulls got castrated. The scrotums and testicles were quickly devoured by the working dogs. When all was said and done, the young ones got released to their awaiting mothers.

SEMINOLE CATTLE DRIVE

The next cattle drive happened in March of 2007. The purpose of that drive was for branding and vaccinations. Once the livestock was rounded into the holding pens, they were led into a hydraulic mechanical holder that pinned the animal, rendering it unmovable. While held down, some animals had their ears tagged. All livestock was vaccinated by a hired veterinarian. These cattle drives were indeed a lot of work but also a lot of fun. Most importantly, they created a sense of community, as Seminole families and tribal members gathered to lend a helping hand to each other.

Among a new breed of cattle owners are the Seminole women. Sam's daughter, Sunshine Frank is among those pioneers. Her desire to step in and continue with such a Seminole tradition is worth honoring. I am proud to have been part of her inauguration when I went with her father to Lorida, Florida to buy her first herd of cattle.

Sam Frank (Panther Clan) and daughter Sunshine Frank (Big Town Clan) ****
Big Cypress Seminole Reservation, ca. 2006

SEMINOLE CATTLE DRIVE

Among the many Seminole Cowboys that welcomed Sunshine into such a male dominant trade was Mr. Richard Bowers Jr. (Panther clan), former president of the Seminole Cattle Association and newly elected president of the Seminole Tribe of Florida. "Mr. Bowers is a third-generation cattle owner, who loves to reminisce about those early years when his grandfather Joe Bowers along with Frank Shore and Dick Bowers became cattle owners. Richard, who started riding horses and working with cattle by the age of four, remembers how his father loaded his horse in the back of his pickup truck and headed to work. Meals for the working cowboys consisted of beef from fresh kill. Those in need were given huge pieces of meat to take home. The rest was given away to needy families. Richard's childhood dream of owning cattle became a reality in 1999 when he purchased his own herd and continued with what has become a family and Seminole tradition.

Today, as President of the Seminole Tribe of Florida, Mr. Bowers has taken Seminole Beef to a higher standard. In 2010, the Seminole Tribe stopped selling their cattle to the highest bidder and began packaging their beef under their own label. Their goal is to supply beef to all of the Seminole-owned Hard Rock Restaurants in the world."[7]

Richard Bowers Jr. (Panther Clan)
President of the Seminole Tribe of Florida and
of the Seminole Cattle Association
Photographed by Gordon O. Wareham (Panther Clan)

255

"Blessing Feast"
Stronghold, Arizona – March 24-25, 2007
Chapter Thirty Eight

In mid February 2007, I received a phone call from Vernon Simmons inviting me to attend a Blessing Feast. Based on the details, I realized that this was not an ordinary feast, but one with a potential of becoming a very significant and historical event. What made it so special was the fact that it was going to be held at the Stronghold in the Dragoon Mountains of Arizona. Among the many sacred Chiricahua Mountains found throughout Apache country, the Stronghold was the most sacred of all, especially to those Chiricahua Apaches from Cochise's band. Filled with eagerness and anticipation, I accepted the invitation.

On March 21, I arrived in Mescalero, New Mexico and began visiting family and friends. It was nice to see that everyone was doing well. Attending the feast was everyone's favorite topic around the reservation. On Friday the 23rd at 5:30am, I arrived at the Simmons' home where I found Vernon, his wife Della and son, Cyrus, along with their granddaughter, waiting and ready to go. Soon after, the two-car caravan began the southwesterly trip across the two states.

Once on Highway I-10, I noticed a huge storm brewing in the western horizon. The sky was black and streaks of lightening were seen every now and then. Under black clouds and a soft rain, we arrived in Wilcox, Arizona in the late morning hours. Unable to check-in due to our early arrival, we decided to go for a ride and see old historical Fort Bowie.

L to R: Cyrus Simmons, Vernon Simmons, Siggy Second-Jumper
Fort Bowie, AZ, ca. 2007
Photographed by Della Simmons

256

BLESSING FEAST

The old Fort was about an hour east of Wilcox. With plenty of room in my Dodge Durango, the five of us drove away. Less than an hour later, we found ourselves looking at Apache Pass cut through the heart of Fort Bowie's general area. Upon arrival, we learned that in order for us to see the old Fort ruins, we had to go on a three-mile round trip hike. With black skies and frequent lightning, we realized it was not going to be an enjoyable experience. Instead, we satisfied ourselves by exploring the old Butterfield Stage Coach Route which cut through the famous Apache Pass, referred to by Mexicans as Puerto Del Dado which means, literally translated, The Doorway of Dice. An apt name, for it was a toss-up whether or not a man could go through the pass without losing his life. White settlers on their way west referred to it as the West's Bloodiest Pass. It was hard to believe that such a quiet place was once filled with chilling Chiricahua war cries. Even harder to believe was the fact that the dry earth I stood on was once soaked with blood, sweat and tears.

Among the many incidents that took place there, none are more memorable than the infamous Bascom Affair. On February 6, 1861, eight men leading a wagon train west were killed by Apaches. Two days before, Lieutenant George Bascom had dishonored Apache leader Cochise by accusing him of theft and kidnapping, a simple misunderstanding that became known as the "Bascom Affair." Such accusation not only angered but prompted Cochise and the Apache Nation to go on the warpath and spread fear and terror for more than a decade across southern Arizona.

While driving along the gravel road, we found a plaque in front of a tree where a number of Apaches were hung during those hostile years. Similar incidents helped shape Arizona's history. Our exploration was cut short by a lightning storm. Once back in Wilcox, everyone wanted to relax in the hotel's heated pool and jacuzzi. Everyone but me, as my restless spirit was not ready to rest. As soon as I dropped the Simmons' off, I found myself driving towards the Cochise Stronghold, located on the eastern slope of the Dragoon Mountains.

Although I had visited such mountain range years earlier, I found myself entering through a town called Sunsites instead of Tombstone. *"What a beautiful sight,"* I thought, as I drove across a valley that resembled a horseshoe. To my right, or to the west, was Cochise Stronghold, named after one the most feared but yet respected Apache leader of all times... Cochise. On my left, or to the east, were the Chiricahua Mountains, the ancestral land of the Chiricahua Apaches. Directly in front of me, in the far distance, the two sacred mountains seemed to blend together. On both sides of the road, the green grass fields were dotted with multi-color wild flowers. I couldn't help but think how many Apache footprints were underneath all that beauty. The enormous amount of rain from the previous day had created marshes among the tall grasses, where a variety of wild ducks seemed to rejoice. After forty minutes of driving under a soft and gentle rain, I entered the outskirts of the Dragoon Mountains. The majestic range was covered in green with dormant grasses, resembling an outdoor carpet. I was amazed to see how the desert showed gratitude to such a gift like water. The beauty and serenity of the place was overwhelming. The only noise heard was coming from my vehicle as I drove across a few creeks that ran across the road.

A few miles later, I came upon the designated area for the Blessing Feast. It consisted of clear and level field, approximately four acres in size. The arbor, or dance arena had been marked by a huge circle of stones. On the western side of the grounds, I found James Kunestsis' camp under a huge oak tree.

Blessing Feast Site ****
Cochise Stronghold, AZ, ca. 2007

He was wrapped in a blanket and standing next to a small burning fire. While talking to him, I saw the arrival of three other Crown Dancing groups from Mescalero.

About an hour later, I drove up the canyon to meet a family which I had made contact with via e-mails prior to our arrival. I found them to be humble and receptive, and most of all delighted with the rain, which they associated with life and the arrival of the Chiricahuas. According to them, a miracle had taken place, as almost four inches of rain had fallen in less than twenty-four hours. That amount of rain had created mini flash floods and caused dry waterfalls to flow again. By the end of my visit, the gentle rain had ceased and the skies began to clear.

I returned to the feast site and found a great number of newly arrived Chiricahuas making camp. Among them were Freddie Kaydahzinne, his wife Edith along with their children Bo and Kristen. What a great feeling it was to be with them and watch everyone with big smiles on their faces. Soon after, the Kaydahzinnes' jumped in my vehicle and I took them to meet the same canyon residents that had so eagerly greeted me. Freddie and his family were treated with joy and kindness. It was clear that a special relationship was about to be born between canyon residents and the Apaches. After our visit, we all headed back to Wilcox and enjoyed each other's company while having dinner at a local restaurant.

The next morning, Saturday, March 24, I woke up fresh and ready to enjoy the first of the two-day feast. Vernon informed me that a tribal bus full of Chiricahua Apaches was heading to the Chiricahua Mountains for a tour of their ancestral homeland. The Simmons' and I decided to join them as we drove out on our own. The five of us arrived at the park about an hour later. Soon after driving into the park, an amazing beauty began to emerge, as the barren desert turned into thick and lush vegetation, wooded canyons and awe-inspiring sandstone cliffs. As we continued our drive, we noticed a drastic change in the landscape.

It consisted of enormous amount of weirdly-shaped rock pinnacles that filled the higher portions of the park. The unique and splendid beauty of these rocks resulted from a volcanic explosion that took place 30 million years ago. For a better view of that unique phenomenon, we drove to Massai's Point. A place named in honor of a legendary Warm Springs-Chiricahua Apache. *"According to Jason Betzinez and James Kaywaykla, both Chiricahua Apaches and P.O.Ws., Massai was with his people when they were forced to move to San Carlos Reservation in 1877. Alphonso and several other children of Massai were born in San Carlos. Massai was among the peaceful Chiricahuas staying at Fort Apache who were rounded up and sent to Florida by General Miles in September of 1886. However, the day before his group reached St Louis, Missouri, he jumped off the train and headed back by himself on foot to his native Warm Spring country in New Mexico. There he hid in the mountains of the Black Range. He raided the Mescalero Indian reservation, stole a young woman, took her back to the mountains and married her the Indian way. They had 4 children. He remained hidden in the mountains for 25 years. Then one day, he and his older son were out hunting near the old Warm Springs Agency, when they saw a horse in the distance. Massai approached the horse, with the boy quite a distance behind him. The boy later said that when Massai was near the horse, he heard a shot. He didn't wait to find out what happened but ran away and went back to his mother. They didn't know if Massai had been killed or wounded, whether he might have escaped and died later. But they never saw him again. Shortly after, his wife and their 4 children came out of the mountains and returned to her own people at Mescalero in 1911[1]. Today some of Massai's descendants are found among the singers of the Warm Springs Crown Dance group of Mescalero.*

L to R: Cyrus Simmons, Vernon Simmons, Siggy Second-Jumper
Massai's Peak, Chiricahua Mountains, AZ. ca.2007
Photographed by Della Simmons

The view from Massai's Point was spectacular. It consisted of a range of mountains with high ridges and towering pinnacles adorned with naturally carved rings. Although I had visited the park years earlier, it simply did not look the same. As a result of the rain, the color of the pinnacles was rich, like those of a wet stone.

The irresistible beauty prompted us to hike some of the trails that cut through the top of the butte. One in particular, led us to an incredible attraction. It consisted of a huge boulder, perhaps the size of a medium size car in the shape of a top. The huge rock sat on a flat surface perfectly balanced. The miraculous site was referred to as Balance Rock. It was hard to understand and accept how such an odd thing could be real. Exhausted from our hike, we sat to rest and talk about God's creation and our ancestors' ways of life.

Vernon Simmons and Siggy Second-Jumper visiting the Homelands of their Ancestors
Massai's Point, Chiricahua Mountains, AZ, ca. 2007
Photographed by Della Simmons

Once rested, we decided to drive around the park and further explore other places of interest. Within a short time, we found a serious of intriguing corridors, some of them leading to perfect hideouts. Another interesting refuge was a huge cave visible from the main road. The cave was certainly big enough to shelter a group of people. It made us all wondered how many Apaches found protection there in their times of need.

Our discovery drive ended at the visitors center. There we found a group of Chiricahuas from Mescalero gathered in the parking lot. Some of them had driven there on their own like us, while others rode in the comfort of a Mescalero tribal bus. The first people we ran into were Carson and Carol Carrillo. After hugging each other, I took the opportunity to take a picture with my friend, mentor and protector, Carson Carrillo.

Siggy Second-Jumper and Carson Carrillo Sr.
Chiricahua Mountains, AZ, ca. 2007
Photographed by C.Carrillo

After spending some time at the park, we drove back to our hotel in Wilcox, where I had lunch. Once energized, I drove out to the Dragoon Mountain to enjoy the first day of the feast. I arrived at the camp grounds close 3:00pm. An hour later, a small group of canyon residents made their way down to meet everyone. Once we met, I headed to the dance arena to join the war singers and dancers, as they prepared for the 4:00pm show.

While sitting on the bench assembling my drum, I noticed that the skies had cleared and the aroma of new life lingered in the air. It was easy to see how each participant was feeling extra special by their happy demeanor. Once everyone was ready, Freddie Kaydahzinne's powerful voice jump-started the war dancers into motion. It was great to see the warriors dance in their traditional outfits as they told their battle stories through their dance. The ground, still moist, quickly displayed hundreds of foot-prints from toe-guarded moccasins, a site not seen in over a century and a quarter in the land of Cochise. To add to the excitement, the dancers began whooping those chilling war cries. In front of us, on the outskirts of the dance arena, Apaches as well as canyon residents sat quietly and enjoyed the historical event.

When the war singing ended, I headed to James' camp to prepare for the evening Crown Dance. Upon my arrival, I found Lynn Hank setting up camp. It was nice to see my old friend and teacher again.

BLESSING FEAST

Once done, Lynn and I walked over to James' camp where we were greeted by the rest of the group. When all preparations were completed, James began to sing.
The only thing heard between singing breaks were the sound of jingles and singing coming from the other three Crown Dance groups. I wondered what it must have felt like for all those sitting outside, when they heard those sacred songs in such a holy place. Upon the completion of transforming our mortal dancers into sacred beings, we headed over to the dance arena.

Our group was the first out. We sat on the benches and waited for our dancers to emerge from the darkness of the night. They entered the arena from the east and began walking towards us. As they got closer, I began to get goose bumps all over my arms and chills down my spine. *"Are my eyes playing tricks on me?"* I wondered. Unlike something I had ever seen before, the dancers looked like true mountain spirits. This particular photo captured their spirit as I saw it that night.

Chiricahua Crown Dancers at the Blessing Feast
James Kunestsis' group performing at their ancestors' homeland.
Cochise Stronghold, AZ, ca.2007
****

BLESSING FEAST

A few moments later, James Kunestsis' voice echoed through the canyon, and with it, a historical event was born. I took a deep breath and began singing my heart out. Our voices we crisp and clear. The dancers were unbelievable; their feet barely touched the ground. I felt an incredible connection between all of us.

A few minutes later, the ladies entered the arena. Their graceful steps quickly fell in rhythm with the beat of our drums. They danced in a clockwise manner making the fringe of their shawls sway back and forth. It was indeed a unique and magical moment, the energy in the air was indescribable. I felt proud and honored to be part of something so special. All dancers danced like each song was the last and we sang as each song was our first. I thanked the Creator for each and every breath I took that night. The following picture captured some of those special moments.

Chiricahua Crown Dancers at the Blessing Feast
James Kunestsis' group performing at their ancestors' homeland.
Cochise Stronghold, AZ, ca.2007
Photographed donated by Vernon Simmons and chosen by him for the book cover

When our session was over, another group made its way into the arena. The men were followed by the other two groups who danced into the early morning hours. That night I stayed in the vehicle and prayed myself to sleep.

In the morning, I was awakened by the sound of chirping birds and the smell of coffee coming from a nearby camp. The weather was beautiful with partly cloudy skies and a gentle cool breeze. With plenty of time on my hands, I decided to drive to Fort Bowie and take the three-mile hike to see the old Fort's ruins.

Once I got there, I decided to further explore the area by driving through the back roads that encircled the fort. My curious nature paid off, as one of the roads led me to the fort's gated side entrance. I got out of my vehicle, jumped over the gate and found myself all alone in complete serenity. The only sound heard came from the flapping of an American flag that flew high on a pole in the center of the fort.

Chiricahua Apaches held here as Prisoners of War in 1886
Fort Bowie ruins, Fort Bowie, AZ, ca. 2007
****

As I walked through the grounds, I observed a multitude of buildings going through various stages of deterioration. None of the structures had roofs on them. All that remained of the original buildings were partial walls. Some were as high as six feet tall while others had crumbled down to inches. Luckily, most of the ruins had plaques in front of them showing and describing what the buildings used to look like and what they were used for. The majority of them belonged to different ranking officers, while others served as various workshops

In the center courtyard, a plaque showed a picture of Geronimo among other Chiricahuas. It was sad but real, there I was, at such a historical place. I stood in silence and thought about the long march my ancestors endured from Cañon de los Embudos to those grounds. How ironic and bizarre, I thought, to be standing on the same grounds that my ancestors once stood upon. After spending some time in prayer, I returned to the hotel in Wilcox for a cleanup and lunch.

264

Once refreshed and energized, I headed out to the Dragoon Mountains for the second and last day of the blessing feast. Upon my arrival, I found many more Apaches present than on the previous day. Among the new faces were Vincent and Carol Kaydahzinne. While talking to them, I noticed that a small crowd had gathered inside the arbor to listen to various guest speakers. Sitting among the crowd was Carson and Carol Carrillo. I sat next to them and quietly enjoyed a picture exhibit. It appeared that someone had put together a series of 8 x 10 laminated photos depicting various cave paintings found throughout the mountain range. The pictures were passed around for everyone to see. I found them to be fascinating and informative.

Soon after, an announcement was made welcoming the next speaker. I sat there and witnessed the arrival of Silas Cochise, the great-grandson of the legendary Chief Cochise. He was wearing brown cowboy boots and hat, blue jeans, and a light blue Guayabera shirt. After attaching a microphone to his shirt, Silas proceeded to address the crowd. He spoke of his great-grandfather, Chief Cochise, and the sacredness in which he held those very own mountains that gave life, joy and refuge to so many Chiricahuas. He mentioned other great leaders such as Mangas Coloradas, Victorio, Chihuahua, Jolsanny, Nana, and Loco. The next topic that Silas spoke about that was heavy in his heart was to know that to this day, the Chiricahua people do not have a place to call home.

L to R: Larry Shay, a Lipan Apache from Mescalero, Siggy Second-Jumper, Silas Cochise, Great Grandson of Chief Cochise. Photographed during the Blessing Feast at Cochise Stronghold, AZ, ca. 2007

265

He concluded with a loud and clear message: *"Be strong, keep your songs and prayers and most of all, keep the beautiful Apache language alive forever."*

When finished, Silas addressed the people in the Apache language. The entire speech was kindly translated to me by Carson; it basically repeated what Mr. Cochise, had said in English. When the speech was over, I felt fortunate and privileged to have been present during such a historical moment.

Chiricahua Apache War Singers at the Blessing Feast - Cochise Stronghold, AZ, ca. 2007
Right rear shows three War Dancers
L to R: on bench: #3: Siggy Second-Jumper, #6 and #7, Bo and Freddie Kaydahzinne.

Shortly after Sila's speech, an announcement was made for all war singers and dancers to make their way into the dance arena. While sitting on the singer's bench, I witnessed something very special. It consisted of our War Dancers standing on a nearby mountain ridge posing for a picture. Dressed in traditional outfits, they proudly stood with their rifles and lances in hand, while wailing war cries. The echo from their whooping along with the discharge of their firearms produced a shock wave that felt like a bolt of lightning had hit the bench we sat on. The powerful experience brought out the Apache in every one of us.

Once all dancers made their way back to the dance arena, Freddie Kaydahzinne addressed the crowd and began singing. His thunderous voice echoed through the canyon as the rest of us singers followed right along. The War Dancers, on the other hand, told their stories with each step they took, as they stayed in rhythm with the beat of our drums.

Who would have thought that eight years after my arrival in Mescalero I would be singing at such a holy event. Not to mention, in the company of direct descendants from some of the most feared Apaches that ever lived. To say that I felt proud for being an Apache and a participant during such a special occasion would be an understatement.

Chiricahua Apache War Singers at Blessing Feast at Cochise Stronghold, AZ, ca. 2007
L to R, sitting on bench, # 1: Silas Cochise, #6 and #7: Bo and Freddie Kaydahzinne, last
singer on right: Siggy Second-Jumper.

Whether another gathering of Chiricahuas of that magnitude would ever happen
again, was unknown. One thing was for sure, that one took place during my lifetime.
Only a fool would not humble himself in front of the Creator for such a gift. With a big
grin on my face, I looked up into the skies and gave thanks.

After many songs and lots of prayers, I headed back to James' camp to begin
preparations for that evening's Fire Dance. Upon my arrival, I found James Kunestsis
and Lynn Hank sitting by the warmth of a camp fire. It was perhaps the mood that
everyone was in that prompted Lynn to reveal some old stories. He spoke of the Dragoon
Mountains and their sacredness to the Chiricahua Apaches. *"It was here that our
ancestors found balance and harmony and our people thrived. This was the place where
total happiness and joy coexisted and children played in peace without worries,"* Lynn
said. He went on to explain how Unsen, the Apache God, had created the Dragoon
Mountains for the Chiricahuas. He based his opinion on the fact that the color of the
rocks and clay that made up the sacred stronghold matched to a blue print the color of the
skin he gave to the Apache people. Further evidence was noted and documented during
times of war, when the Chiricahuas hid in the canyons from the soldiers. Countless
military reports from the Mexican and U.S armies told how Apaches simply disappeared
during pursuit, once they reached their sacred stronghold.

On the other hand, Apache oral stories spoke of how Apaches blended in
perfectly with the canyon walls, to the point where the soldiers would not see them, even
though they were literally inches away.

267

"That in itself was proof that Apaches were indeed in their natural habitat and Gods chosen place for them to live," Lynn said.

Perhaps inspired by Lynn, James Kunestsis began to reveal a story that was told to him by his Dad, the late Berle Kanseah. Berle's grandfather, Jasper Kanseah, was Geronimo's nephew and his youngest warrior. *"Jasper was an orphan, who was raised by his aunts. He spent most of his early childhood roaming alone through different camps. Jasper did not play much with other kids his age; instead he preferred to be with the warriors. One day during a movement when Geronimo and his group decided to return to San Carlos, young Jasper was left behind all alone. Half way through the trip Geronimo noticed that his nephew was missing. Geronimo turned around and picked up the lonely boy. Together they rode on Geronimo's horse all the way to the San Carlos reservation. Soon after relocating, Jasper along with an older boy by the name of David Kazhe were promoted to the rank of warrior. Jasper will always be known as Geronimo's youngest warrior at the time of surrender in 1886. He was approximately thirteen years of age. Jasper Kanseah endured the long twenty-seven years of imprisonment. He was among the group that chose to move to Mescalero, where his body and spirit forever rest,"* James concluded

After the stories were told, we began with the preparations for the last evening of the Blessing Feast. Once done, the entire group came out of the arbor and the Crown Dancers lined up before they made their way to the dance arena. It was at that moment that I asked James Kunestsis for permission to capture this rare moment for this book and as a testament of time.

Chiricahua Crown Dancers at the Blessing Feast
James Kunestsis' group performing at their ancestors' homeland.
Cochise Stronghold, AZ, ca.2007
Photographed by author

After capturing our group's image, I thought about the famous postcard that showed the Chiricahua warriors "hostiles" meeting with General G. Crook at Cañon de los Embudos, Mexico in 1886. It has been said that somehow everyone, Apaches and soldiers knew the significance of capturing that moment on film on that fateful day.

Council meeting between General Crook and Geronimo's band of Chiricahuas
Cañon De Los Embudos, Mexico, March, 1886
Courtesy of the St. Augustine Historical Society Library

It remains the only photograph ever taken of any Native American with the enemy on the field. Just like that day in 1886, James and I knew how significant it was to capture our historical moment in March of 2007.

That night, we were the second group out. We stood behind the singers from the Warm Springs' group and watched their Crown Dancers perform. The energy in the air was contagious. Those Crown Dancers danced like they were possessed, their moves brought whooping sounds from all of us. When that group's session ended, we shook hands with them, sat on the benches, and waited for our dancers to make their way in.

Shortly after, James' voice echoed through the canyon sending chills down my spine. Next to me sat Lynn Hank, his clear voice was easy for me to follow and understand. During our last song, I gave thanks to the Creator for all His gifts. Soon after, we found ourselves shaking hands with another incoming group. As the night fell, I realized that it was truly over.

The next morning everyone began to break camp. By noon, a caravan of vehicles began heading back east towards Mescalero, New Mexico. Needless to say, the main topic of conversation around the reservation was about the success of the feast. On Wednesday the 28th, after an incredible week of enjoyment among family and friends, I found myself back in Florida reminiscing on my life's journey and events.

Bloodline Continue
Chapter Thirty Nine

Three months after the Blessing Feast, I found myself returning to New Mexico in the company of my children. After landing in El Paso, Texas, we rented a car and drove straight to the place that meant so much to us, Monticello Canyon. After spending a few days of fun and enjoyment, we headed up to The Mescalero Apache Reservation.

We arrived at our family's house in Second Canyon late that afternoon. The next day we set out to visit friends. One in particular was Lynn Hank's family. I wanted my children to experience the same type of love and warmth that I had received from the Hanks' over the years. Upon our arrival, we were greeted by Lynn's mom, Mrs. Adrianne M. Hank. Not surprisingly, she welcomed my children as if they were her own. To add to the joy, my children met Adrianne's granddaughter, Savannah Hank. It was no surprise to see Savannah embrace my Emily and Lance as if they were her siblings. Within minutes, they were out the door and into the hills, where they ran and played.

L to R: Emily, Adrianne, Savannah and Lance ****
Adrianne Hanks' Home, Mescalero Apache Reservation, NM, ca. 2007

While sitting on a couch and feeling comfortable, I asked Adrianne to share with me some of her stories from White Tail. I was eager to hear how she felt while growing up in such a special place. With a grin on her face and a sense of pride, Adrianne began to reminisce about the early years of her life.

As a child, Adrianne was raised by her great grandmother Oskissay (Goth-Kayzhn) from the Kazhe family. Oskissay married Jewett Tissnolthtos (1866-1936). Tissnolthtos was Geronimo's warrior and surrendered with him in 1886. He was Eugene Chihuahua's uncle. "Tissnolthtos and Oskissay had 5 children while living in Fort Sill, three of them died there.[1]"

270

One of the surviving children was Henrietta, born (1896-?) a.k.a. Keesah. "Tissnolthtos also had 4 children by another wife, name not recalled, who was the sister of Clarence Bailtso and of Bey-gil-clay-ih who married Albert Chatto, the Scout.

Tissnolthtos and Oskissay were among the Chiricahuas that relocated to Mescalero in 1913, where they had 2 more children: Gladys, born in 1913, and Leila born in 1915. While living in Mescalero, Keesah married Tom Duffy (1883-?)," "They had the following children, Austin, born in 1916, and Rosaline, born in 1917[1]." Tom found employment at Mescalero; there he built a modest two bedroom house just below the Feast Grounds. "Subsequently Tom Duffy married Christine Kozinne. Their daughter was Narcissus Duffy Gayton.[1]"

Even though, Adrianne moved back and forth from Mescalero to White Tail, her favorite place was White Tail, a place she called her *"Playground."* Adrianne's favorite past time was playing with grass dolls, which she pulled around in a wooden box, imitating a wagon. To accommodate her dolls, she made miniature furniture, such as tables and chairs out of rocks.

As she got older, she developed a love for horses, which she rode bareback all over white Tail. Some of the places she rode her horse to were Roger's Pasture, Snake Tank, and # 1 Cow Camp. All that fun ended when Adrianne entered the 6th grade and was forced to attend Indian School. Her family had two choices, Albuquerque or Santa Fe. Adrianne was sent to Albuquerque where she attended from the 6th to the 12th grade. There, she ran into an old White Tail school teacher by the name of Carlton Webb. Mr. Webb became her band teacher.

The children were only allowed to come home once a year. Adrianne remembered how much she looked forward to returning home during those summer breaks. It was during that time that she took advantage of her favorite past time; riding horses. *"Once I got on that horse, I was gone all day; sometimes getting back home at night time. I still remember how tired I used to be at the end of those days,"* Adrianne said. In time she became known as the *"Horse Woman."* Even though she wasn't an adult, she rode like one. A summer day did not go by, where Adrianne didn't race someone from White Tail. *"I used to outrun them all, including the boys,"* she proudly said with a big grin on her face.

She spoke of how plentiful food was, *"I remembered always having bread on hand and drinking water from anywhere."* Adrianne said. Her comments brought memories of my own childhood as I remembered doing the same thing when riding horses. Adrianne's family grew tomatoes, meat was mostly hunted deer or butcher cattle from the family's share. Other goods came from the school garden. There, Mrs. Callahan, the school teacher's wife, grew beans, potatoes, squash, carrots, corn, pumpkins and turnips. Next to the garden were rows of apple trees. The Chiricahua women in the community helped cann the goods. The school kept some, and the Apaches kept the rest. Those goods were stored for the winter months. Staples were provided by the Government. A book of stamps was used to monitor the rations. *"I never knew what a hungry day was,"* said Adrianne.

After learning about Adrianne's childhood days, she began reminiscing about the Maiden's Puberty ceremonies that took place at White Tail. She began by telling me that all the feasts held at White Tail were extra special, by the simple fact that the place was so incredibly beautiful. She went on to explain in great detail all the arrangements needed to successfully conduct a Puberty Sunrise Feast. It was *"a true family affair,"* as Adrianne described it.

The preparations began years before the two-day (Chiricahua style) or four-day celebration (Mescalero style). It involved the gathering of herbs, hides and beads. Once all the necessary items were gathered, the females in the family made a pattern for the dress along with bead colors and designs. Because the Maidens' dresses were so personal, each family implemented their own patterns and designs. Every detail, however small had a special meaning to that particular family and/or Maiden. As a result I was unable to reveal a lot of the particulars given to me by Adrianne pertaining to her family's medicine. To this day, the Hanks' have maintained their traditional ways by celebrating their family feasts at White Tail, a privilege my son and I experienced in August of 2010.

When Adrianne finished revealing such intimate stories, I realized how much work went into making a Puberty Ceremony a reality. I felt honored for having participated in so many of them as a singer with the Crown Dancers. I would like to thank all the families who allowed me to take part in such a sacred affair. Before leaving Adrianne's home, I thanked her for sharing such special moments and for the love and warmth that she so eagerly gave us.

After leaving Adrianne's home, my children expressed how much fun they had and how they were looking forward to another visit. Shortly after, we arrived at the Feast Grounds, just in time to assemble my drum and join Freddie Kaydahzinne and the boys for some War Singing and Dancing.

When our session ended, I reported to James' camp to begin preparations for that evening's Fire Dance. As usual I was welcomed with open arms. It was good to see my old pals again. Our preparations and performance went on as usual. The next morning we headed to Second Canyon to visit our aunt Lorraine. We stayed there for most of the day until the time came to head to the Feast Grounds again.

Upon entering the sacred grounds something magical happened, when my son Lance asked the following question. *"Dad, can I sing with you guys?"* I found myself repeating Freddie Kaydahzinne's words when I first asked him the same question. *"What makes you think you can sing these songs?"* I asked. *"I don't know Dad, something came over me and I want to sing with you,"* he replied. *"Very well, tomorrow we will work on the making of your drum and stick,"* I said, as I let him know how proud his desire to sing made me feel. That evening I sang like never before, as I felt the Creator's blessings upon me. I felt proud knowing that my boy wanted to be part of something so special and sacred. When our session came to an end, we headed to our hotel for the night.

The next day after lunch, we drove to Lorraine's home in hopes to find all the necessary components to assemble an Apache drum. A few hours later, Lance had his own drum, which consisted of a small metal bucket, a piece of buckskin and a few strips of rubber. The next and final step was the making of the drumstick. After hiking a couple hundred yards into Second Canyon, we came across a cluster of fresh green oaks growing in a shaded area. There, Lance and I sat, carved and molded his drumstick. During that process, I told him of the responsibilities associated with such position, duties he understood and accepted.

Late that afternoon, we drove to the Feast Grounds and straight to James' camp. Upon our arrival, we found that everyone was already inside the tepee. As a result I was not able to ask James if it was ok to have Lance sing along with us. Not knowing what to do, I proceeded to enter the tepee with Lance by my side.

Not surprisingly, we were both greeted with enthusiasm and respect. That evening, things felt different for me, as having Lance next to me was no small deed. I thought about the first time I walked into the tepee with Carson and wondered if Lance felt the same way. Although he knew just about everyone there, he still showed signs of nervousness. Our preparations went on as normal, but they were far from usual to me. There, for the first time, my boy sat next to me with his drum on hand. His piercing black eyes expressed his excitement, while mine revealed pride through tears of joy. With a sense of relief, I looked at my son knowing that for at least one more generation those sacred songs would be preserved.

As my mind wondered, I began to think about my own mortality and my children's future. Indeed, I had come a long way, but my greatest accomplishment was the fact that I had paved the road for my descendants to travel on if they ever wanted to be part of their ancestral ways of life.

My deep thoughts were interrupted when James began beating on his drum, thus signaling the beginning of the ceremony. A short time later, our group began to walk towards the Feast Grounds where I found my daughter Emily and her cousin Hailey Ahidley waiting for our arrival. Our group stood in the eastern entrance and waited for James to give the signal to march in. As the night fell, our voices echoed throughout the Canyon. Encouraging smiles from Emily and Hailey let me know that Lance and I were doing well. Between pauses, my mind wondered with questions and thoughts. *"How lucky can one man be?"* I thought about my long journey and all my accomplishments, but none compared to having my children with me in such a place and time. I thanked the Creator for all his gifts. About an hour later, our session came to an end and the next group made their way into the arena. From there we headed to the hotel where we called it a night.

The next day my boy was eager to sing again. We arrived at James' camp early that afternoon. While Lance sat and talked with the other singers, I headed over to James, as I wanted to apologize for having brought my son into the tepee without his prior consent. *"No need to apologize, Lance is your son and therefore one of us. He will always be welcome here,"* James kindly replied. Nearly choked with emotions, I barely said thanks. With a grin on my face, I returned to the arbor, where I found the rest of the group chatting, eating and having a good time. After a good meal, we all headed into the tepee and began our preparations for the fourth and final evening of the feast.

A few minutes later, James approached my son and proceeded to bless him and his drum with the sacred pollen. Watching that was one of the proudest moments of my life. I thanked the Creator for allowing me to live one more day to see my son officially inaugurated into our group.

That night, inside that tepee with Lance by my side, I understood and saw clearly what I was put on this earth to do. I thought about my long journey and what, if anything, I had brought to the people that had given so much. The first thing that came to my mind was the most precious gift of all, blood. In a very minute way, my two children represented an infusion to the bloodline of a dying breed. Like a dying man counting his last breaths, The Warm Springs-Chiricahuas are destined to be an extinct group. Unless other descendants like my children come forward to strengthen the blood, we will soon cease to exist.

Once done, we made our way to the Feast Grounds. We sat on the benches and waited for the Crown Dancers as they made their way into the arena. Sitting next to me on my right was Vernon Simmons, the oldest member of our singing group.

BLOODLINE CONTINUES

To my left sat Lance, the youngest. Before singing our first song, I switched positions and allowed my son to sit next to Vernon. Song after song, I watched Vernon lean over to his left and sing into Lance's ear, just like he had done for me over the years. Some songs were easy for Lance to pick up, while others left him with a blank look on his face, reminding me of my earlier days. Needless to say, it was one of the most memorable evenings of any feast I had ever been part of.

When our session was over we all shook hands and walked away. While driving to our hotel, I thought how significant the last two nights had been. Not only was I thankful for the many gifts and blessings bestowed upon me by the Creator, but for all the love and warmth that I had received from the Chiricahuas and Mescaleros.

Indeed I had come a long way, not once did I give up on my ancestors. My families' broken loop has been mended. Today I find myself with inner peace and no longer searching for what others perceived as a past obsession. Those old photographs of my ancestors no longer appear sad when I look at them. Despite past government efforts to annihilate the Apaches and Seminoles, they failed to succeed.

I am proud to be a Chiricahua descendant and honored to call the Seminoles my friends. This document will endure long after I'm gone. I hope that my story will help and inspire my descendants as well as others to stay connected or seek a reconnection with their ancestors' heritage and culture.

I am just thankful for having lived long enough to finish this project. I will no longer look to the past. From now on, I will devote myself with the same intensity used to find my roots, to preserve and promote the welfare of today's living descendants. May the Creator give us light and strength in our times of need. May we always be humble and thankful for His gifts.

References

1. Griswold G. (1958-1962) *The Fort Sill Apache Tribal Origins and Antecedents*; Director US Army Field Artillery and Fort Sill Museum, Ft. Sill, OK.

2. Jumper B.M., Gallagher P., Labree G. (1998) *Legends of the Seminoles*, Sarasota: Pineapple Press.

3. Welsh H. *The Apache Prisoners in Ft. Marion, St. Augustine Florida. (1887)* Indian Rights Association, Office of the Indian Rights Association, Philadelphia.

4. Anonymous. Plaque under statue of Crown Dancers. Inn of the Mountain Gods Resort and Casina, Mescalero, New Mexico.

5. Seminole Tribe of Florida. (2007) V. Mitchell & E. Leiba E. (Eds.) *Celebrating 50 Years of the Signing of our Constitution and Corporate Charter.* Seminole Communications, p. 6-7.

6. Noel, J. videographer (2005). Exploratory Mining Permit Public Hearing. Personal video recording of meeting. Monticello Fire Station, Monticello, New Mexico.

7. Seminole Tribe of Florida Inc. CD. (2010) *Seminole Cattle. A way of life for the Seminole People.*

8. Robert S. Ove and Henrietta Stockel; (1997) *Geronimo's kids*, Texas, A & M University Press.

9. Jose Barreiro (1989), *Indians of Cuba*, Cultural Survival Quarterly, Vol, 13, no. 3, pp. 56-60

10. * = Photographed by Jack Wood

11. **= Photographed by Jack Noel

12. **** = Photographed by author

CPSIA information can be obtained at www.ICGtesting.com
Printed in the USA
239339LV00001B/1/P